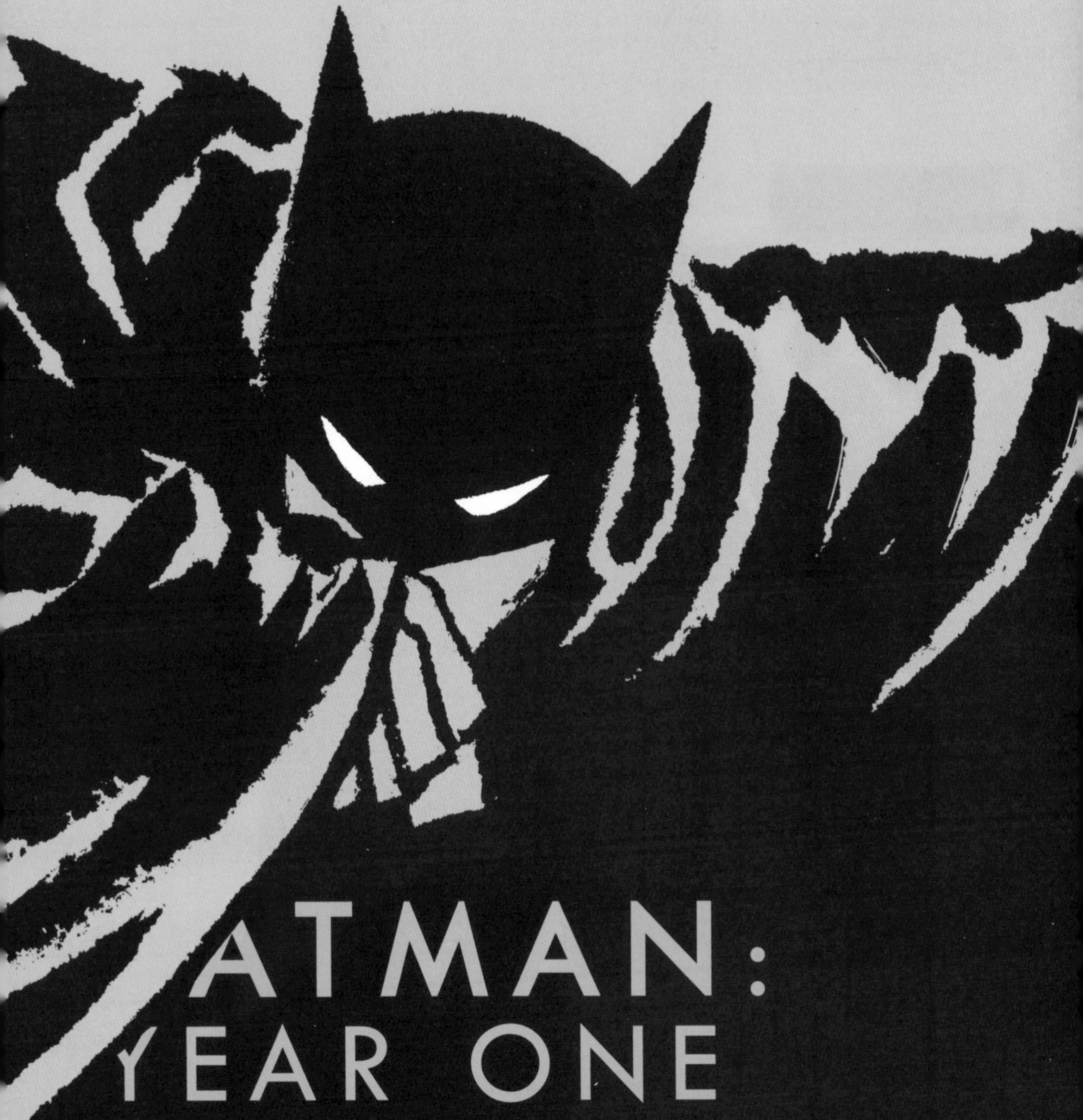

ATMAN:
YEAR ONE

FRANK MILLER

WRITER

DAVID MAZZUCCHELLI

ILLUSTRATOR

RICHMOND LEWIS

COLORIST

TODD KLEIN

LETTERING

BATMAN CREATED BY BOB KANE.

ADAPTED FROM THE WORKS OF BOB KANE, BILL FINGER AND JERRY ROBINSON.

BATMAN: YEAR ONE

Published by DC Comics. Cover, introductions and compilation Copyright © 2005 DC Comics. All Rights Reserved.
Originally published in single magazine form as BATMAN 404-407. Copyright © 1986, 1987 DC Comics. All Rights Reserved.
All characters, their distinctive likenesses and related elements featured in this publication are trademarks of DC Comics. The stories, characters and incidents featured in this publication are entirely fictional. DC Comics does not read or accept unsolicited submissions of ideas, stories or artwork. DC Comics, 1700 Broadway, New York, NY 10019 • A Warner Bros. Entertainment Company Printed by Transcontinental Interglobe, Beauceville, QC, Canada. 11/28/14. Tenth Printing. ISBN: 978-1-4012-0752-6

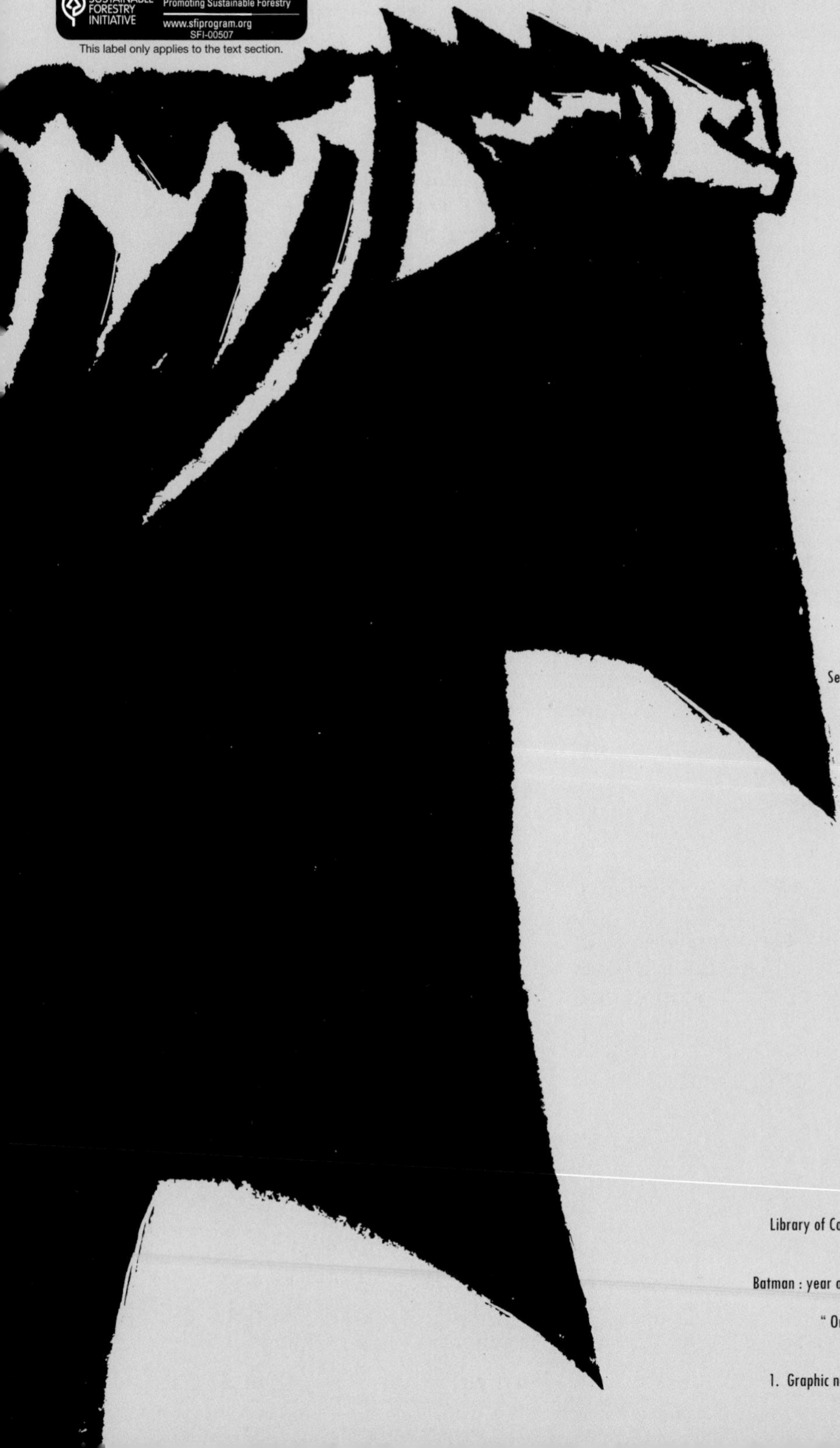

Cover art by David Mazzucchelli.

Library of Congress Cataloging-in-Publication Data

Miller, Frank, 1957-
Batman : year one / Frank Miller, David Mazzucchelli,
pages cm
" Originally published in single magazine
form in Batman 404-407."
ISBN 978-1-4012-0752-6
1. Graphic novels. I. Mazzucchelli, David. II. Title.
PN6728.B36 M547 2012
741.5'973—dc23
2012376780

THE CRIME BLOTTER

by Slam Bradley

OOPS! SHE DID IT AGAIN!

■Gossip diva Vicki Vale got her legendary, notoriously firm, shapely fanny tossed into the hoosegow yet again after trying to lift an estimated $11,320.00 worth of merchandise from the Sprang. The cutie klepto pled guilty. After paying for the loot and promising on a whole big heap of bibles to seek counseling, she got off with a wink and nod to the judge.

Leave us say the dame knows how to wink.

One juror says she even blew a kiss to the horny old fart.

You can't make this crap up!

THE PERP LIKED PISTACHIO

■How that little snot pulled off this heist is anybody's guess. I know what my own guess is, but you can figure that out for yourself. I just report this stuff:

It was like somebody's bad idea for a joke. Like some dumbass screenwriter's idea for a crowd-pleasing gag that every last dimwit on the planet would laugh at. But only the dimwits. For Christ sake, it was a goddam doughnut shop. In the middle of the night. And yeah, of course the joint was full of Gotham City cops, more even than you'll find in most saloons. So in waltzes this punk – he is, as of this writing, still unidentified, but I'll get to that in a minute – and this punk, he bellies up to the counter, orders himself a pistachio puff and a cup of joe. Then instead of paying a two-buck bill for the chow, the punk tells the poor sap working the register that he's packing heat. "You know the drill," he says, right in front of a baker's dozen of Gotham's Finest.

The cops don't need you, and man, they expect the same.

So the poor sap clerk empties the register and he empties the joint's safebox and

gives with a since-declared fifteen grand. Cash. And Sergeant Novick - yeah, that Novick, the one who's still squeezing all the printer's ink he can out of that one time he did something right and saved a kid – well, it looks like Hero Cop Novick didn't notice any of what was going down, on account of how fixated he was on his Chocolate Chip Crunch Special.

The security camera showed some kind of exchange between the perp and the good sergeant before the perp walked out, unidentified. Easy as you please. Scot-free. The exchange seemed pleasant enough.

And it just so happens our hero cop just bought his girlfriend an eight grand boob job. Fancy that.

Must've won the lottery.

Right. Sure.

FUGGEDABOUTIT

■22-year-old paralegal Stacy Lynch withdrew charges of gang rape in the notorious Robinson Park incident, that now, she says, despite witnesses, never happened.

In her press conference, it was observed that Lynch was missing her right index finger.

Prosecutor Harvey Dent could barely keep his lunch down. Hell. He looked like he was about to give birth to something really ugly.

What a town. You gotta love it.

ON A MORE SERIOUS NOTE

■Our very serious Mayor confronted the city legislature yesterday, taking no prisoners in his brave campaign to eliminate ATM fees.

What a man. What a champ.

What a town.

INTRODUCTION

In 1986 the editorial board of DC Comics decided that their heroes, some of whom were nearly a half-century old, had become dated. A massive revamping was clearly in order, and the place to begin was with the company's three most popular and enduring characters—Superman, Wonder Woman and Batman. The writers and artists assigned to the task had quick and clear ideas about how to update Superman and Wonder Woman, but Batman was a problem. He was fine just as he was. The origin that Bob Kane and Bill Finger had created in 1939 was a perfect explanation of how and why Batman came to be, why he continued his obsessive crusade, and,

perhaps more important, it mirrored the fears, frustrations and hopes of a readership coping with the realities of 20th-century urban life.

So, DC's editors decided, Batman's origin should not be changed. But it might be improved. It could be given depth, complexity, a wider context. Details could be added to give it focus and credibility. Bruce Wayne's struggles to become the thing he was trying to create, the Batman, could be dramatized. And, finally, all the storytelling techniques that comic book creators had developed in those 50 years could be applied to realize the potential of the basic material.

The question then was, who would do all this?

Frank Miller volunteered. Miller was generally acknowledged to be the best writer-artist to enter comics since

the early 1960s; indeed, some said he was the best ever. When he was a beginner at DC's chief competitor, Marvel Comics, he had re-created a minor character called Daredevil and produced a series that was at once faithful to established continuity, dazzlingly innovative and immensely popular. At DC, he had done an extended graphic novel titled RONIN, which incorporated Japanese and European influences into a personal vision of a horrifying future and, more recently, he had collaborated with Lynn Varley and Klaus Janson to produce the phenomenal BATMAN: THE DARK KNIGHT RETURNS, which portrayed an aging Batman driven out of retirement by a society running amok and his own inner needs. Having done Batman's omega, Miller was willing and anxious to do Batman's alpha.

But he chose to abandon his role as artist; he wanted to function as writer only. His collaborator of choice was David Mazzucchelli. Mazzucchelli, though only a few years into the field, had already acquired a reputation as

one of comics' extraordinary talents. He had an absolute command of composition, a powerful sense of visual drama and an unerring eye for the telling details that bring a scene to life.

Miller and Mazzucchelli complemented each other perfectly. With the help of colorist Richmond Lewis, herself a gifted artist, and letterer Todd Klein, they produced the definitive version of one of popular culture's enduring stories. Originally published in four parts, BATMAN: YEAR ONE is presented here as the organic whole that Frank Miller and David Mazzucchelli mean it to be—a graphic novel that combines a familiar urban myth with an unmistakably modern sensibility and brilliant storytelling.

—DENNY O'NEIL
March 1988

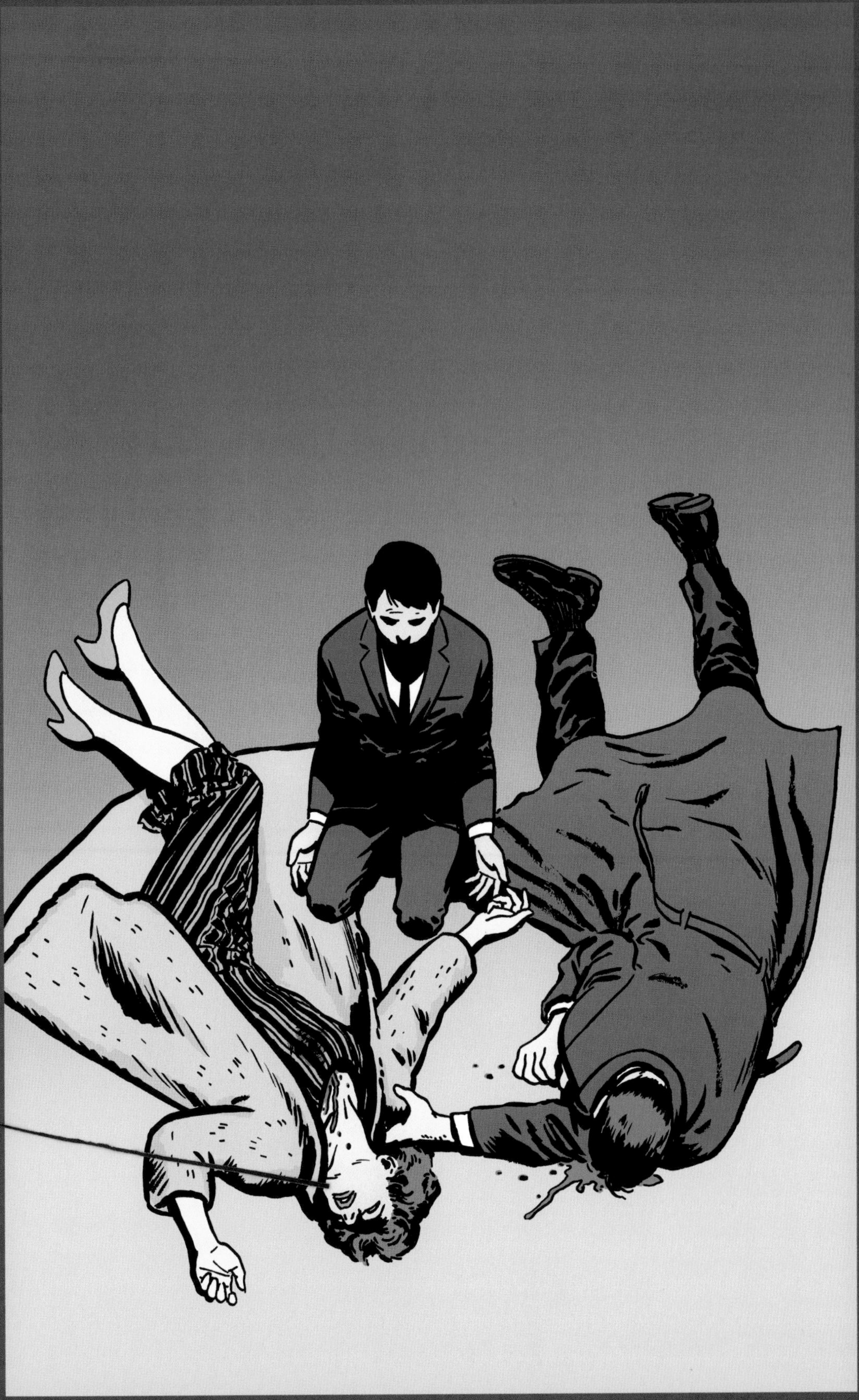

He will become the
greatest crimefighter
the world has ever known...

It won't be easy.

CHAPTER ONE:
WHO I AM
HOW I COME TO BE

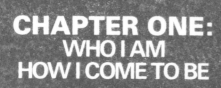

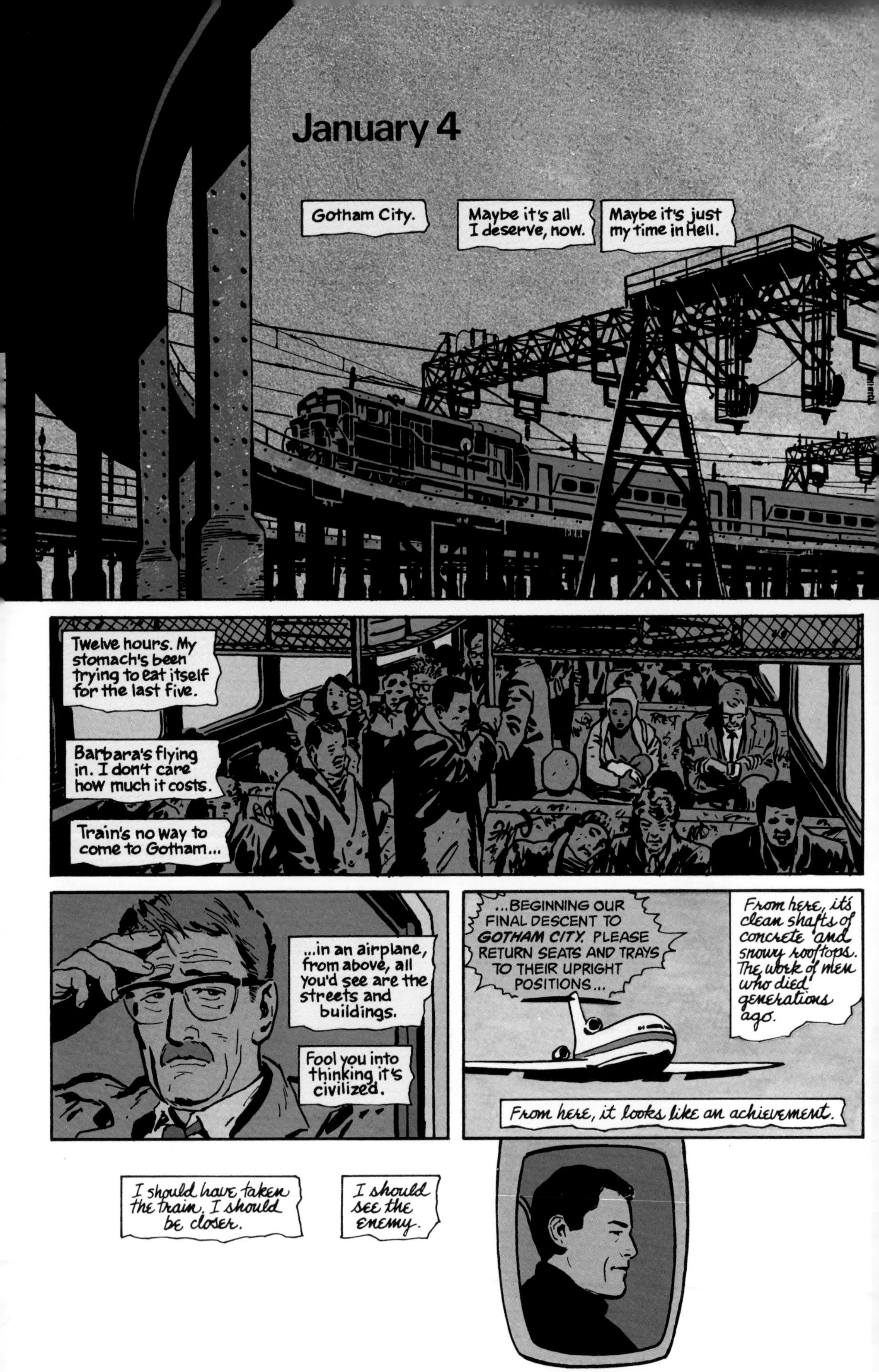
January 4
Gotham City.
Maybe it's all I deserve, now.
Maybe it's just my time in Hell.
Twelve hours. My stomach's been trying to eat itself for the last five.
Barbara's flying in. I don't care how much it costs.
Train's no way to come to Gotham...
...in an airplane, from above, all you'd see are the streets and buildings.
Fool you into thinking it's civilized.
...BEGINNING OUR FINAL DESCENT TO *GOTHAM CITY.* PLEASE RETURN SEATS AND TRAYS TO THEIR UPRIGHT POSITIONS...
From here, it's clean shafts of concrete and snowy rooftops. The work of men who died generations ago.
From here, it looks like an achievement.
I should have taken the train. I should be closer.
I should see the enemy.

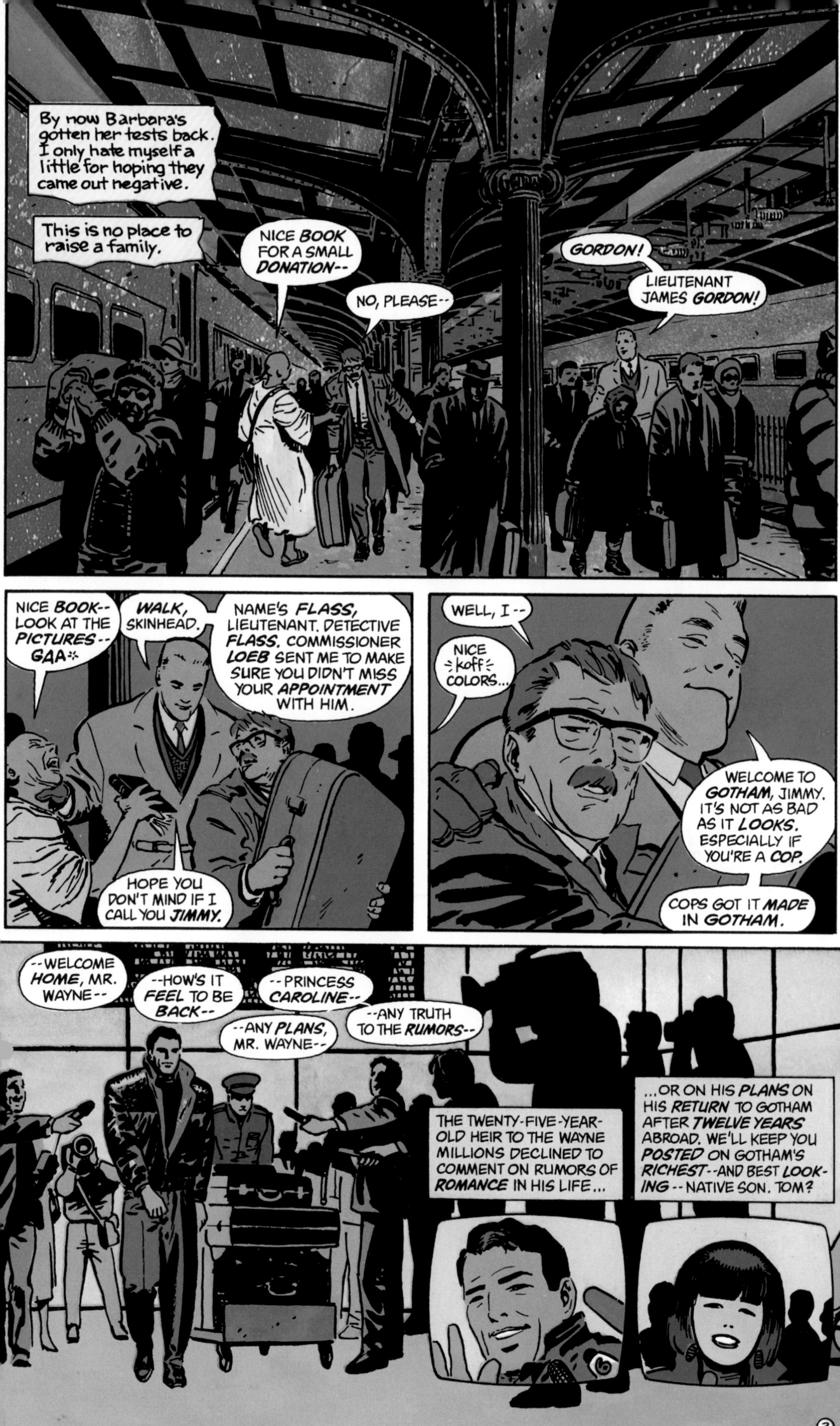

By now Barbara's gotten her tests back. I only hate myself a little for hoping they came out negative.
This is no place to raise a family.
NICE BOOK FOR A SMALL DONATION--
NO, PLEASE--
GORDON!
LIEUTENANT JAMES GORDON!
NICE BOOK-- LOOK AT THE PICTURES-- GAA*
WALK, SKINHEAD.
NAME'S FLASS, LIEUTENANT. DETECTIVE FLASS. COMMISSIONER LOEB SENT ME TO MAKE SURE YOU DIDN'T MISS YOUR APPOINTMENT WITH HIM.
HOPE YOU DON'T MIND IF I CALL YOU JIMMY.
WELL, I--
NICE koff COLORS...
WELCOME TO GOTHAM, JIMMY. IT'S NOT AS BAD AS IT LOOKS. ESPECIALLY IF YOU'RE A COP.
COPS GOT IT MADE IN GOTHAM.
--WELCOME HOME, MR. WAYNE--
--HOW'S IT FEEL TO BE BACK--
--PRINCESS CAROLINE--
--ANY PLANS, MR. WAYNE--
--ANY TRUTH TO THE RUMORS--
THE TWENTY-FIVE-YEAR-OLD HEIR TO THE WAYNE MILLIONS DECLINED TO COMMENT ON RUMORS OF ROMANCE IN HIS LIFE...
...OR ON HIS PLANS ON HIS RETURN TO GOTHAM AFTER TWELVE YEARS ABROAD. WE'LL KEEP YOU POSTED ON GOTHAM'S RICHEST--AND BEST LOOKING--NATIVE SON. TOM?

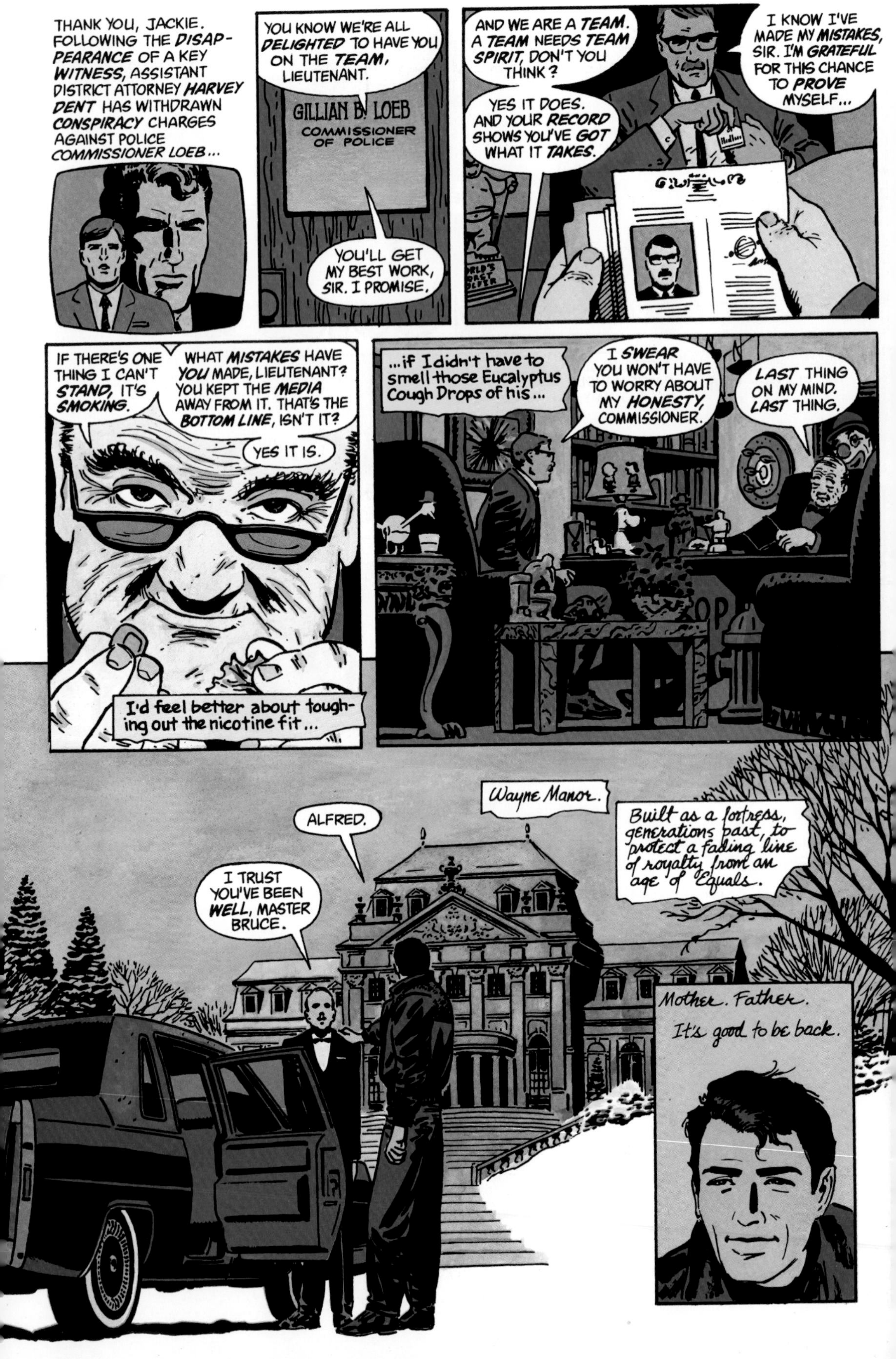
THANK YOU, JACKIE. FOLLOWING THE DISAPPEARANCE OF A KEY WITNESS, ASSISTANT DISTRICT ATTORNEY HARVEY DENT HAS WITHDRAWN CONSPIRACY CHARGES AGAINST POLICE COMMISSIONER LOEB...
YOU KNOW WE'RE ALL DELIGHTED TO HAVE YOU ON THE TEAM, LIEUTENANT.
GILLIAN B. LOEB
COMMISSIONER OF POLICE
YOU'LL GET MY BEST WORK, SIR. I PROMISE.
AND WE ARE A TEAM. A TEAM NEEDS TEAM SPIRIT, DON'T YOU THINK?
YES IT DOES. AND YOUR RECORD SHOWS YOU'VE GOT WHAT IT TAKES.
I KNOW I'VE MADE MY MISTAKES, SIR. I'M GRATEFUL FOR THIS CHANCE TO PROVE MYSELF...
IF THERE'S ONE THING I CAN'T STAND, IT'S SMOKING.
WHAT MISTAKES HAVE YOU MADE, LIEUTENANT? YOU KEPT THE MEDIA AWAY FROM IT. THAT'S THE BOTTOM LINE, ISN'T IT?
YES IT IS.
I'd feel better about toughing out the nicotine fit...
...if I didn't have to smell those Eucalyptus Cough Drops of his...
I SWEAR YOU WON'T HAVE TO WORRY ABOUT MY HONESTY, COMMISSIONER.
LAST THING ON MY MIND. LAST THING.
Wayne Manor.
ALFRED.
Built as a fortress, generations past, to protect a fading line of royalty from an age of Equals.
I TRUST YOU'VE BEEN WELL, MASTER BRUCE.
Mother. Father.
It's good to be back.

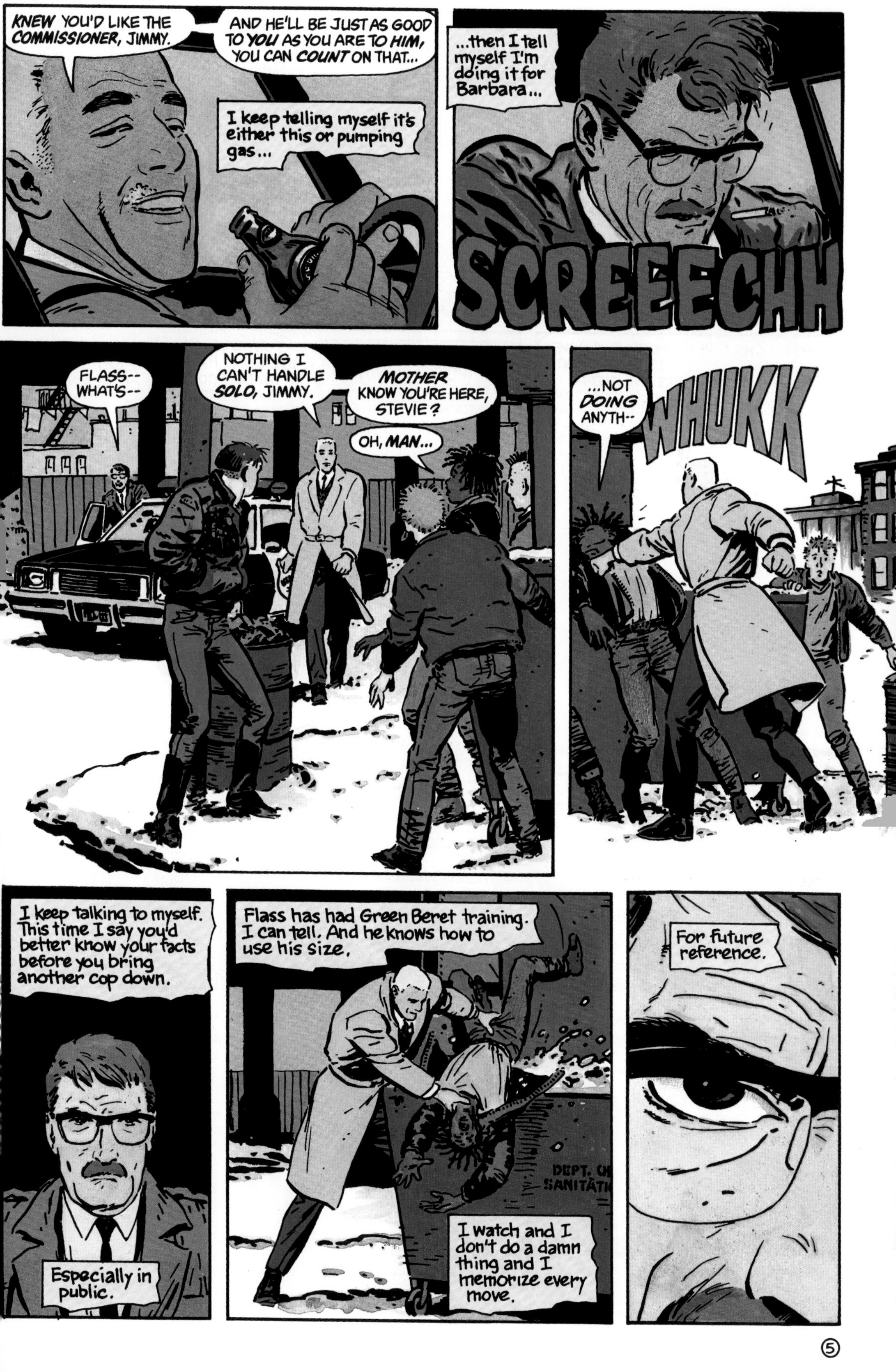

KNEW YOU'D LIKE THE COMMISSIONER, JIMMY.
AND HE'LL BE JUST AS GOOD TO YOU AS YOU ARE TO HIM, YOU CAN COUNT ON THAT...
I keep telling myself it's either this or pumping gas...
...then I tell myself I'm doing it for Barbara...
SCREEECHH
FLASS-- WHAT'S--
NOTHING I CAN'T HANDLE SOLO, JIMMY.
MOTHER KNOW YOU'RE HERE, STEVIE?
OH, MAN...
...NOT DOING ANYTH--
WHUKK
I keep talking to myself. This time I say you'd better know your facts before you bring another cop down.
Especially in public.
Flass has had Green Beret training. I can tell. And he knows how to use his size.
I watch and I don't do a damn thing and I memorize every move.
For future reference.

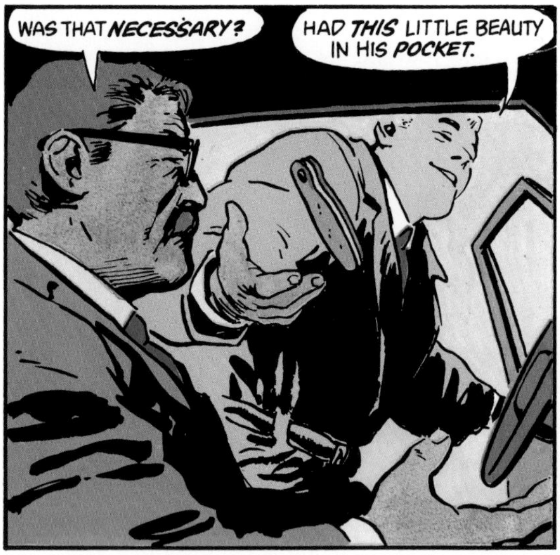
WAS THAT *NECESSARY?*
HAD *THIS* LITTLE BEAUTY IN HIS *POCKET.*

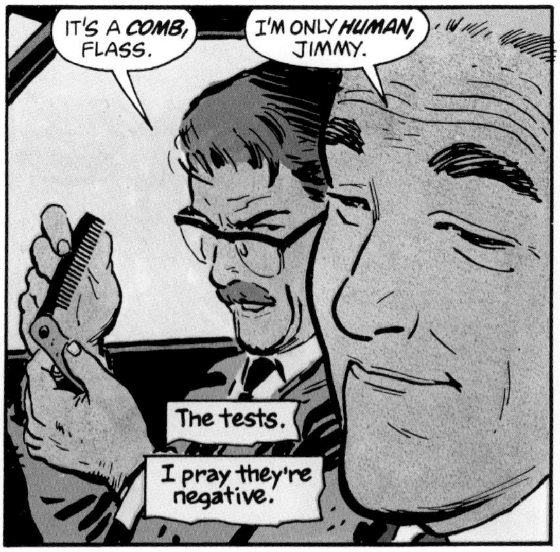
IT'S A *COMB,* FLASS.
I'M ONLY *HUMAN,* JIMMY.
The tests.
I pray they're negative.

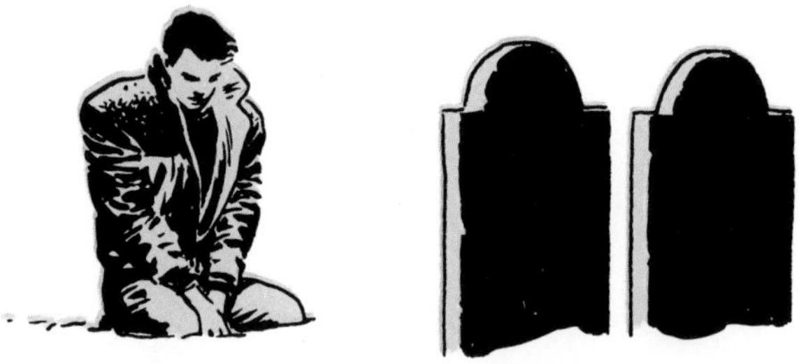

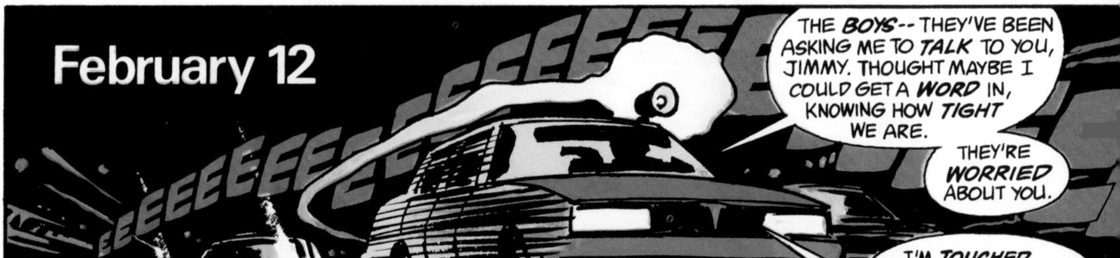
February 12
THE *BOYS*-- THEY'VE BEEN ASKING ME TO *TALK* TO YOU, JIMMY. THOUGHT MAYBE I COULD GET A *WORD* IN, KNOWING HOW *TIGHT* WE ARE.
THEY'RE *WORRIED* ABOUT YOU.
I'M *TOUCHED,* FLASS. BUT RIGHT NOW *I'M* WORRIED--ABOUT A *HOMICIDE.* TURN *LEFT.*

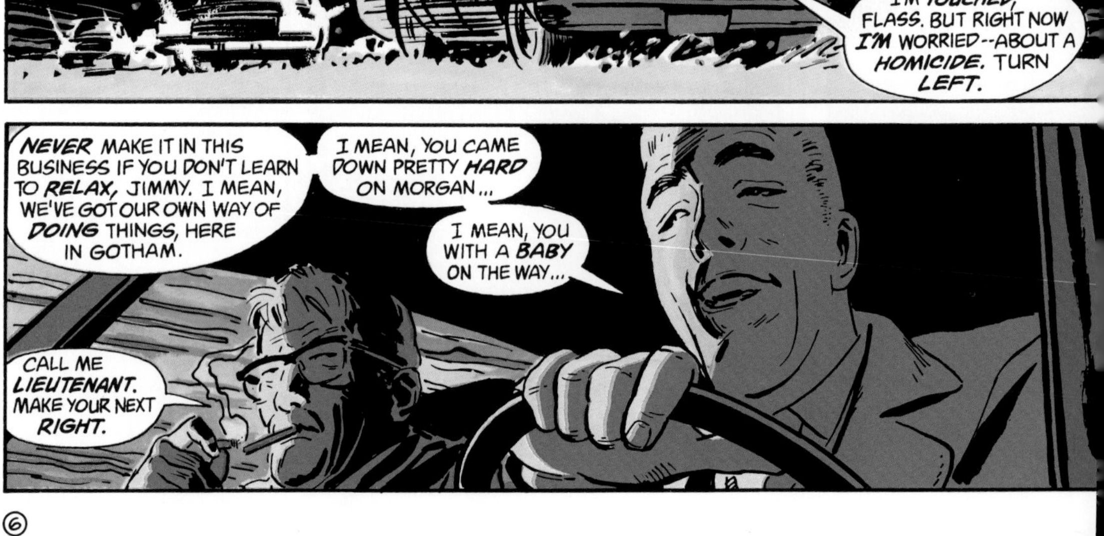
NEVER MAKE IT IN THIS BUSINESS IF YOU DON'T LEARN TO *RELAX,* JIMMY. I MEAN, WE'VE GOT OUR OWN WAY OF *DOING* THINGS, HERE IN GOTHAM.
I MEAN, YOU CAME DOWN PRETTY *HARD* ON MORGAN...
I MEAN, YOU WITH A *BABY* ON THE WAY...
CALL ME *LIEUTENANT.* MAKE YOUR NEXT *RIGHT.*

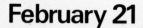

February 21

I'm not ready.

I have the means, the skill -- but not the method...

...no. That's not true. I have hundreds of methods.

But something's missing. Something isn't right.

I have to wait.

I have to wait.

February 26

...SO FATHER DONELLEY, HE SLIPS GORDON A FIFTY WITH THE HANDSHAKE...

GILLIAN B. L
COMMISSIONER
OF POLICE

...AND *GORDON,* HE LOOKS AT IT LIKE HIS *HAND'S* GOT A *DISEASE.* THEN HE *THROWS* THE FIFTY IN THE PADRE'S *FACE.*

GIVES THE *SQUAD* A TWO-HOUR *LECTURE.* PUTS *SCHELL* ON *PROBATION.*

HE'S JUST NOT FITTING *IN,* GILL.

I HAD SUCH HOPES FOR THAT BOY...

I COULD GET THE *BOYS* TOGETHER-- SOFTEN HIM *UP.*

NO. NOT WHILE I'M IN *TOWN.* THERE'S ENOUGH HEAT ON ME AS IT *IS.*

NO. YOU'LL ABSOLUTELY HAVE TO *WAIT* UNTIL I'M AT THE *CONFERENCE* IN *WASHINGTON*...TWO WEEKS, FLASS...

March 11

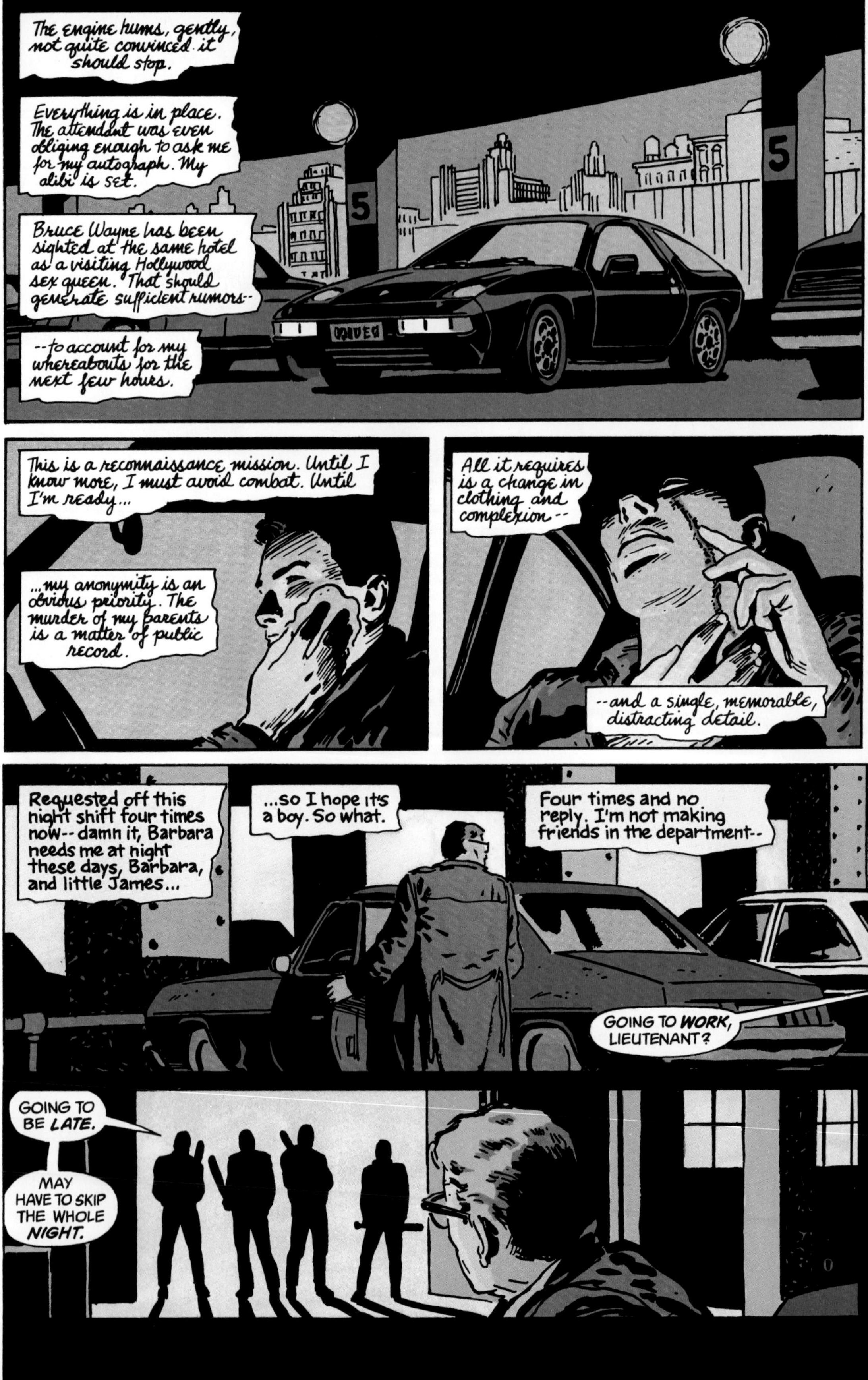

The engine hums, gently, not quite convinced it should stop.
Everything is in place. The attendant was even obliging enough to ask me for my autograph. My alibi is set.
Bruce Wayne has been sighted at the same hotel as a visiting Hollywood sex queen. That should generate sufficient rumors-
--to account for my whereabouts for the next few hours.
This is a reconnaissance mission. Until I know more, I must avoid combat. Until I'm ready...
...my anonymity is an obvious priority. The murder of my parents is a matter of public record.
All it requires is a change in clothing and complexion--
--and a single, memorable, distracting detail.
Requested off this night shift four times now-- damn it, Barbara needs me at night these days, Barbara, and little James...
...so I hope it's a boy. So what.
Four times and no reply. I'm not making friends in the department--
GOING TO WORK, LIEUTENANT?
GOING TO BE LATE.
MAY HAVE TO SKIP THE WHOLE NIGHT.

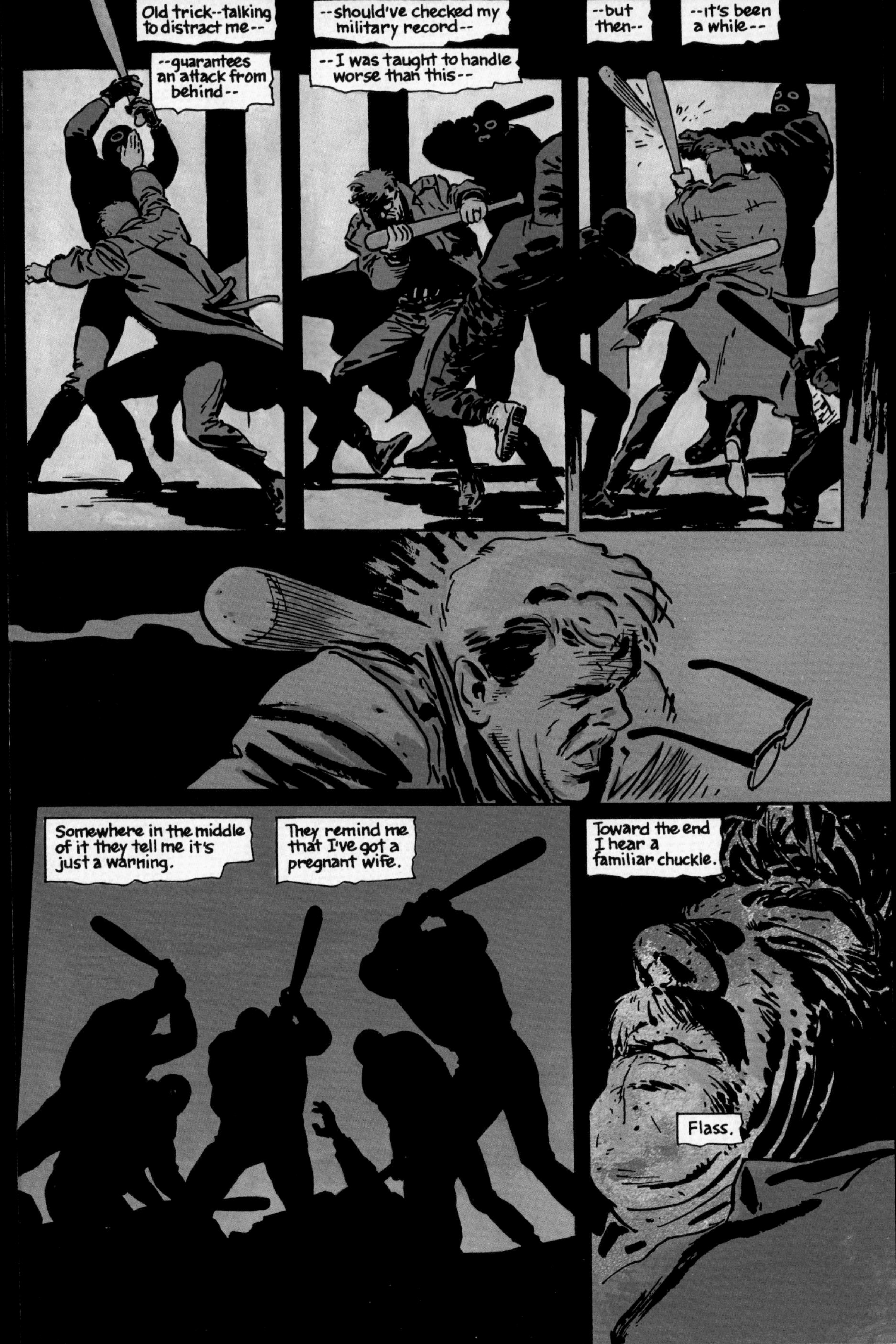
Old trick--talking to distract me--
--guarantees an attack from behind--
--should've checked my military record--
--I was taught to handle worse than this--
--but then--
--it's been a while--
Somewhere in the middle of it they tell me it's just a warning.
They remind me that I've got a pregnant wife.
Toward the end I hear a familiar chuckle.
Flass.

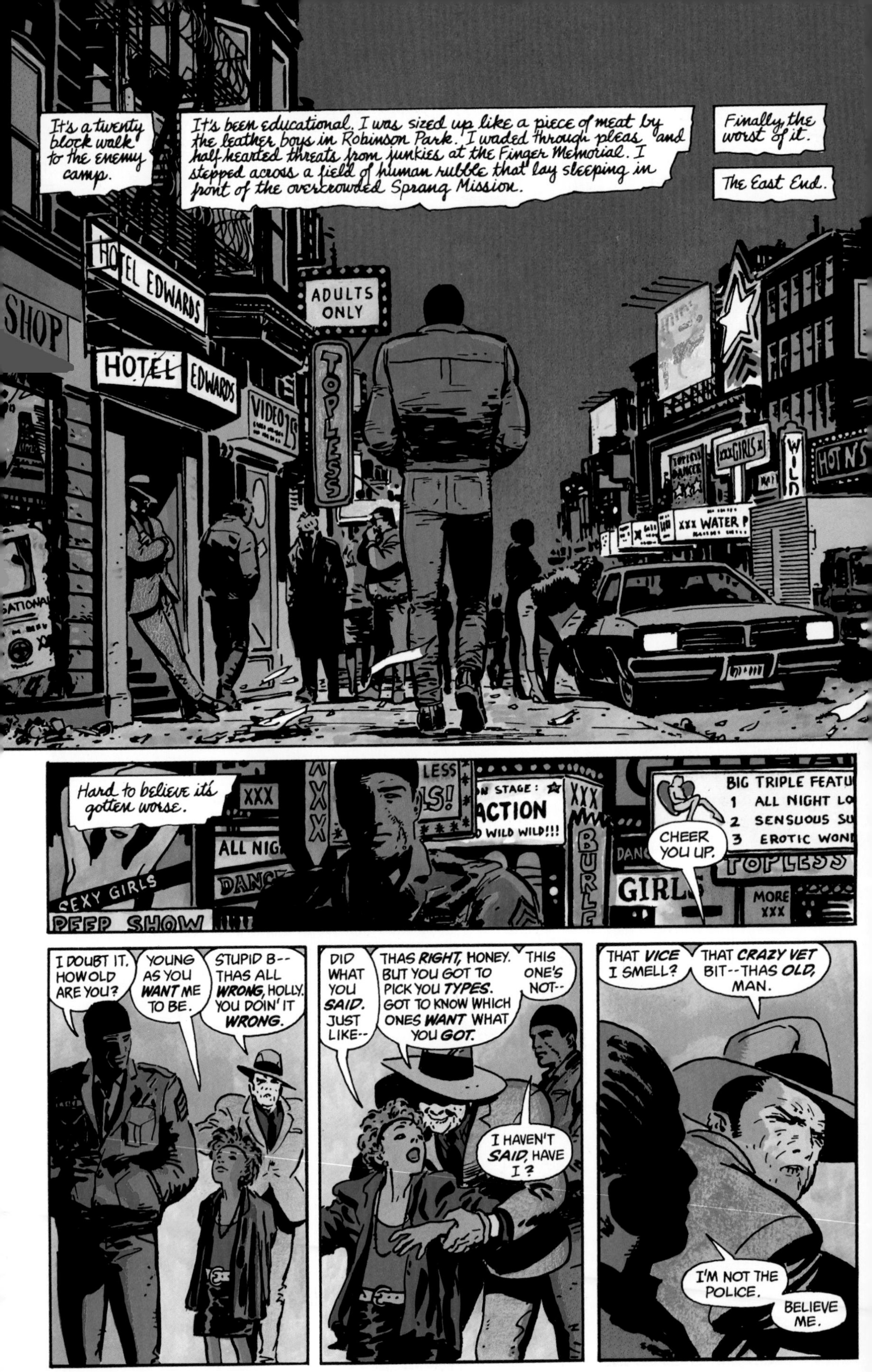

It's a twenty block walk to the enemy camp.
It's been educational. I was sized up like a piece of meat by the leather boys in Robinson Park. I waded through pleas and half hearted threats from junkies at the Finger Memorial. I stepped across a field of human rubble that lay sleeping in front of the overcrowded Sprang Mission.
Finally the worst of it.
The East End.
HOTEL EDWARDS
ADULTS ONLY
TOPLESS
SHOP
HOTEL EDWARDS
XXX WATER
Hard to believe it's gotten worse.
CHEER YOU UP.
BIG TRIPLE FEATU
1 ALL NIGHT LO
2 SENSUOUS SU
3 EROTIC WON
ACTION
WILD WILD!!!
XXX
SEXY GIRLS
PEEP SHOW
GIRLS
TOPLESS
MORE XXX
I DOUBT IT. HOW OLD ARE YOU?
YOUNG AS YOU WANT ME TO BE.
STUPID B-- THAS ALL WRONG, HOLLY. YOU DOIN' IT WRONG.
DID WHAT YOU SAID. JUST LIKE--
THAS RIGHT, HONEY. BUT YOU GOT TO PICK YOU TYPES. GOT TO KNOW WHICH ONES WANT WHAT YOU GOT.
THIS ONE'S NOT--
I HAVEN'T SAID, HAVE I?
THAT VICE I SMELL?
THAT CRAZY VET BIT--THAS OLD, MAN.
I'M NOT THE POLICE.
BELIEVE ME.

YOU STILL *HERE?* *TOLD* YOU TO *GO,* HOLLY.

HE HADN'T *SAID.*

WE TALK THIS OVER *LATER,* SWEET CHUNKS.

NO...

...I THINK YOU'RE *FINISHED* WITH HER.

I'm provoking him.

I really shouldn't.

MAN, YOU *PUSHIN.* YOU ON THE *EDGE.*

YOU LOOKIN' FOR A *NEW SCAR. THAS* RIGHT. JUS TELL ME *WHERE,* MAN...

OH. GEEZ...CAN'T BE *VICE.* WE'RE PAID *UP.* JUST SOME *IDIOT* OUT TO GET HIMSELF *KILLED.*

SELINA... DON'T STOP *NOW...*

SHUT UP, SKUNK.

YOU KNOW WHAT I HATE *MOST* ABOUT *MEN,* SKUNK?

PLEASE, SELINA... *TELL* ME... WHY YOU *HATE* US SO... OH, *PLEASE...*

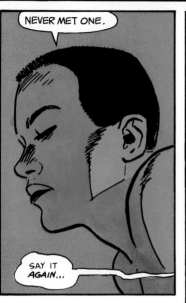

NEVER MET ONE.

SAY IT *AGAIN...*

His eyes keep flicking away from the girls to me. He turns away for a second --

-- a dead giveaway --

-- he's pretty fast --

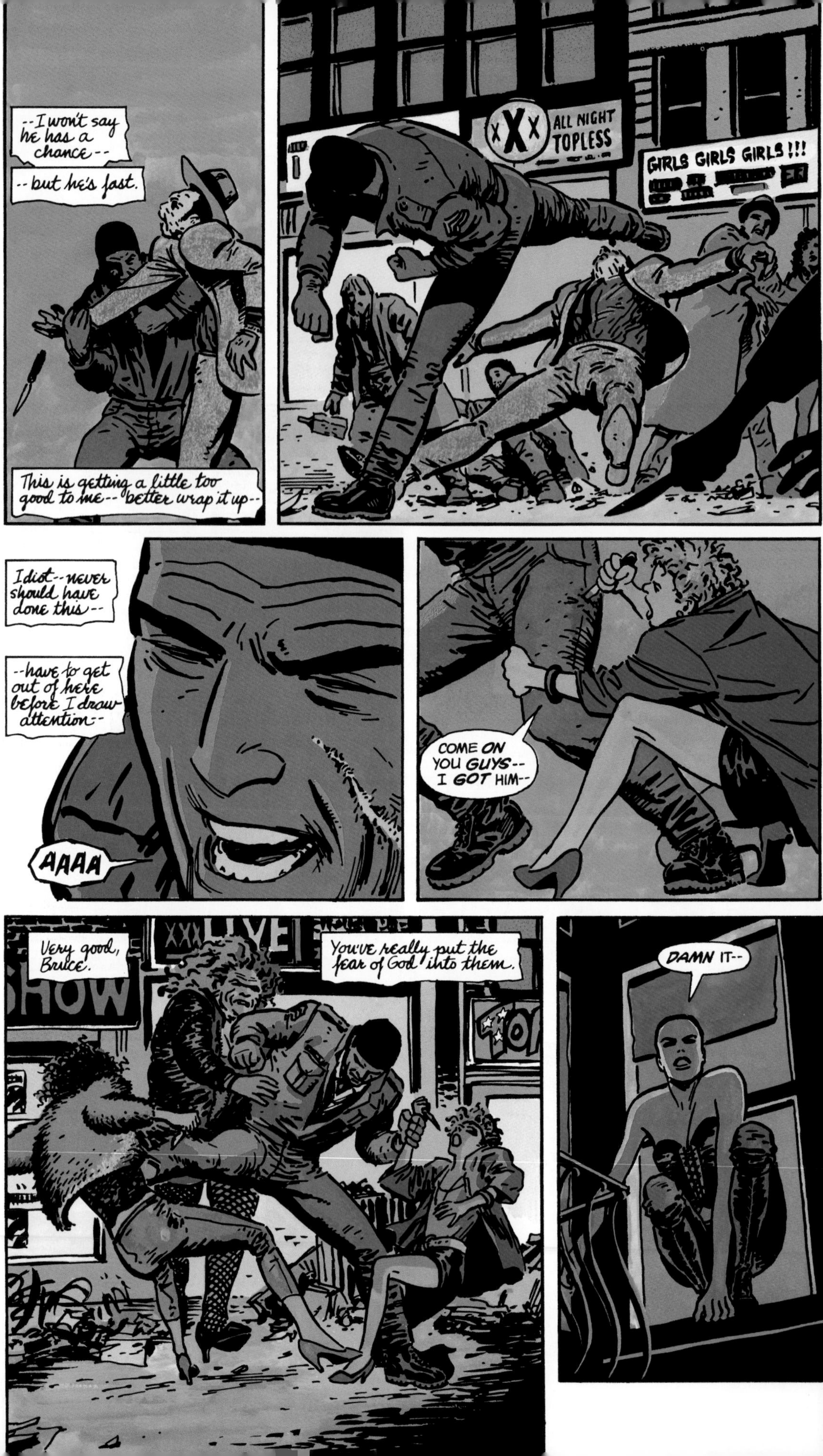
--I won't say he has a chance--
--but he's fast.
This is getting a little too good to me-- better wrap it up--
ALL NIGHT TOPLESS
GIRLS GIRLS GIRLS!!!
Idiot--never should have done this--
--have to get out of here before I draw attention--
AAAA
COME ON YOU GUYS-- I GOT HIM--
Very good, Bruce.
You've really put the fear of God into them.
DAMN IT--

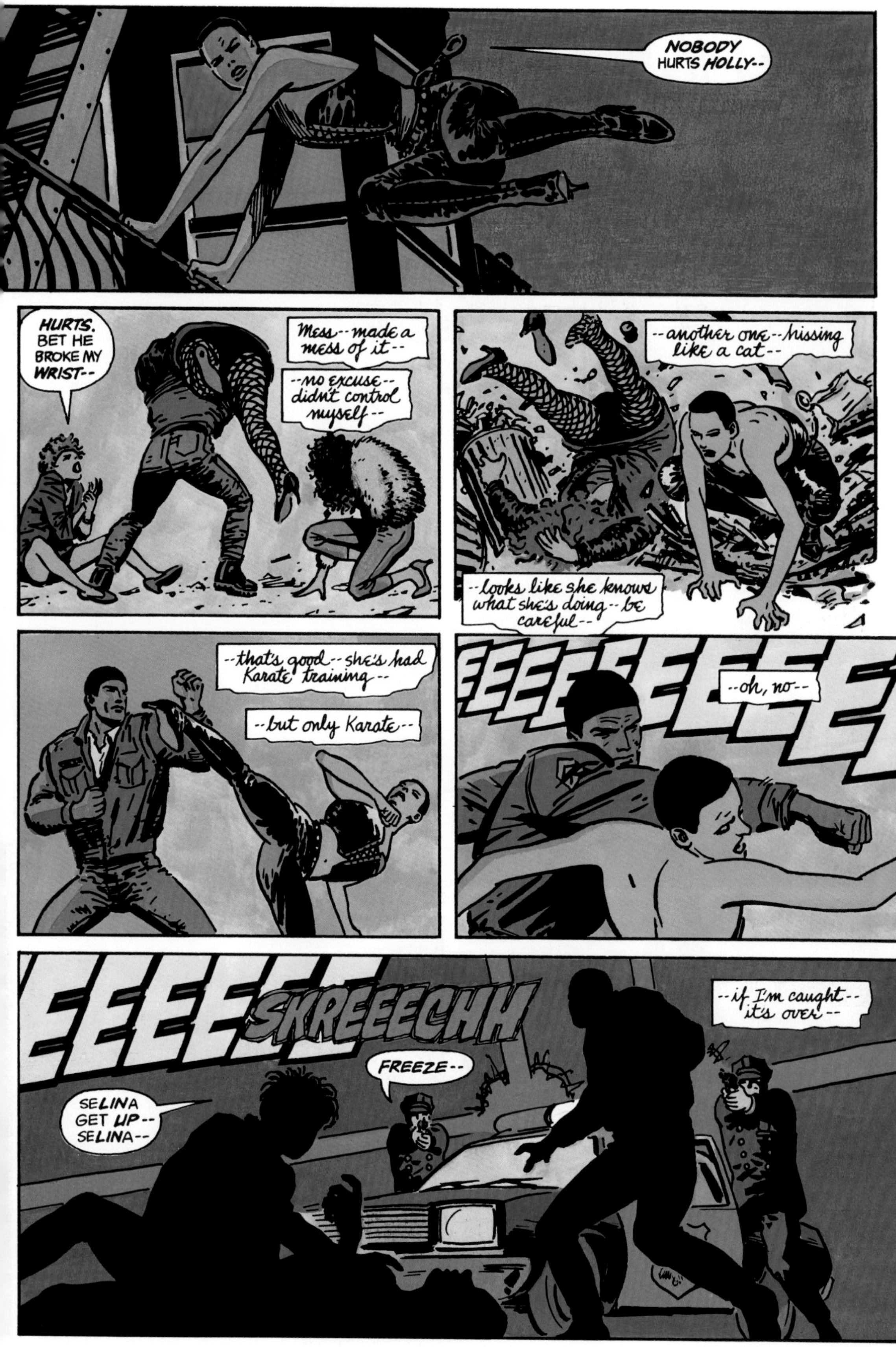
NOBODY HURTS HOLLY--
HURTS. BET HE BROKE MY WRIST--
Mess--made a mess of it--
--no excuse--didn't control myself--
--another one--hissing like a cat--
--looks like she knows what she's doing--be careful--
--that's good--she's had Karate training--
--but only Karate--
EEEEEEEEE
--oh, no--
EEEEEE
SKREEECHH
--if I'm caught--it's over--
FREEZE--
SELINA GET UP--SELINA--

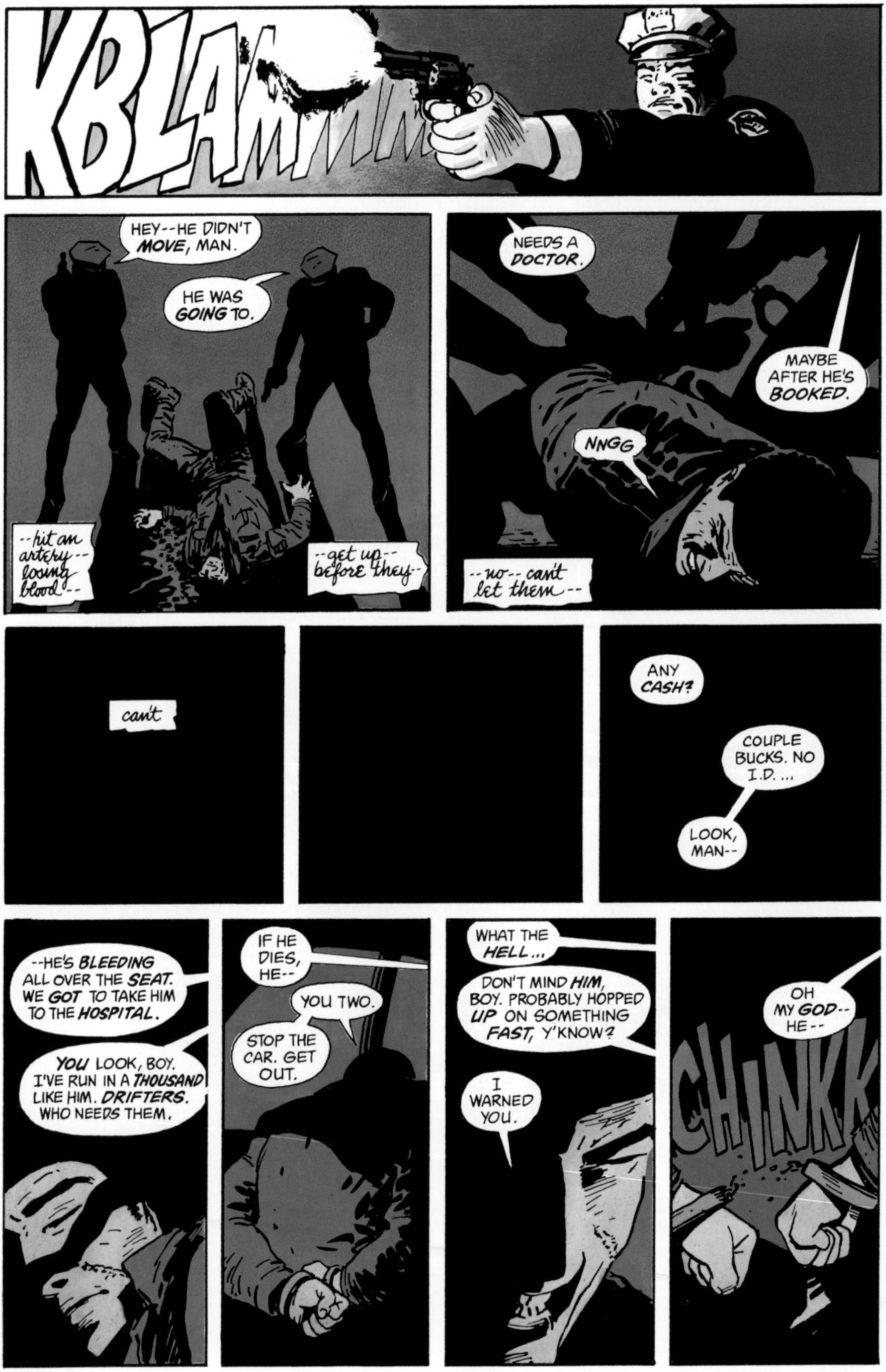
KBLAMMM
HEY--HE DIDN'T MOVE, MAN.
HE WAS GOING TO.
--hit an artery--losing blood--
--get up--before they--
NEEDS A DOCTOR.
MAYBE AFTER HE'S BOOKED.
NNGG
--no--can't let them--
can't
ANY CASH?
COUPLE BUCKS. NO I.D. ...
LOOK, MAN--
--HE'S BLEEDING ALL OVER THE SEAT. WE GOT TO TAKE HIM TO THE HOSPITAL.
YOU LOOK, BOY. I'VE RUN IN A THOUSAND LIKE HIM. DRIFTERS. WHO NEEDS THEM.
IF HE DIES, HE--
YOU TWO.
STOP THE CAR. GET OUT.
WHAT THE HELL...
DON'T MIND HIM, BOY. PROBABLY HOPPED UP ON SOMETHING FAST, Y'KNOW?
I WARNED YOU.
OH MY GOD--HE--
CHINKK

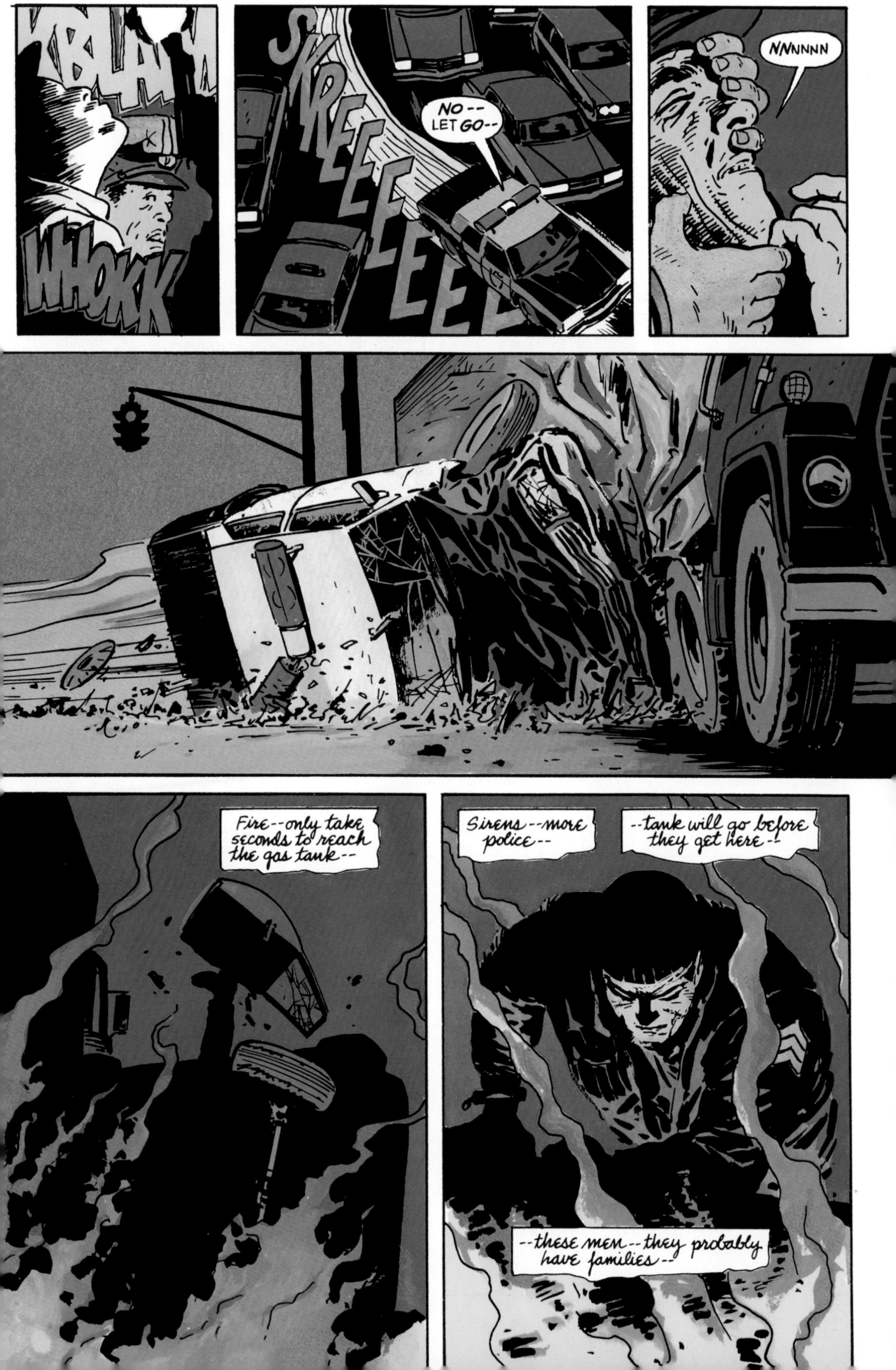
BLAM
WHOKK
SKREEEEEEE
NO -- LET GO--
NNNNNN
Fire--only take seconds to reach the gas tank--
Sirens--more police--
--tank will go before they get here--
--these men--they probably have families--

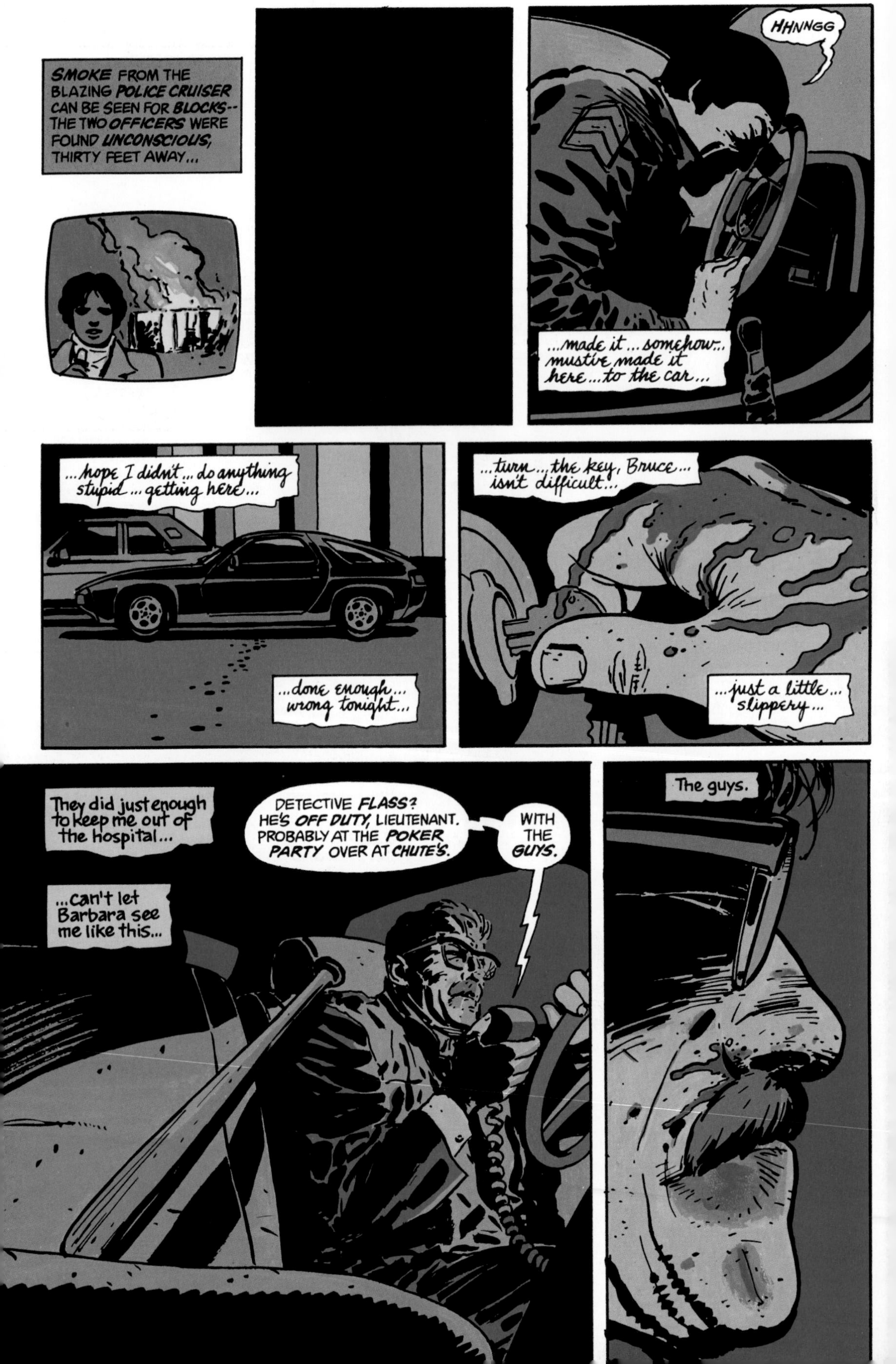
SMOKE FROM THE BLAZING POLICE CRUISER CAN BE SEEN FOR BLOCKS-- THE TWO OFFICERS WERE FOUND UNCONSCIOUS, THIRTY FEET AWAY...
HHNNGG
...made it ...somehow... mustive made it here ...to the car...
...hope I didn't ... do anything stupid ... getting here...
...done enough... wrong tonight...
...turn ... the key, Bruce... isn't difficult...
...just a little... slippery...
They did just enough to keep me out of the hospital...
...can't let Barbara see me like this...
DETECTIVE FLASS? HE'S OFF DUTY, LIEUTENANT. PROBABLY AT THE POKER PARTY OVER AT CHUTE'S.
WITH THE GUYS.
The guys.

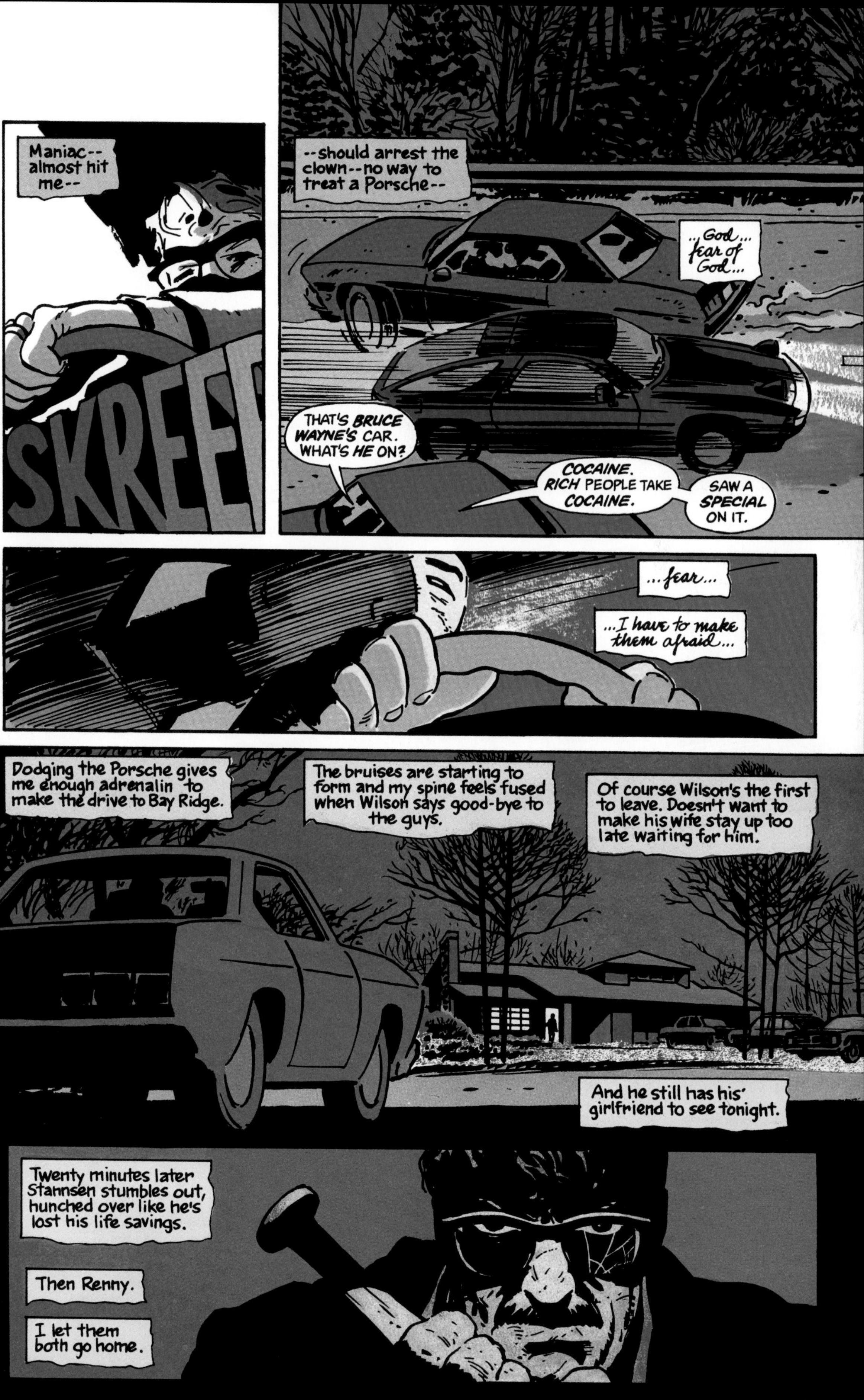

Maniac--almost hit me--
SKREEE
--should arrest the clown--no way to treat a Porsche--
...God... fear of God...
THAT'S BRUCE WAYNE'S CAR. WHAT'S HE ON?
COCAINE. RICH PEOPLE TAKE COCAINE.
SAW A SPECIAL ON IT.
...fear...
...I have to make them afraid...
Dodging the Porsche gives me enough adrenalin to make the drive to Bay Ridge.
The bruises are starting to form and my spine feels fused when Wilson says good-bye to the guys.
Of course Wilson's the first to leave. Doesn't want to make his wife stay up too late waiting for him.
And he still has his' girlfriend to see tonight.
Twenty minutes later Stannsen stumbles out, hunched over like he's lost his life savings.
Then Renny.
I let them both go home.

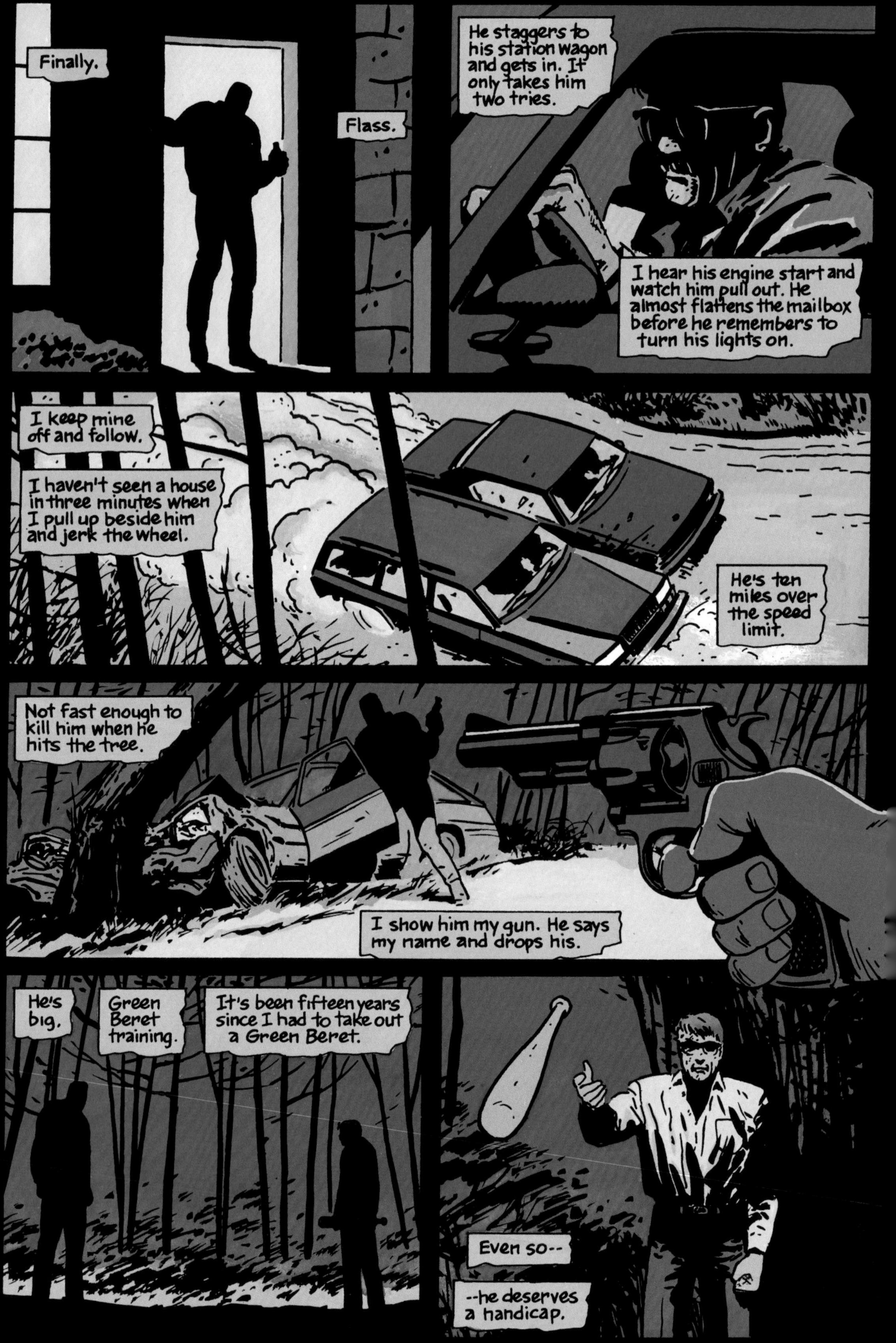
Finally.
Flass.
He staggers to his station wagon and gets in. It only takes him two tries.
I hear his engine start and watch him pull out. He almost flattens the mailbox before he remembers to turn his lights on.
I keep mine off and follow.
I haven't seen a house in three minutes when I pull up beside him and jerk the wheel.
He's ten miles over the speed limit.
Not fast enough to kill him when he hits the tree.
I show him my gun. He says my name and drops his.
He's big.
Green Beret training.
It's been fifteen years since I had to take out a Green Beret.
Even so--
--he deserves a handicap.

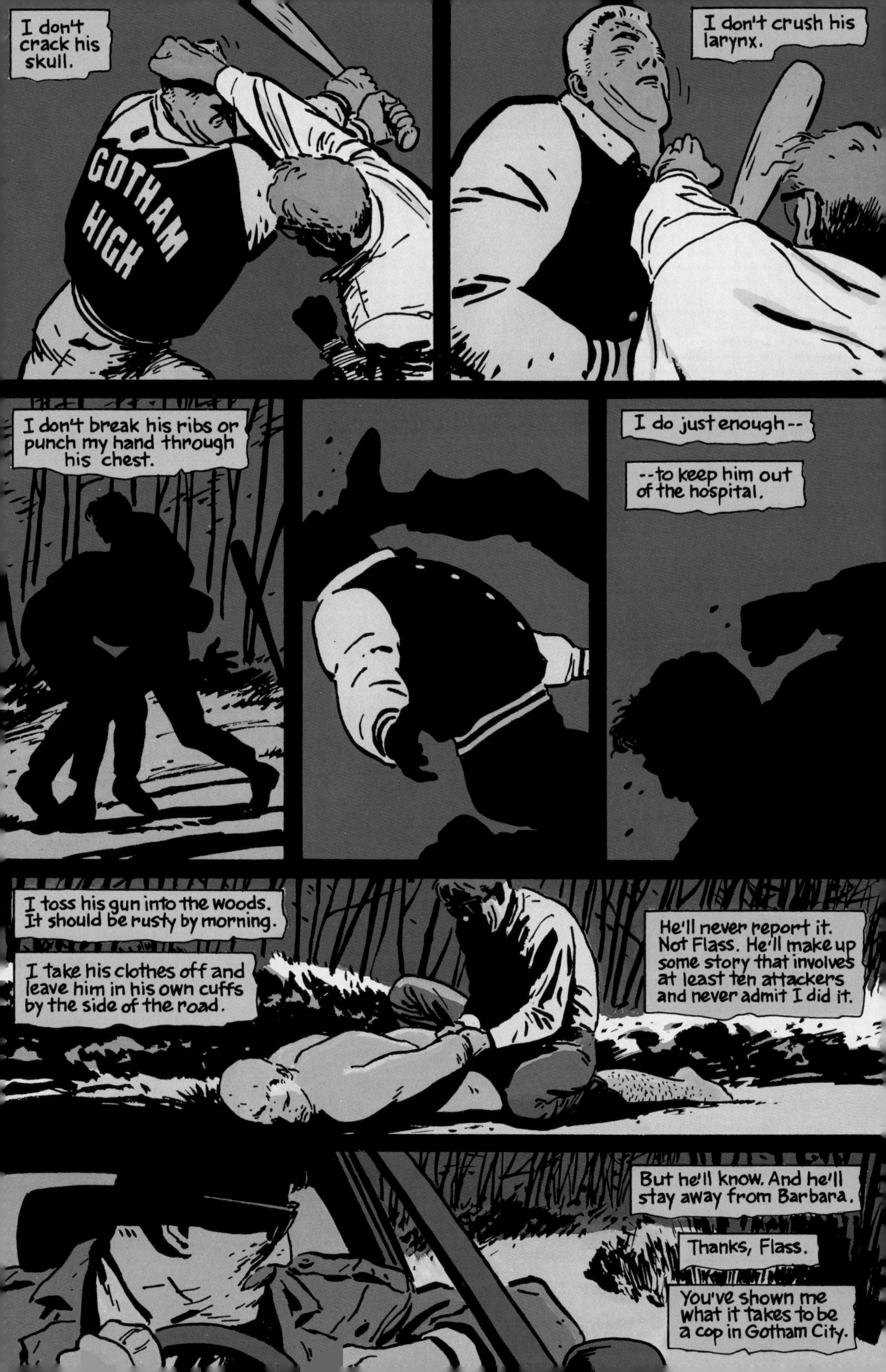

I don't crack his skull.
I don't crush his larynx.
GOTHAM HIGH
I don't break his ribs or punch my hand through his chest.
I do just enough--
--to keep him out of the hospital.
I toss his gun into the woods. It should be rusty by morning.
I take his clothes off and leave him in his own cuffs by the side of the road.
He'll never report it. Not Flass. He'll make up some story that involves at least ten attackers and never admit I did it.
But he'll know. And he'll stay away from Barbara.
Thanks, Flass.
You've shown me what it takes to be a cop in Gotham City.

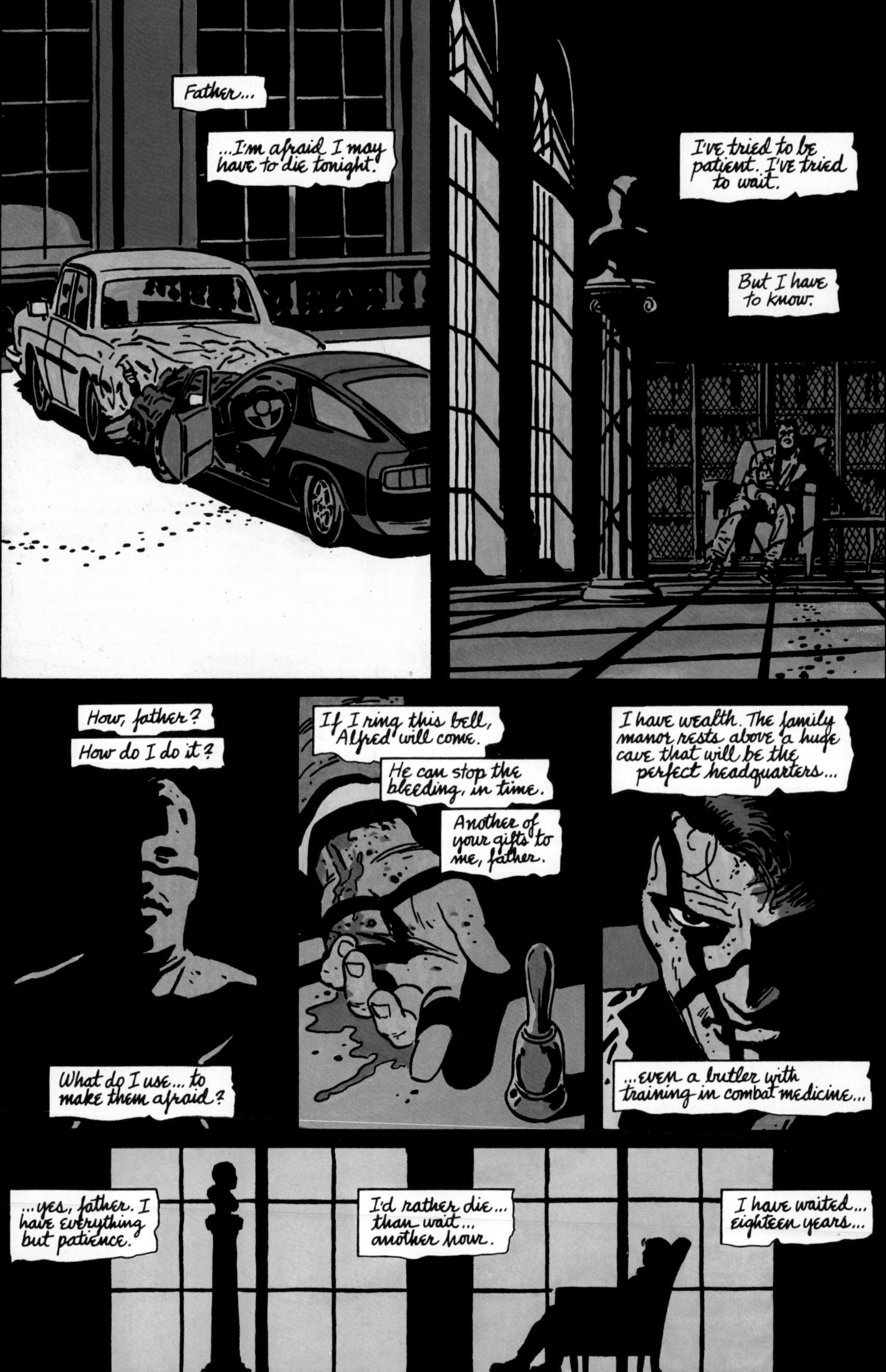
Father...
...I'm afraid I may have to die tonight.
I've tried to be patient. I've tried to wait.
But I have to know.
How, father?
How do I do it?
What do I use... to make them afraid?
If I ring this bell, Alfred will come.
He can stop the bleeding, in time.
Another of your gifts to me, father.
I have wealth. The family manor rests above a huge cave that will be the perfect headquarters...
...even a butler with training in combat medicine...
...yes, father. I have everything but patience.
I'd rather die... than wait... another hour.
I have waited... eighteen years...

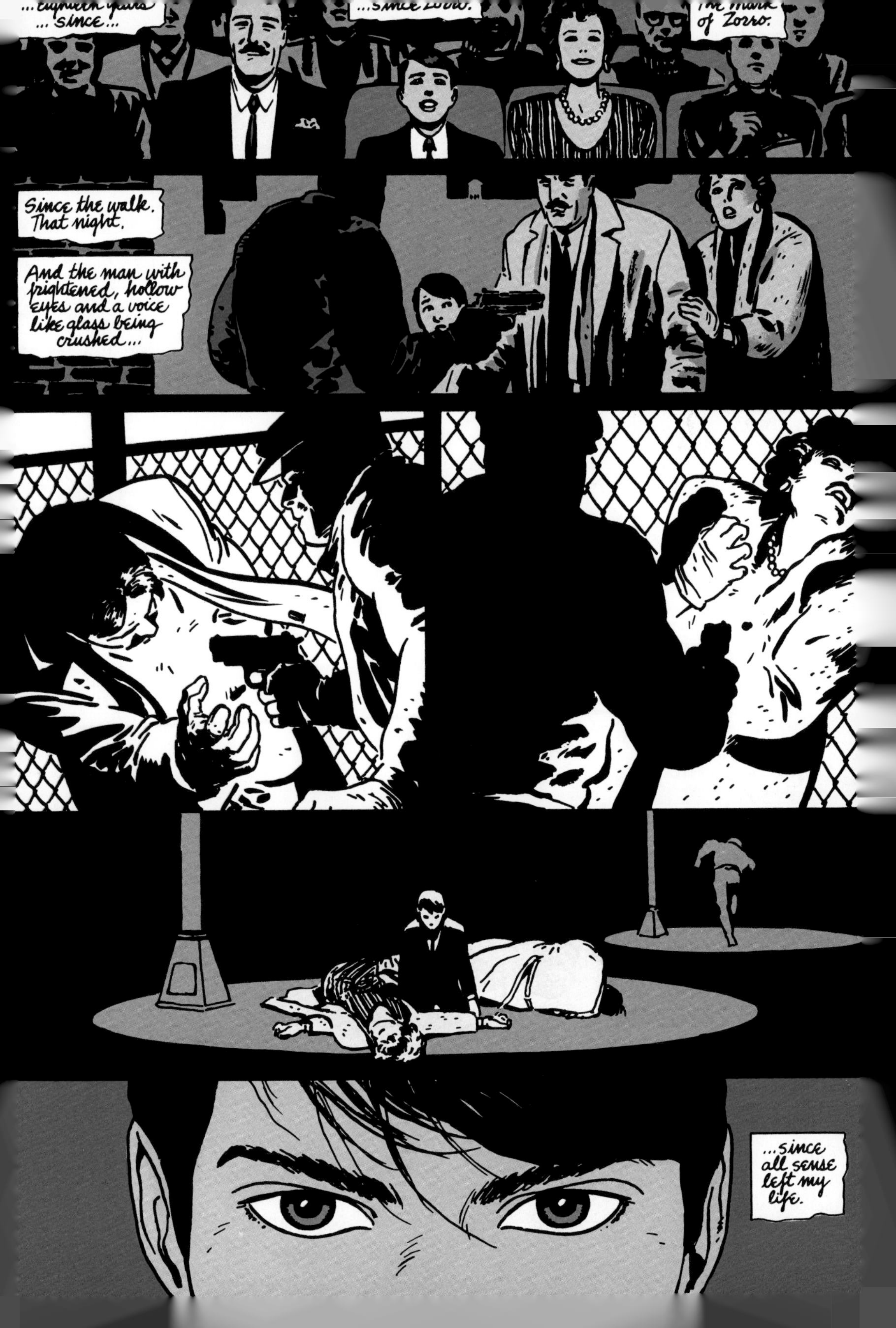
... since...
of Zorro.
Since the walk. That night.
And the man with frightened, hollow eyes and a voice like glass being crushed...
...since all sense left my life.

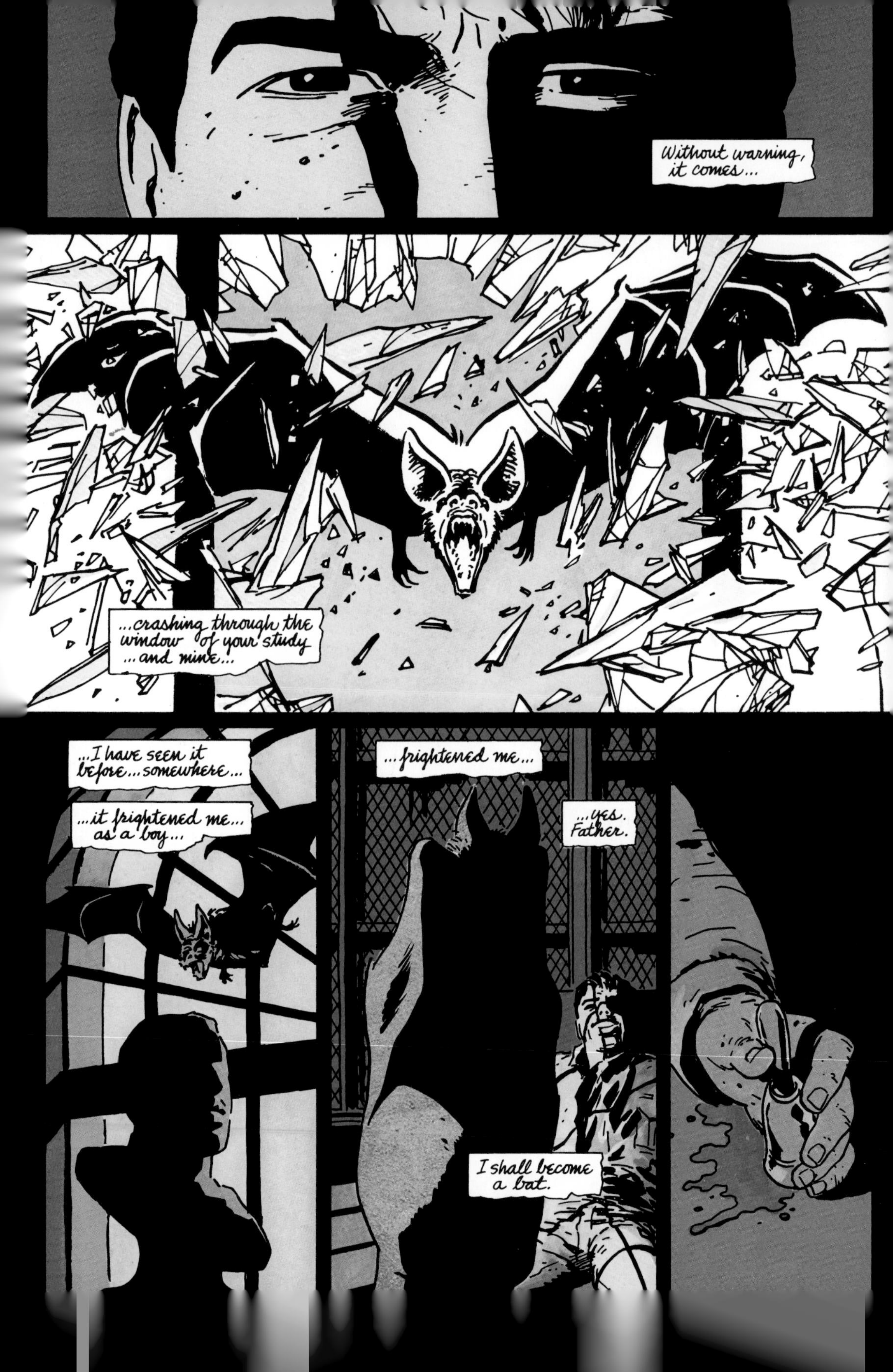
Without warning, it comes...
...crashing through the window of your study ...and mine...
...I have seen it before...somewhere...
...it frightened me... as a boy...
...frightened me...
...yes. Father.
I shall become a bat.

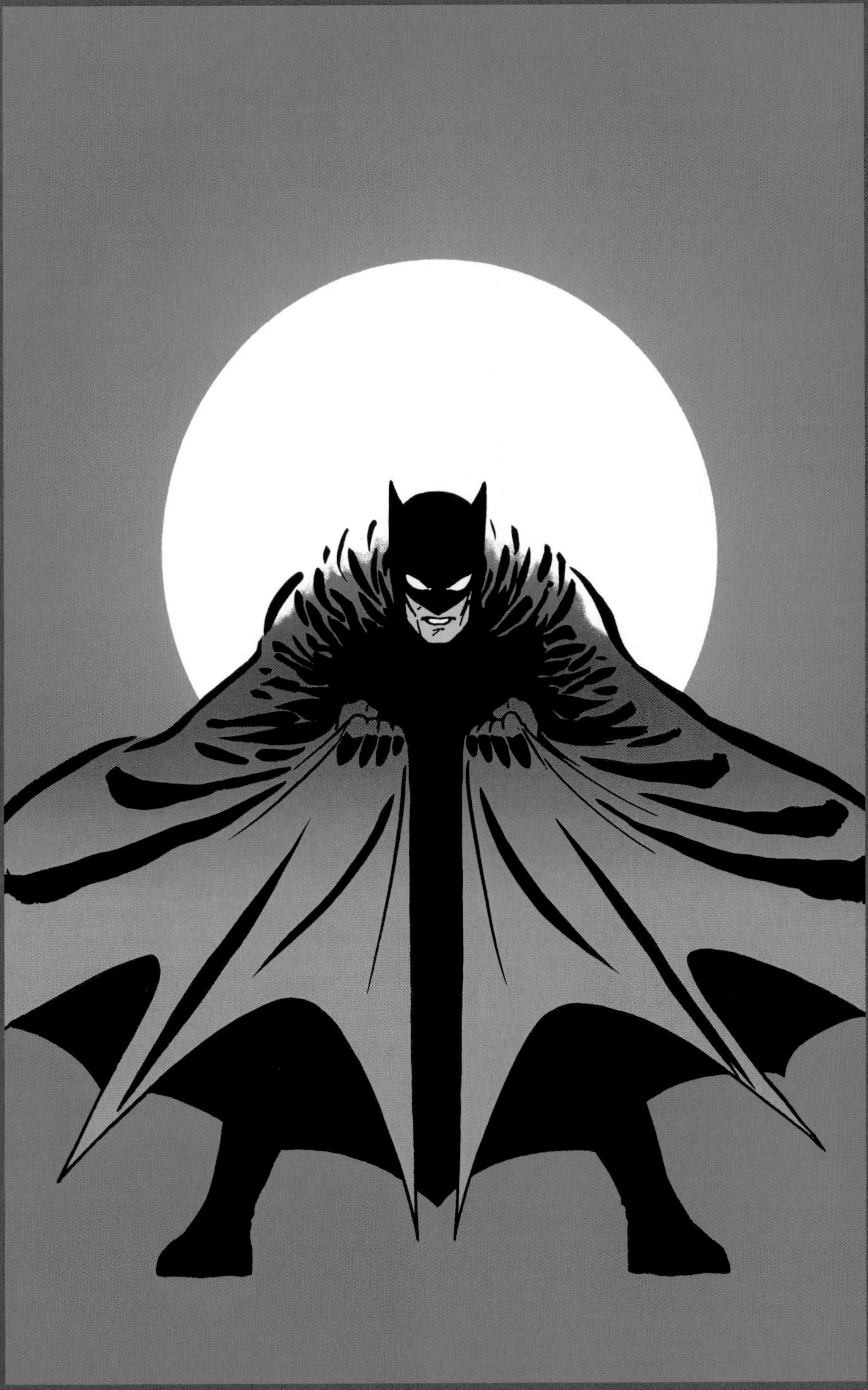

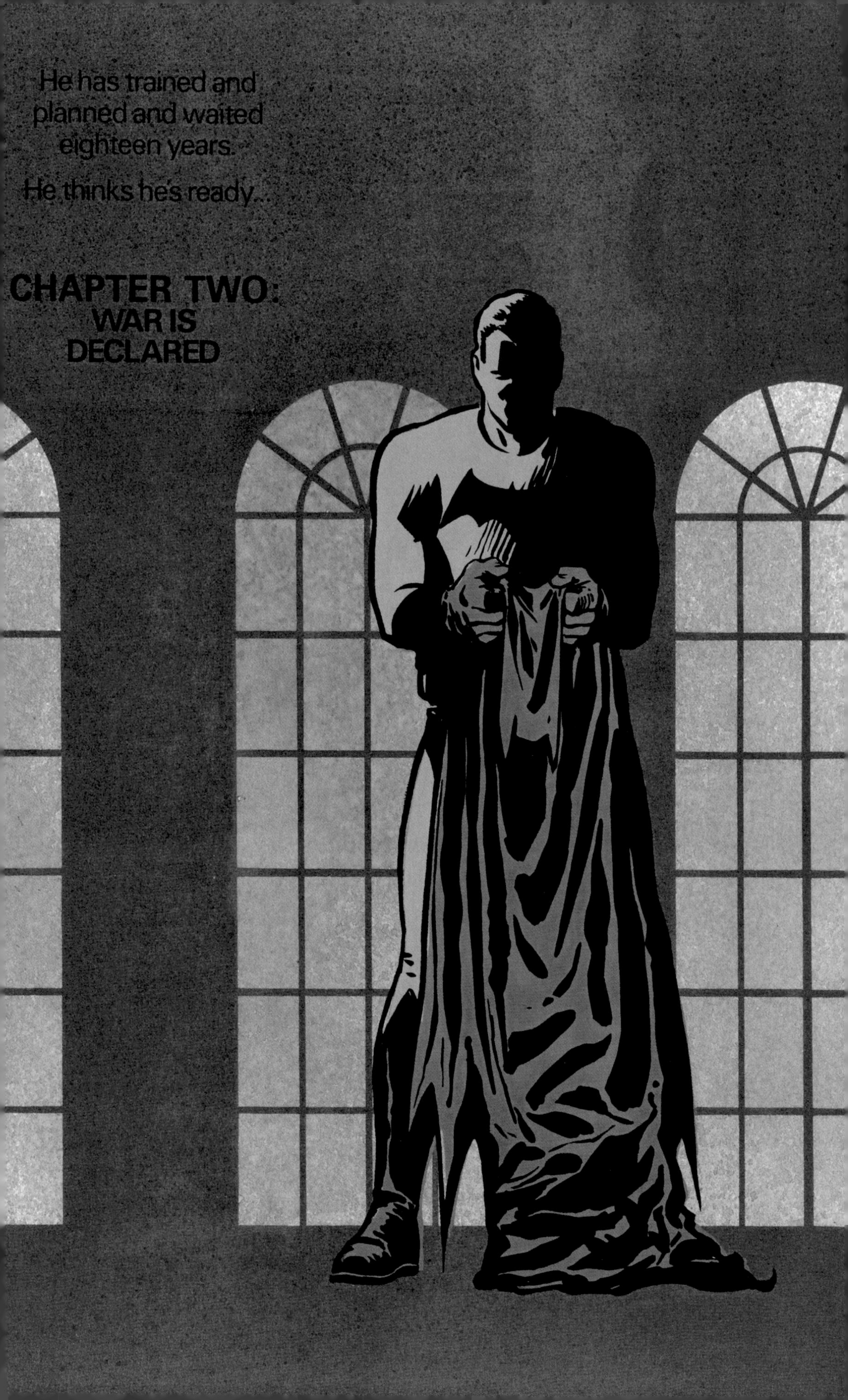
He has trained and planned and waited eighteen years.
He thinks he's ready...
CHAPTER TWO:
WAR IS DECLARED

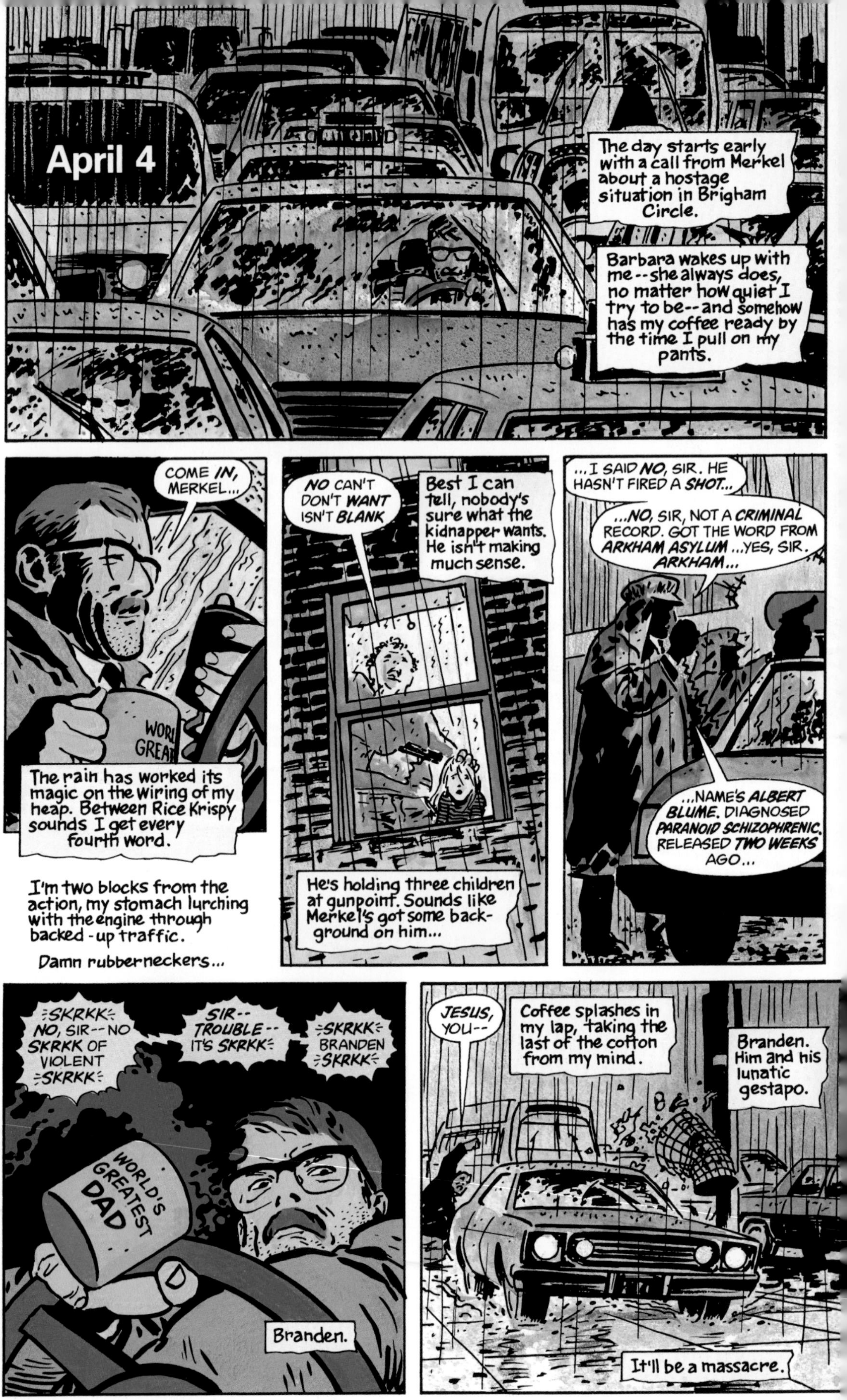
April 4
The day starts early with a call from Merkel about a hostage situation in Brigham Circle.
Barbara wakes up with me--she always does, no matter how quiet I try to be--and somehow has my coffee ready by the time I pull on my pants.
COME IN, MERKEL...
WORLD GREAT
The rain has worked its magic on the wiring of my heap. Between Rice Krispy sounds I get every fourth word.
I'm two blocks from the action, my stomach lurching with the engine through backed-up traffic.
Damn rubberneckers...
NO CAN'T DON'T WANT ISN'T BLANK
Best I can tell, nobody's sure what the kidnapper wants. He isn't making much sense.
He's holding three children at gunpoint. Sounds like Merkel's got some background on him...
...I SAID NO, SIR. HE HASN'T FIRED A SHOT...
...NO, SIR, NOT A CRIMINAL RECORD. GOT THE WORD FROM ARKHAM ASYLUM ...YES, SIR. ARKHAM...
...NAME'S ALBERT BLUME. DIAGNOSED PARANOID SCHIZOPHRENIC. RELEASED TWO WEEKS AGO...
SKRKK NO, SIR--NO SKRKK OF VIOLENT SKRKK
SIR--TROUBLE--IT'S SKRKK
SKRKK BRANDEN SKRKK
WORLD'S GREATEST DAD
Branden.
JESUS, YOU--
Coffee splashes in my lap, taking the last of the cotton from my mind.
Branden. Him and his lunatic gestapo.
It'll be a massacre.

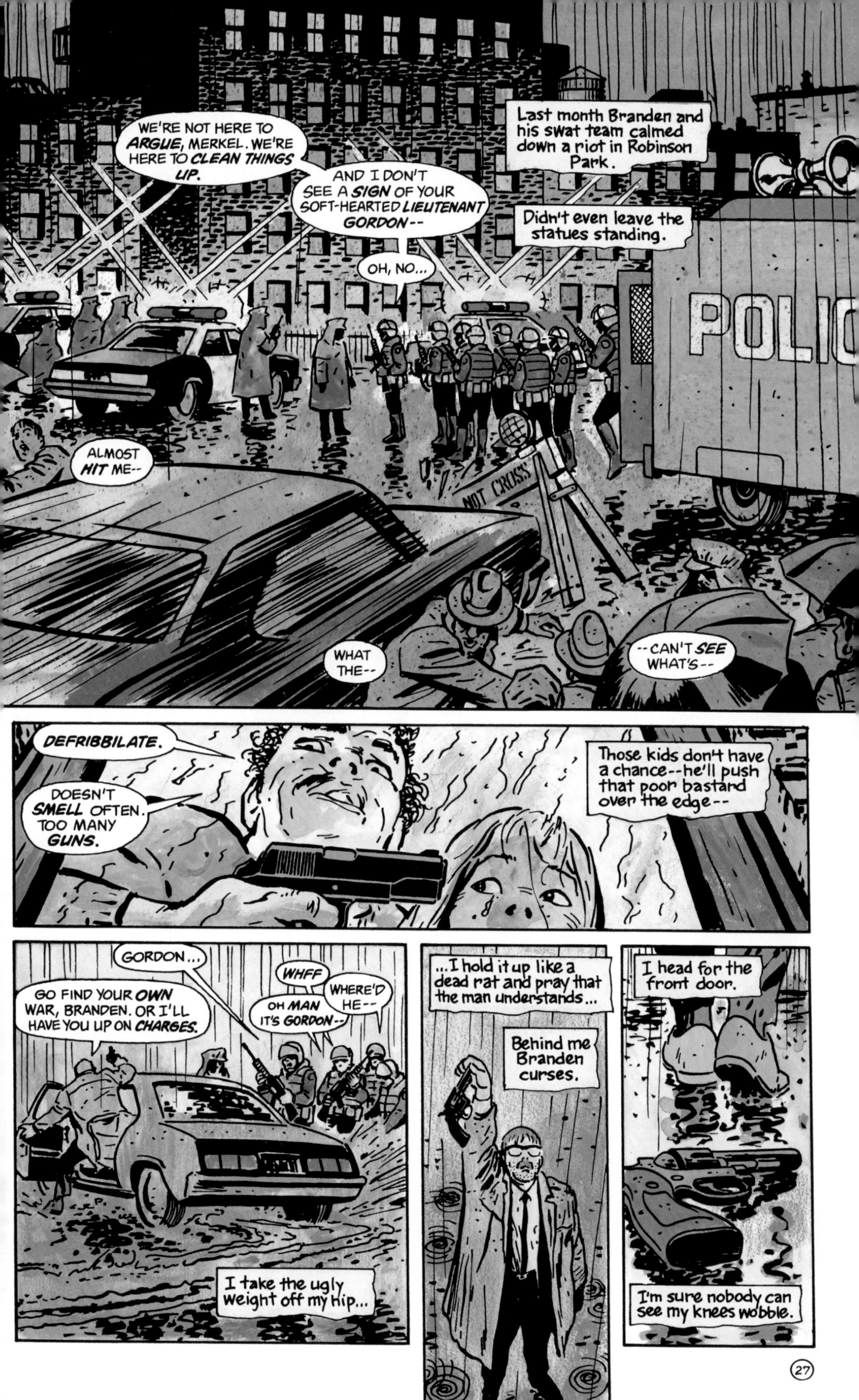
WE'RE NOT HERE TO ARGUE, MERKEL. WE'RE HERE TO CLEAN THINGS UP.
AND I DON'T SEE A SIGN OF YOUR SOFT-HEARTED LIEUTENANT GORDON--
OH, NO...
Last month Branden and his swat team calmed down a riot in Robinson Park.
Didn't even leave the statues standing.
POLIC
ALMOST HIT ME--
NOT CROSS
WHAT THE--
--CAN'T SEE WHAT'S--
DEFRIBBILATE.
DOESN'T SMELL OFTEN. TOO MANY GUNS.
Those kids don't have a chance--he'll push that poor bastard over the edge--
GORDON...
GO FIND YOUR OWN WAR, BRANDEN. OR I'LL HAVE YOU UP ON CHARGES.
WHFF
OH MAN IT'S GORDON--
WHERE'D HE--
I take the ugly weight off my hip...
...I hold it up like a dead rat and pray that the man understands...
Behind me Branden curses.
I head for the front door.
I'm sure nobody can see my knees wobble.

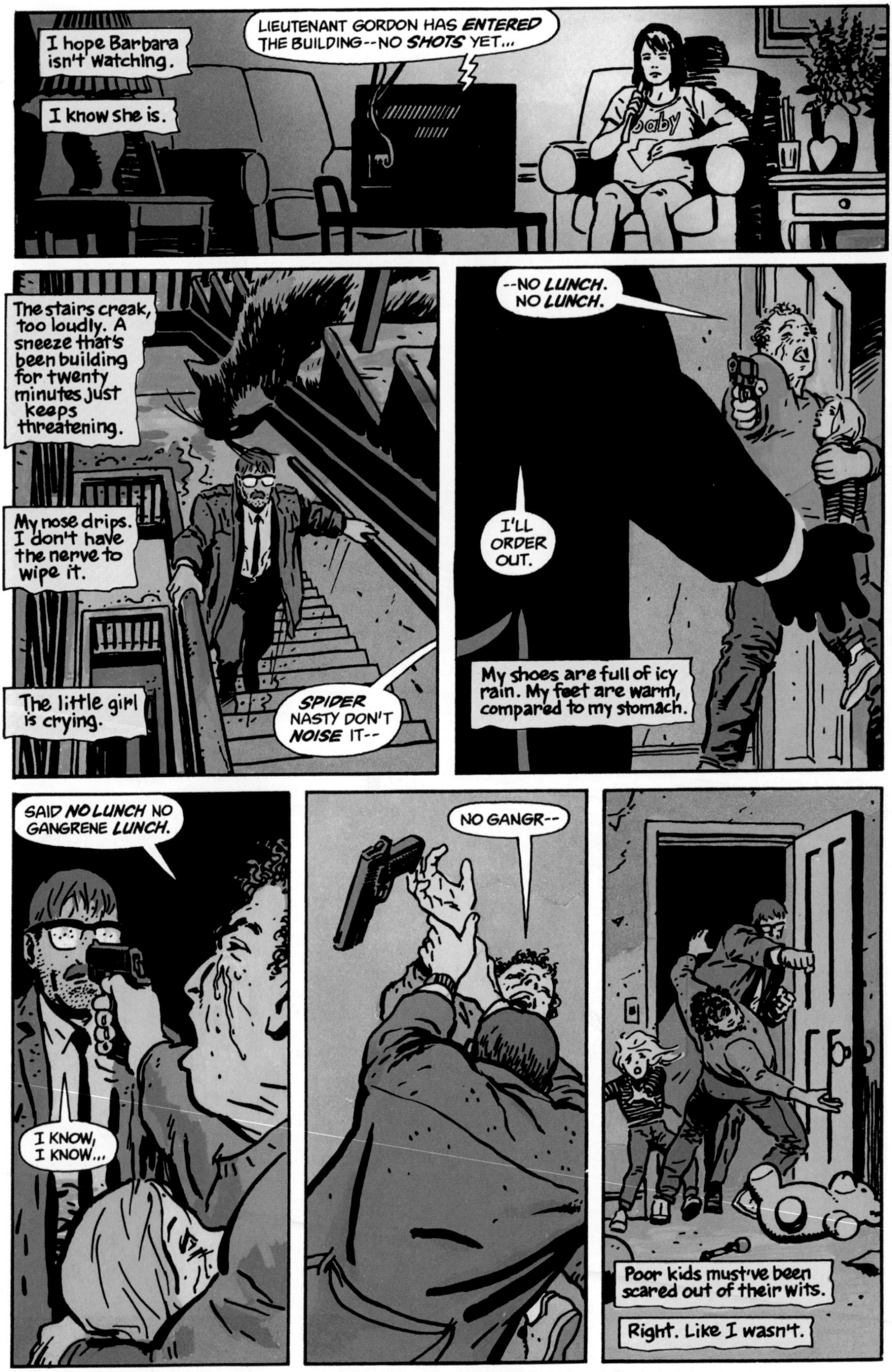
I hope Barbara isn't watching.
LIEUTENANT GORDON HAS ENTERED THE BUILDING--NO SHOTS YET...
I know she is.
baby
The stairs creak, too loudly. A sneeze that's been building for twenty minutes just keeps threatening.
My nose drips. I don't have the nerve to wipe it.
The little girl is crying.
SPIDER NASTY DON'T NOISE IT--
--NO LUNCH. NO LUNCH.
I'LL ORDER OUT.
My shoes are full of icy rain. My feet are warm, compared to my stomach.
SAID NO LUNCH NO GANGRENE LUNCH.
I KNOW, I KNOW...
NO GANGR--
Poor kids must've been scared out of their wits.
Right. Like I wasn't.

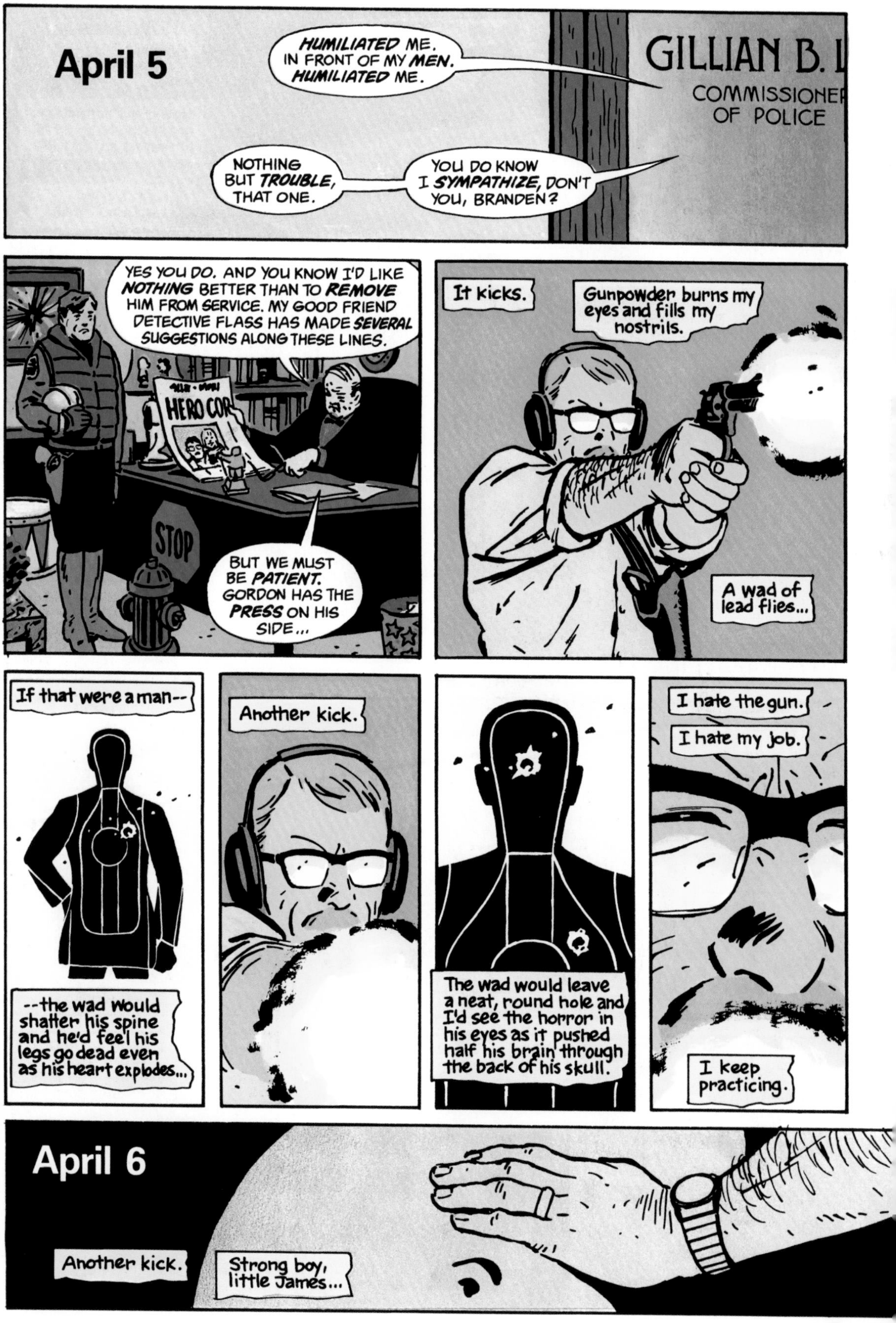
April 5
HUMILIATED ME. IN FRONT OF MY MEN. HUMILIATED ME.
GILLIAN B. L
COMMISSIONER OF POLICE
NOTHING BUT TROUBLE, THAT ONE.
YOU DO KNOW I SYMPATHIZE, DON'T YOU, BRANDEN?
YES YOU DO. AND YOU KNOW I'D LIKE NOTHING BETTER THAN TO REMOVE HIM FROM SERVICE. MY GOOD FRIEND DETECTIVE FLASS HAS MADE SEVERAL SUGGESTIONS ALONG THESE LINES.
HERO COP
STOP
BUT WE MUST BE PATIENT. GORDON HAS THE PRESS ON HIS SIDE...
It kicks.
Gunpowder burns my eyes and fills my nostrils.
A wad of lead flies...
If that were a man--
--the wad would shatter his spine and he'd feel his legs go dead even as his heart explodes...
Another kick.
The wad would leave a neat, round hole and I'd see the horror in his eyes as it pushed half his brain through the back of his skull.
I hate the gun.
I hate my job.
I keep practicing.
April 6
Another kick.
Strong boy, little James...

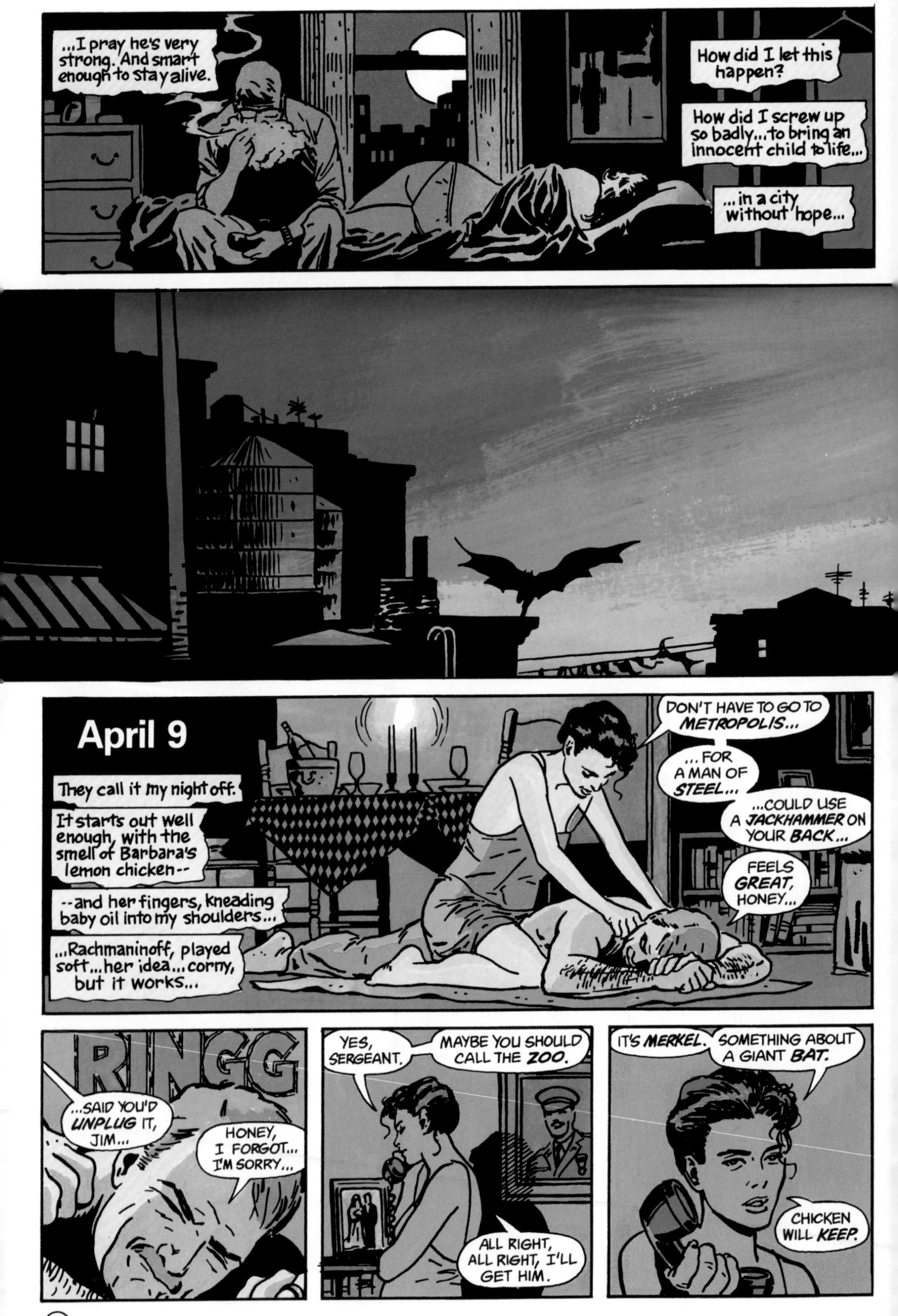

...I pray he's very strong. And smart enough to stay alive.
How did I let this happen?
How did I screw up so badly...to bring an innocent child to life...
...in a city without hope...
April 9
They call it my night off.
It starts out well enough, with the smell of Barbara's lemon chicken--
--and her fingers, kneading baby oil into my shoulders...
...Rachmaninoff, played soft...her idea...corny, but it works...
DON'T HAVE TO GO TO METROPOLIS...
...FOR A MAN OF STEEL...
...COULD USE A JACKHAMMER ON YOUR BACK...
FEELS GREAT, HONEY...
RINGG
...SAID YOU'D UNPLUG IT, JIM...
HONEY, I FORGOT... I'M SORRY...
YES, SERGEANT.
MAYBE YOU SHOULD CALL THE ZOO.
ALL RIGHT, ALL RIGHT, I'LL GET HIM.
IT'S MERKEL.
SOMETHING ABOUT A GIANT BAT.
CHICKEN WILL KEEP.

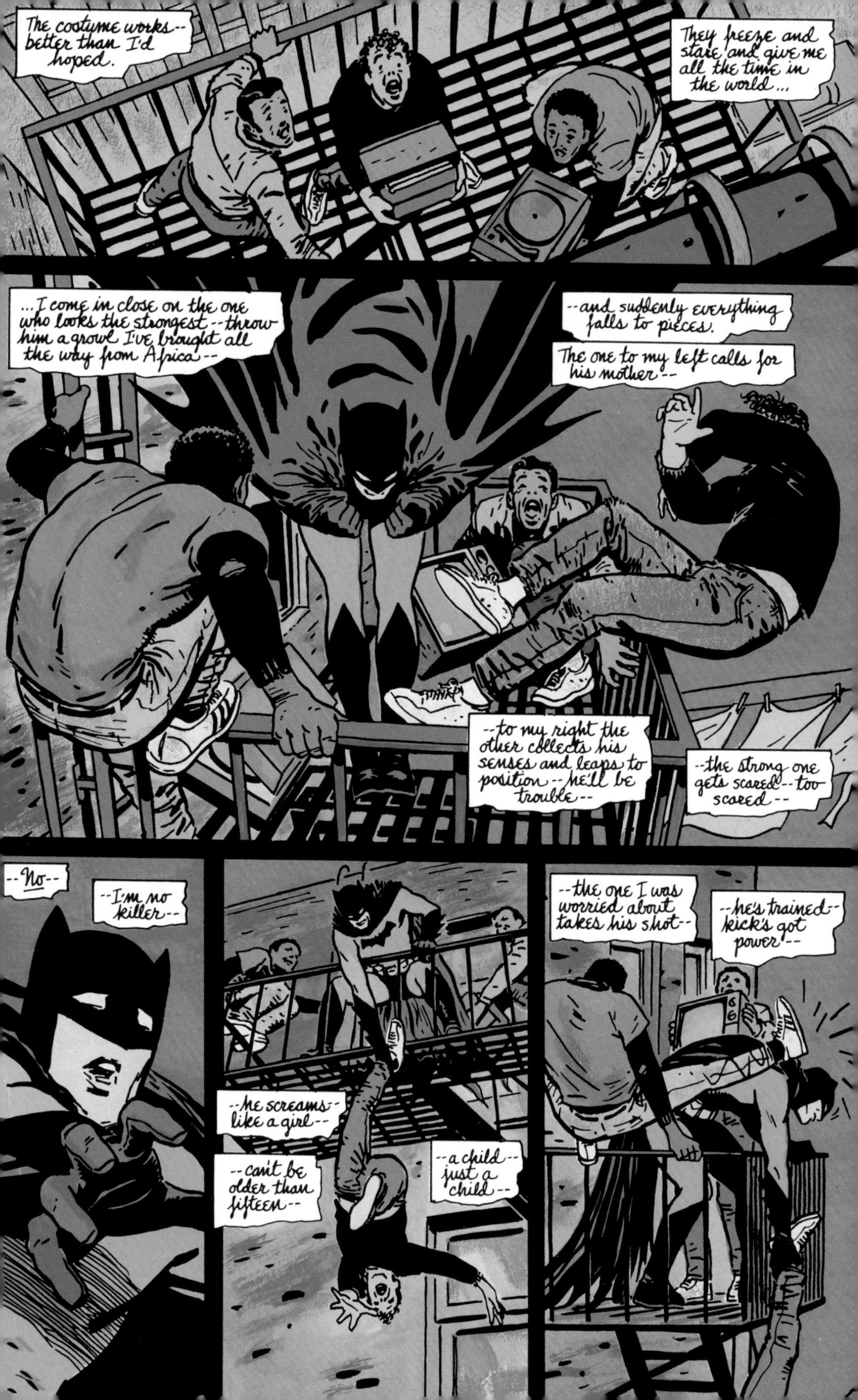
The costume works-- better than I'd hoped.
They freeze and stare and give me all the time in the world...
...I come in close on the one who looks the strongest--throw him a growl I've brought all the way from Africa--
--and suddenly everything falls to pieces.
The one to my left calls for his mother--
--to my right the other collects his senses and leaps to position--he'll be trouble--
--the strong one gets scared--too scared--
--No--
--I'm no killer--
--he screams--like a girl--
--can't be older than fifteen--
--a child--just a child--
--the one I was worried about takes his shot--
--he's trained--kick's got power--

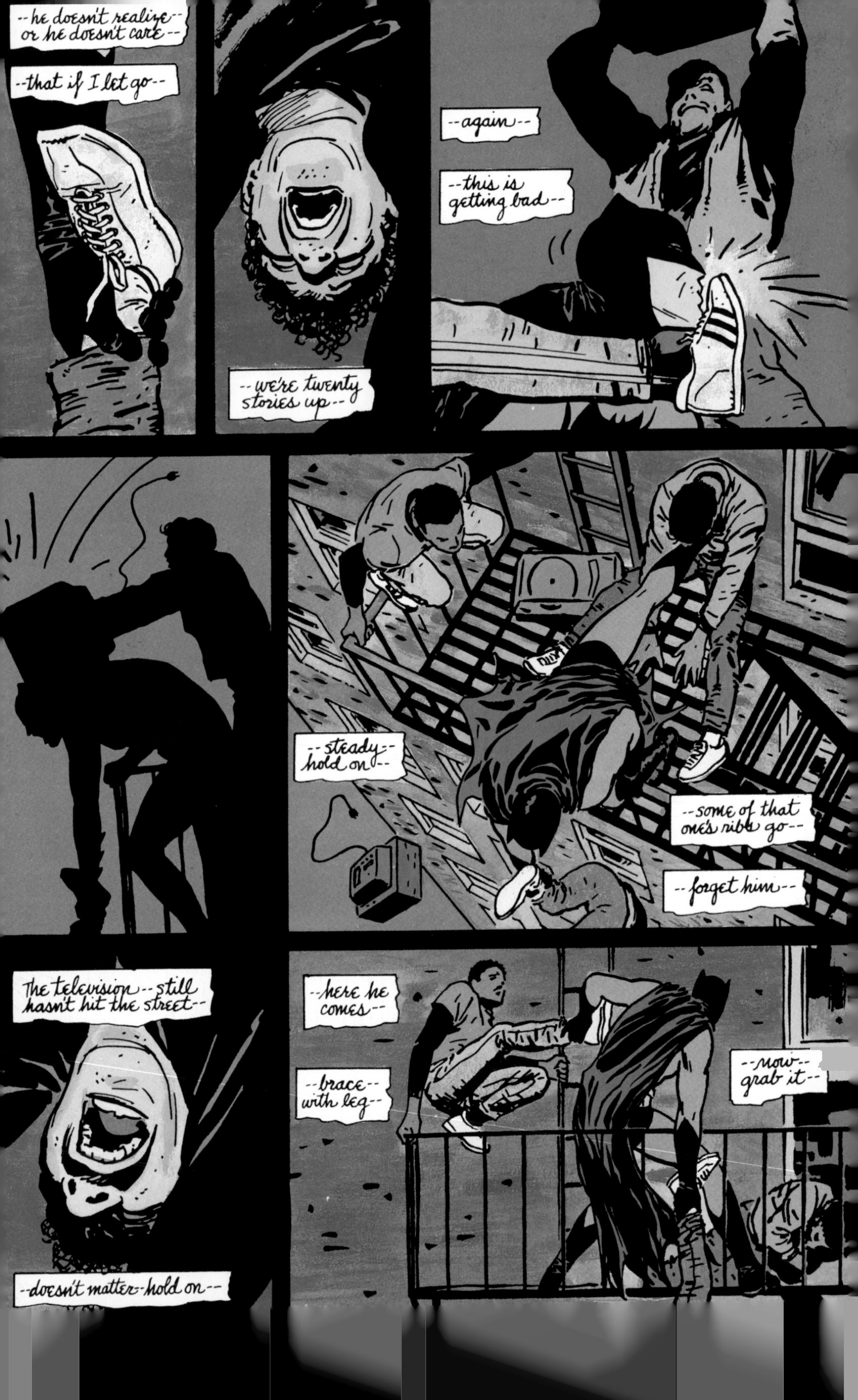
--he doesn't realize--
or he doesn't care--
--that if I let go--
--we're twenty stories up--
--again--
--this is getting bad--
--steady--
hold on--
--some of that one's ribs go--
--forget him--
The television--still hasn't hit the street--
--doesn't matter-hold on--
--here he comes--
--brace with leg--
--now--
grab it--

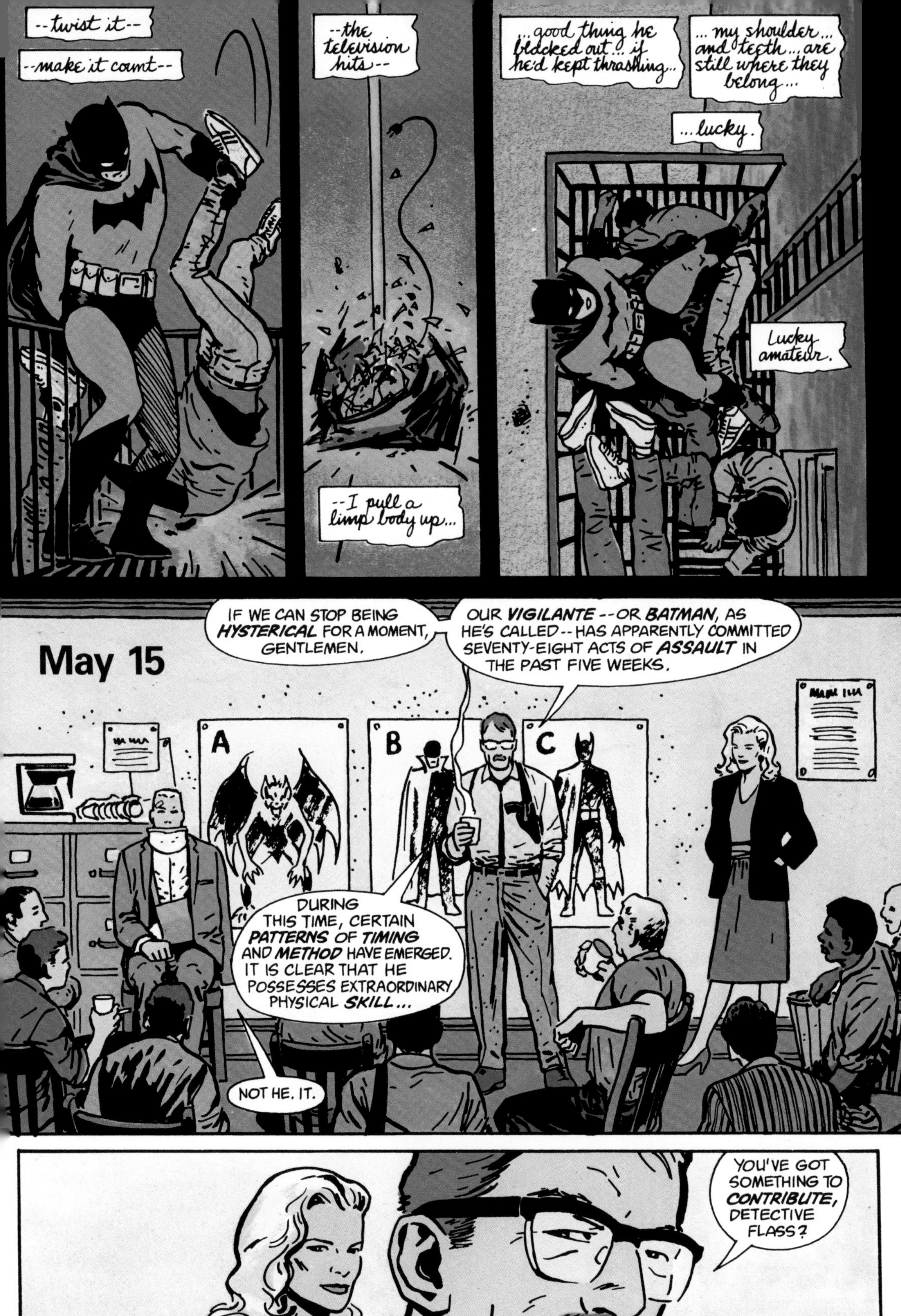

--twist it--
--make it count--
--the television hits--
--I pull a limp body up...
...good thing he blacked out... if he'd kept thrashing...
...my shoulder... and teeth... are still where they belong...
...lucky.
Lucky amateur.
May 15
IF WE CAN STOP BEING HYSTERICAL FOR A MOMENT, GENTLEMEN.
OUR VIGILANTE--OR BATMAN, AS HE'S CALLED--HAS APPARENTLY COMMITTED SEVENTY-EIGHT ACTS OF ASSAULT IN THE PAST FIVE WEEKS.
A
B
C
DURING THIS TIME, CERTAIN PATTERNS OF TIMING AND METHOD HAVE EMERGED. IT IS CLEAR THAT HE POSSESSES EXTRAORDINARY PHYSICAL SKILL...
NOT HE. IT.
YOU'VE GOT SOMETHING TO CONTRIBUTE, DETECTIVE FLASS?

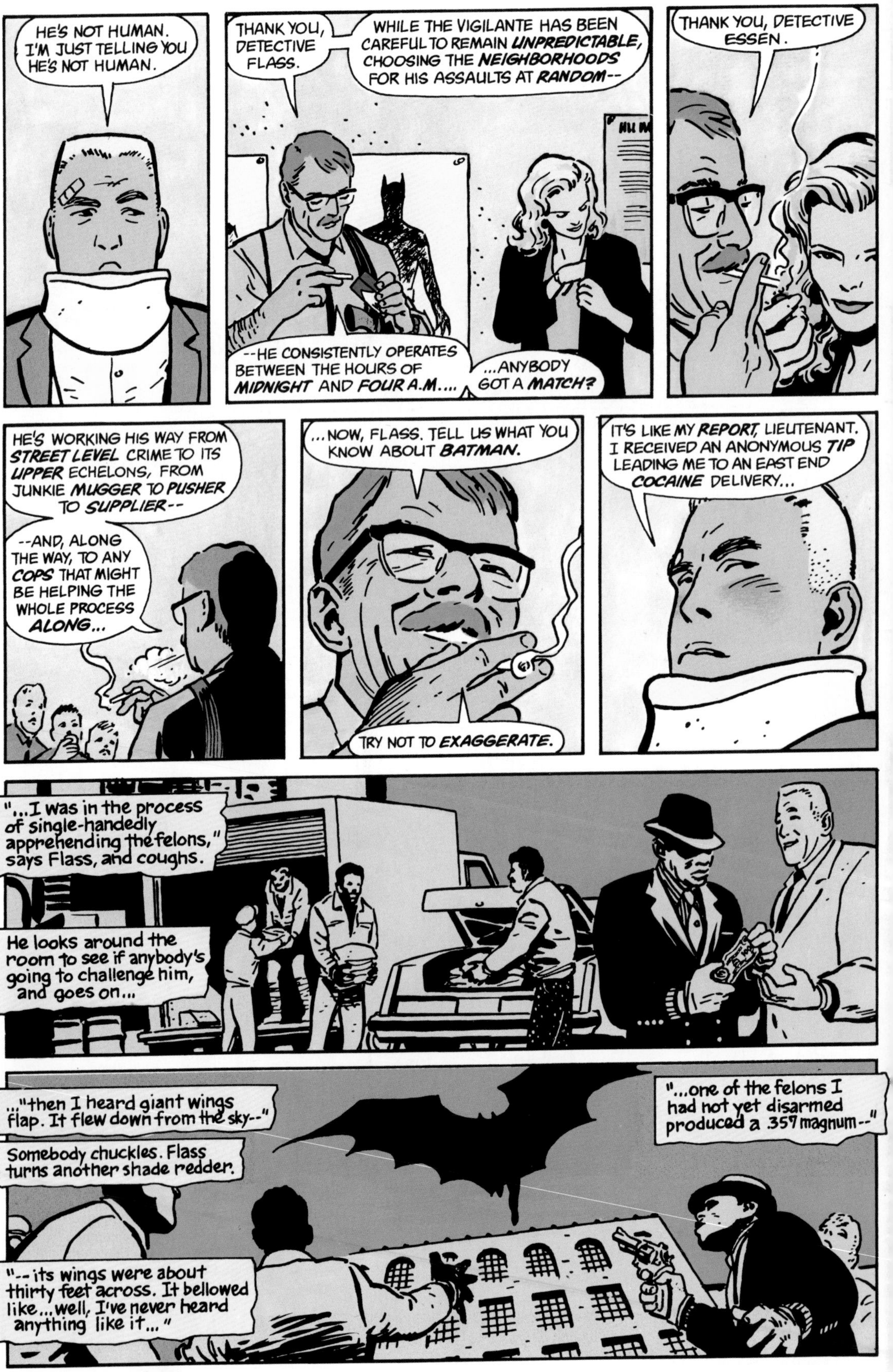
HE'S NOT HUMAN. I'M JUST TELLING YOU HE'S NOT HUMAN.
THANK YOU, DETECTIVE FLASS.
WHILE THE VIGILANTE HAS BEEN CAREFUL TO REMAIN UNPREDICTABLE, CHOOSING THE NEIGHBORHOODS FOR HIS ASSAULTS AT RANDOM--
--HE CONSISTENTLY OPERATES BETWEEN THE HOURS OF MIDNIGHT AND FOUR A.M....
...ANYBODY GOT A MATCH?
THANK YOU, DETECTIVE ESSEN.
HE'S WORKING HIS WAY FROM STREET LEVEL CRIME TO ITS UPPER ECHELONS, FROM JUNKIE MUGGER TO PUSHER TO SUPPLIER--
--AND, ALONG THE WAY, TO ANY COPS THAT MIGHT BE HELPING THE WHOLE PROCESS ALONG...
...NOW, FLASS. TELL US WHAT YOU KNOW ABOUT BATMAN.
TRY NOT TO EXAGGERATE.
IT'S LIKE MY REPORT, LIEUTENANT. I RECEIVED AN ANONYMOUS TIP LEADING ME TO AN EAST END COCAINE DELIVERY...
"...I was in the process of single-handedly apprehending the felons," says Flass, and coughs.
He looks around the room to see if anybody's going to challenge him, and goes on...
..."then I heard giant wings flap. It flew down from the sky--"
Somebody chuckles. Flass turns another shade redder.
"...one of the felons I had not yet disarmed produced a .357 magnum--"
"--its wings were about thirty feet across. It bellowed like...well, I've never heard anything like it..."

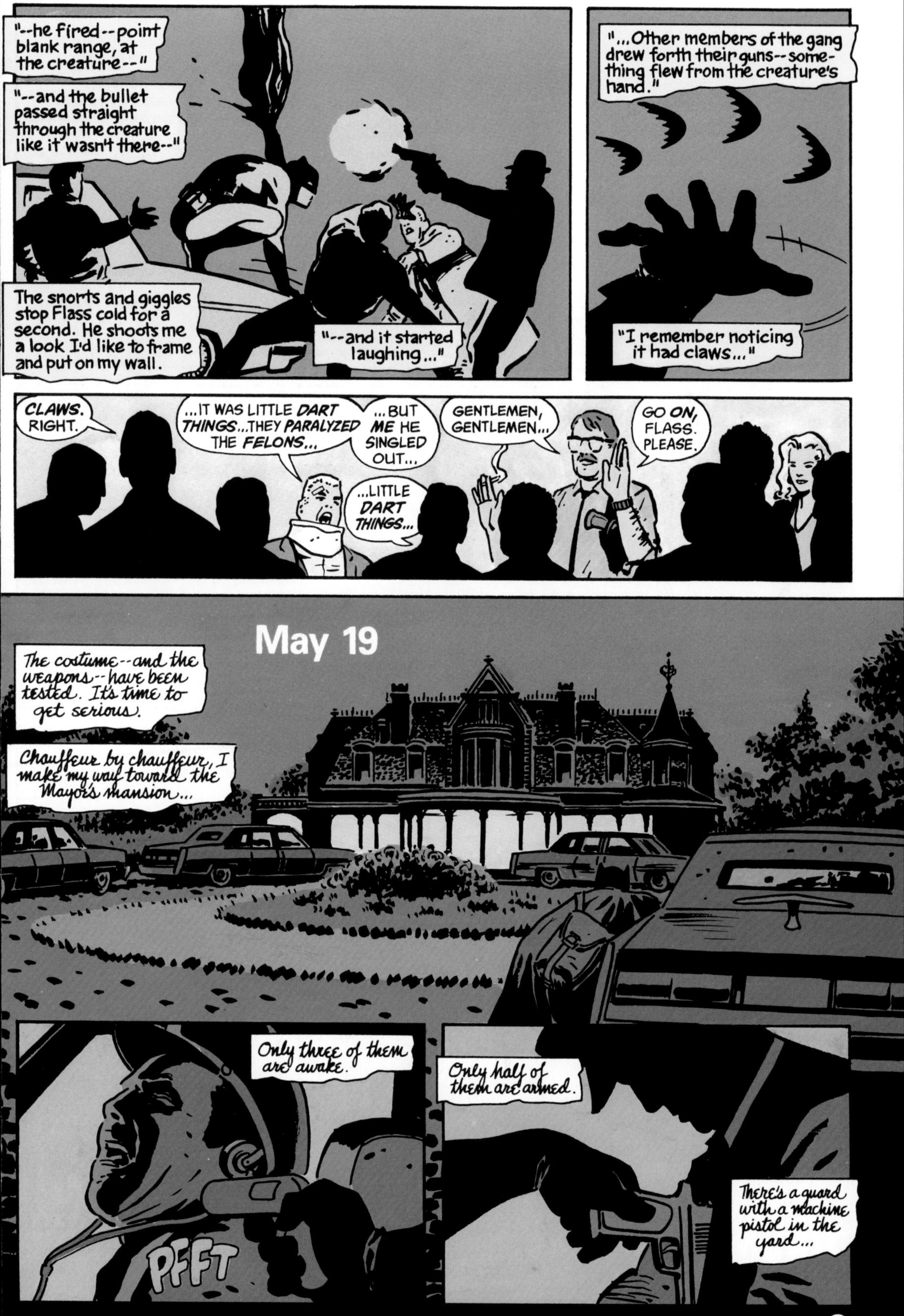
"--he fired--point blank range, at the creature--"
"--and the bullet passed straight through the creature like it wasn't there--"
The snorts and giggles stop Flass cold for a second. He shoots me a look I'd like to frame and put on my wall.
"--and it started laughing..."
"...Other members of the gang drew forth their guns--something flew from the creature's hand."
"I remember noticing it had claws..."
CLAWS. RIGHT.
...IT WAS LITTLE DART THINGS...THEY PARALYZED THE FELONS...
...BUT ME HE SINGLED OUT...
...LITTLE DART THINGS...
GENTLEMEN, GENTLEMEN...
GO ON, FLASS. PLEASE.
May 19
The costume--and the weapons--have been tested. It's time to get serious.
Chauffeur by chauffeur, I make my way toward the Mayor's mansion...
Only three of them are awake.
PFFT
Only half of them are armed.
There's a guard with a machine pistol in the yard...

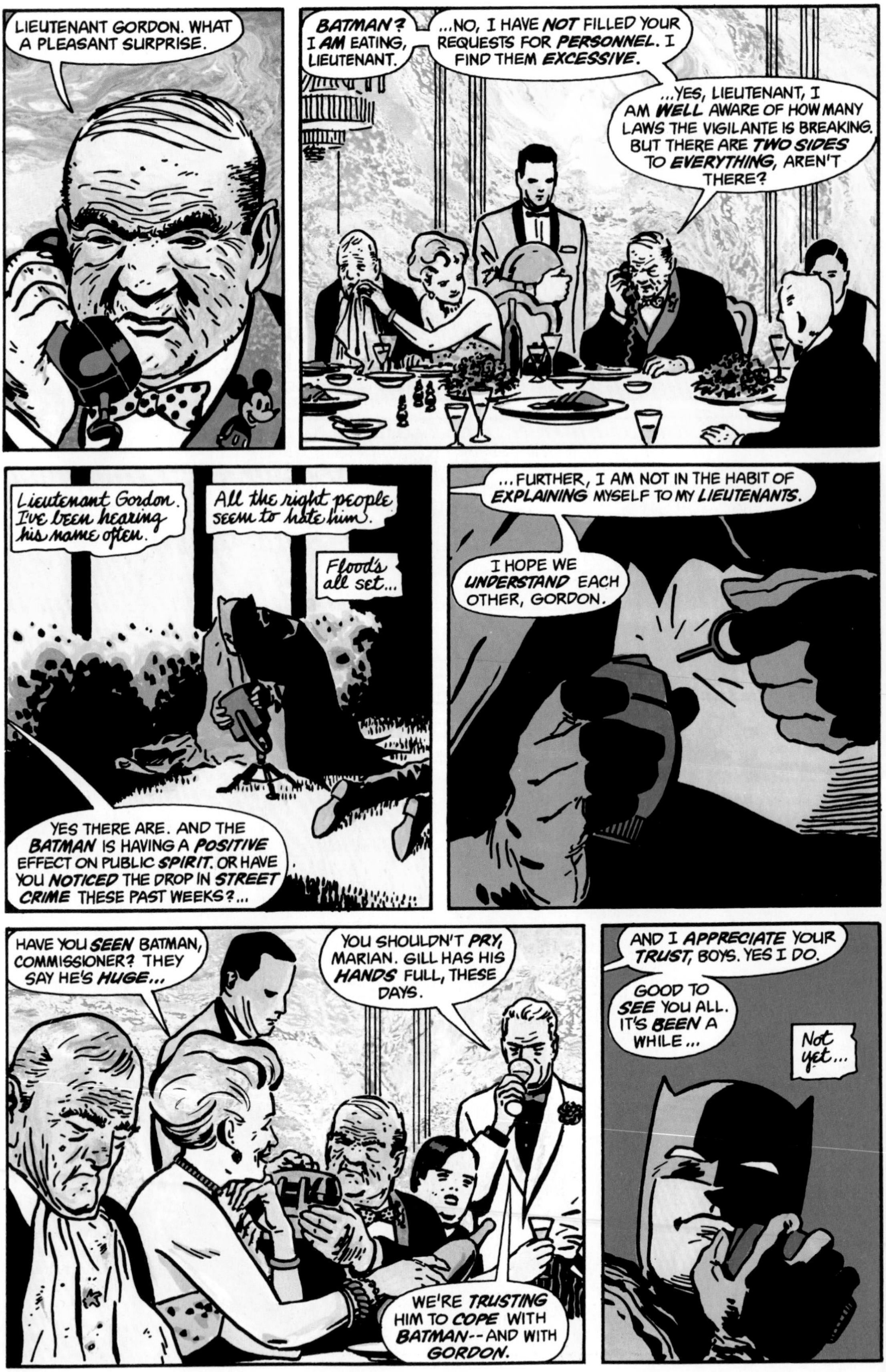
LIEUTENANT GORDON. WHAT A PLEASANT SURPRISE.
BATMAN? I AM EATING, LIEUTENANT.
...NO, I HAVE NOT FILLED YOUR REQUESTS FOR PERSONNEL. I FIND THEM EXCESSIVE.
...YES, LIEUTENANT, I AM WELL AWARE OF HOW MANY LAWS THE VIGILANTE IS BREAKING. BUT THERE ARE TWO SIDES TO EVERYTHING, AREN'T THERE?
Lieutenant Gordon. I've been hearing his name often.
All the right people seem to hate him.
Flood's all set...
YES THERE ARE. AND THE BATMAN IS HAVING A POSITIVE EFFECT ON PUBLIC SPIRIT. OR HAVE YOU NOTICED THE DROP IN STREET CRIME THESE PAST WEEKS?...
...FURTHER, I AM NOT IN THE HABIT OF EXPLAINING MYSELF TO MY LIEUTENANTS.
I HOPE WE UNDERSTAND EACH OTHER, GORDON.
HAVE YOU SEEN BATMAN, COMMISSIONER? THEY SAY HE'S HUGE...
YOU SHOULDN'T PRY, MARIAN. GILL HAS HIS HANDS FULL, THESE DAYS.
WE'RE TRUSTING HIM TO COPE WITH BATMAN--AND WITH GORDON.
AND I APPRECIATE YOUR TRUST, BOYS. YES I DO.
GOOD TO SEE YOU ALL. IT'S BEEN A WHILE...
Not yet...

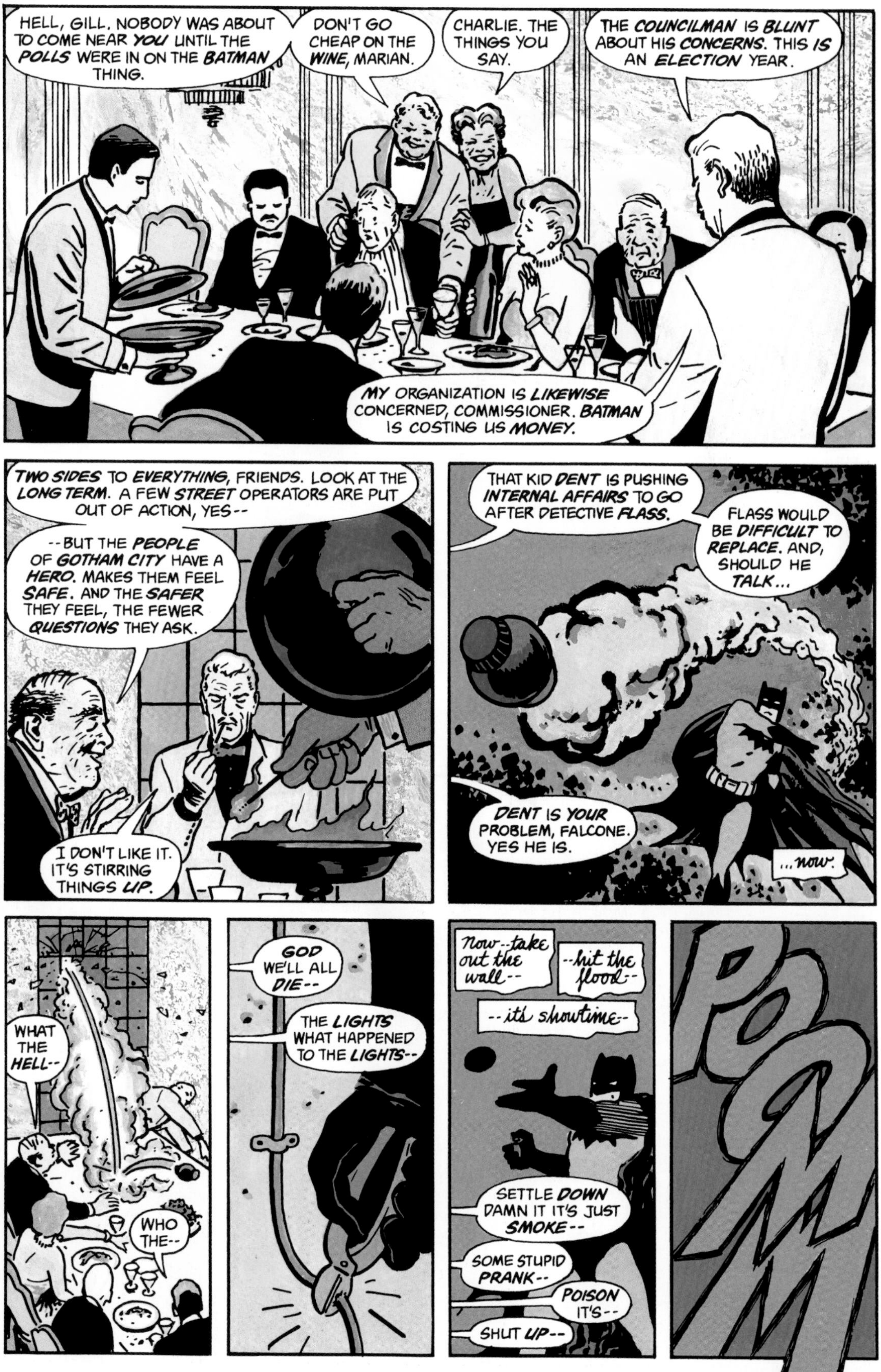
HELL, GILL. NOBODY WAS ABOUT TO COME NEAR YOU UNTIL THE POLLS WERE IN ON THE BATMAN THING.
DON'T GO CHEAP ON THE WINE, MARIAN.
CHARLIE. THE THINGS YOU SAY.
THE COUNCILMAN IS BLUNT ABOUT HIS CONCERNS. THIS IS AN ELECTION YEAR.
MY ORGANIZATION IS LIKEWISE CONCERNED, COMMISSIONER. BATMAN IS COSTING US MONEY.
TWO SIDES TO EVERYTHING, FRIENDS. LOOK AT THE LONG TERM. A FEW STREET OPERATORS ARE PUT OUT OF ACTION, YES--
--BUT THE PEOPLE OF GOTHAM CITY HAVE A HERO. MAKES THEM FEEL SAFE. AND THE SAFER THEY FEEL, THE FEWER QUESTIONS THEY ASK.
I DON'T LIKE IT. IT'S STIRRING THINGS UP.
THAT KID DENT IS PUSHING INTERNAL AFFAIRS TO GO AFTER DETECTIVE FLASS.
FLASS WOULD BE DIFFICULT TO REPLACE. AND, SHOULD HE TALK...
DENT IS YOUR PROBLEM, FALCONE. YES HE IS.
...now.
WHAT THE HELL--
WHO THE--
GOD WE'LL ALL DIE--
THE LIGHTS WHAT HAPPENED TO THE LIGHTS--
now--take out the wall--
--hit the flood--
--it's showtime--
SETTLE DOWN DAMN IT IT'S JUST SMOKE--
SOME STUPID PRANK--
POISON IT'S--
SHUT UP--
POOM

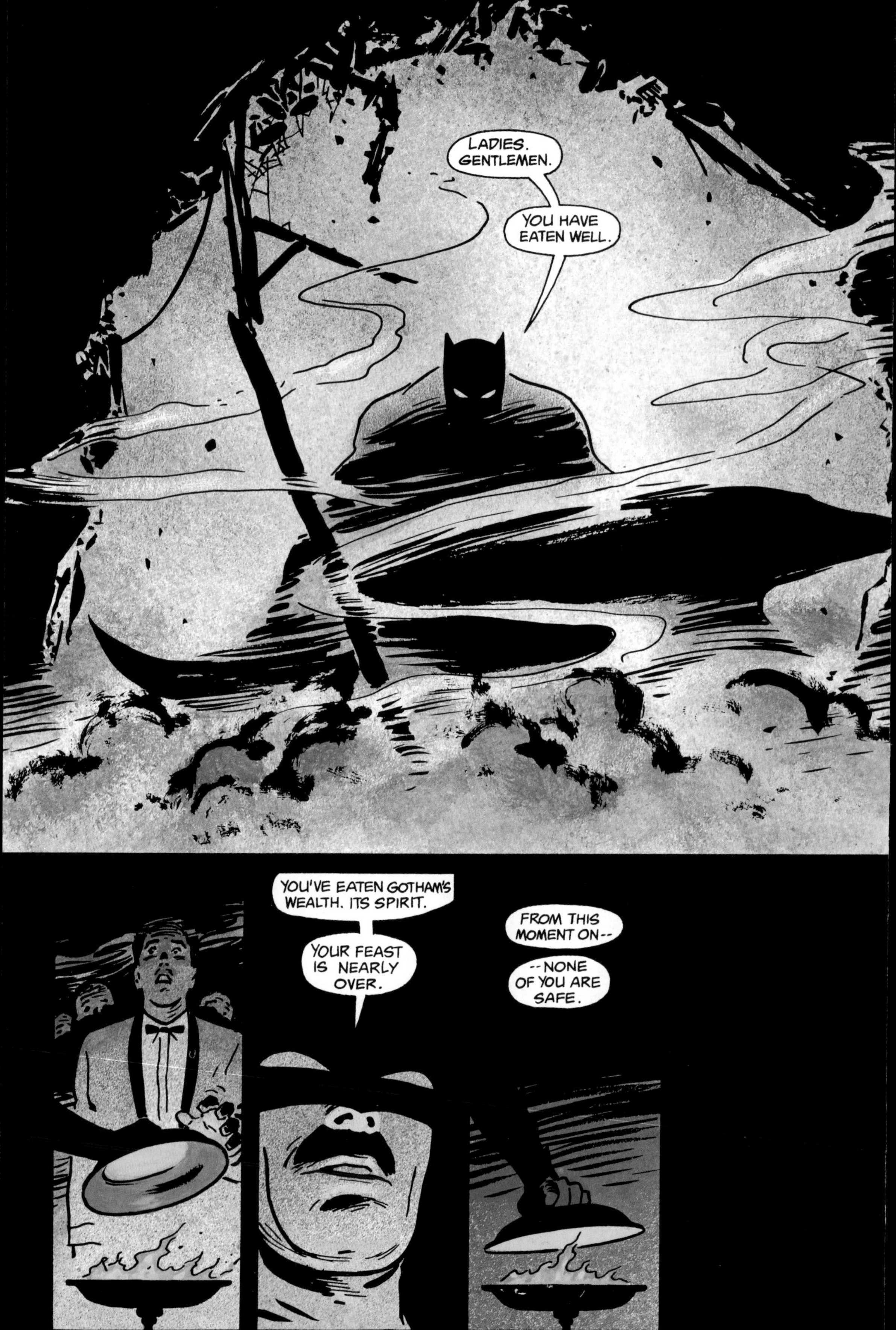
LADIES. GENTLEMEN.
YOU HAVE EATEN WELL.
YOU'VE EATEN GOTHAM'S WEALTH. ITS SPIRIT.
YOUR FEAST IS NEARLY OVER.
FROM THIS MOMENT ON--
--NONE OF YOU ARE SAFE.

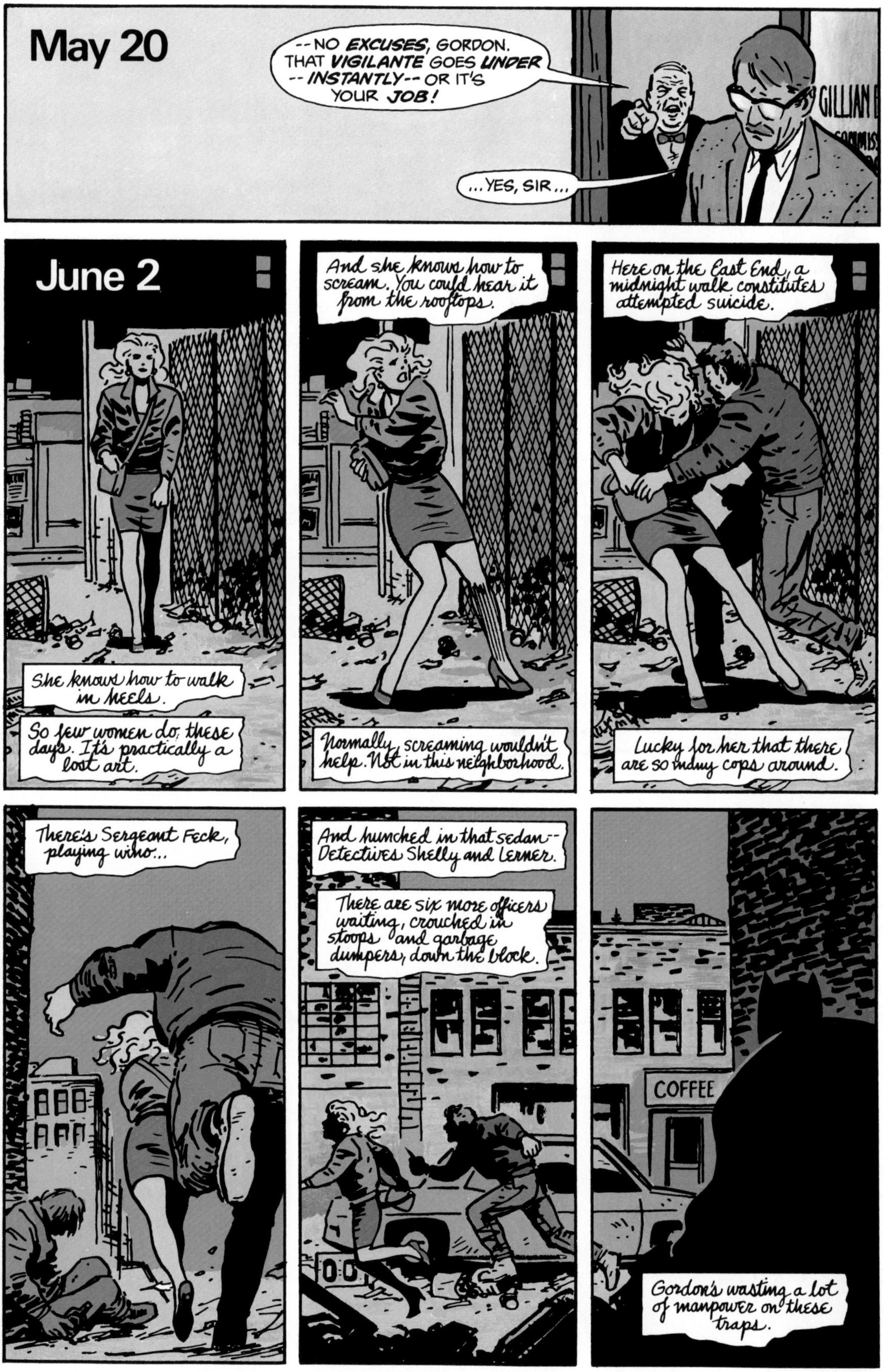
May 20
--NO EXCUSES, GORDON. THAT VIGILANTE GOES UNDER --INSTANTLY-- OR IT'S YOUR JOB!
...YES, SIR...
June 2
She knows how to walk in heels.
So few women do, these days. It's practically a lost art.
And she knows how to scream. You could hear it from the rooftops.
Normally, screaming wouldn't help. Not in this neighborhood.
Here on the East End, a midnight walk constitutes attempted suicide.
Lucky for her that there are so many cops around.
There's Sergeant Feck, playing wino...
And hunched in that sedan-- Detectives Shelly and Lerner.
There are six more officers waiting, crouched in stoops and garbage dumpers, down the block.
COFFEE
Gordon's wasting a lot of manpower on these traps.

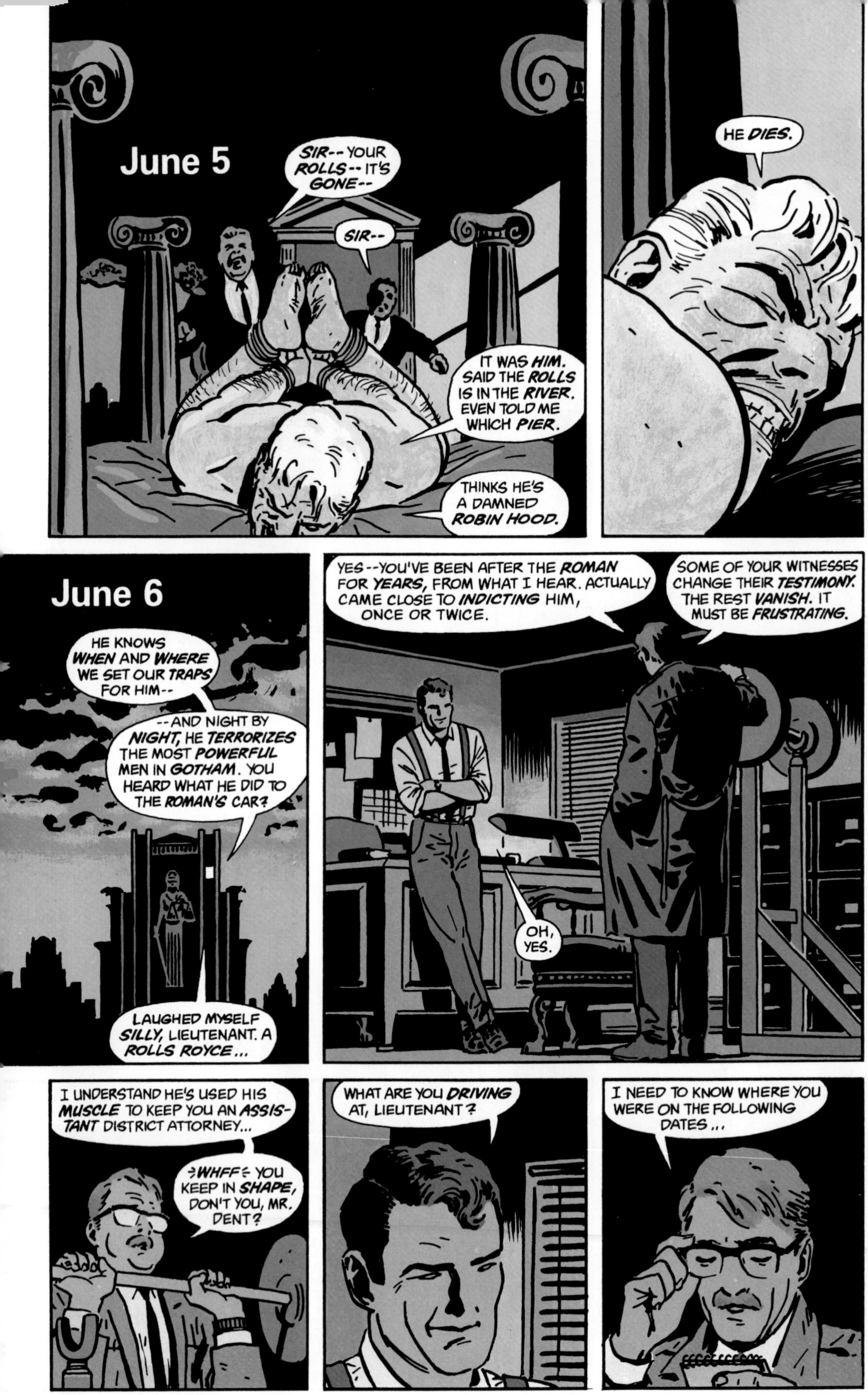

June 5
SIR-- YOUR ROLLS-- IT'S GONE--
SIR--
IT WAS HIM. SAID THE ROLLS IS IN THE RIVER. EVEN TOLD ME WHICH PIER.
THINKS HE'S A DAMNED ROBIN HOOD.
HE DIES.
June 6
HE KNOWS WHEN AND WHERE WE SET OUR TRAPS FOR HIM--
--AND NIGHT BY NIGHT, HE TERRORIZES THE MOST POWERFUL MEN IN GOTHAM. YOU HEARD WHAT HE DID TO THE ROMAN'S CAR?
LAUGHED MYSELF SILLY, LIEUTENANT. A ROLLS ROYCE...
YES--YOU'VE BEEN AFTER THE ROMAN FOR YEARS, FROM WHAT I HEAR. ACTUALLY CAME CLOSE TO INDICTING HIM, ONCE OR TWICE.
SOME OF YOUR WITNESSES CHANGE THEIR TESTIMONY. THE REST VANISH. IT MUST BE FRUSTRATING.
OH, YES.
I UNDERSTAND HE'S USED HIS MUSCLE TO KEEP YOU AN ASSISTANT DISTRICT ATTORNEY...
WHFF YOU KEEP IN SHAPE, DON'T YOU, MR. DENT?
WHAT ARE YOU DRIVING AT, LIEUTENANT?
I NEED TO KNOW WHERE YOU WERE ON THE FOLLOWING DATES...

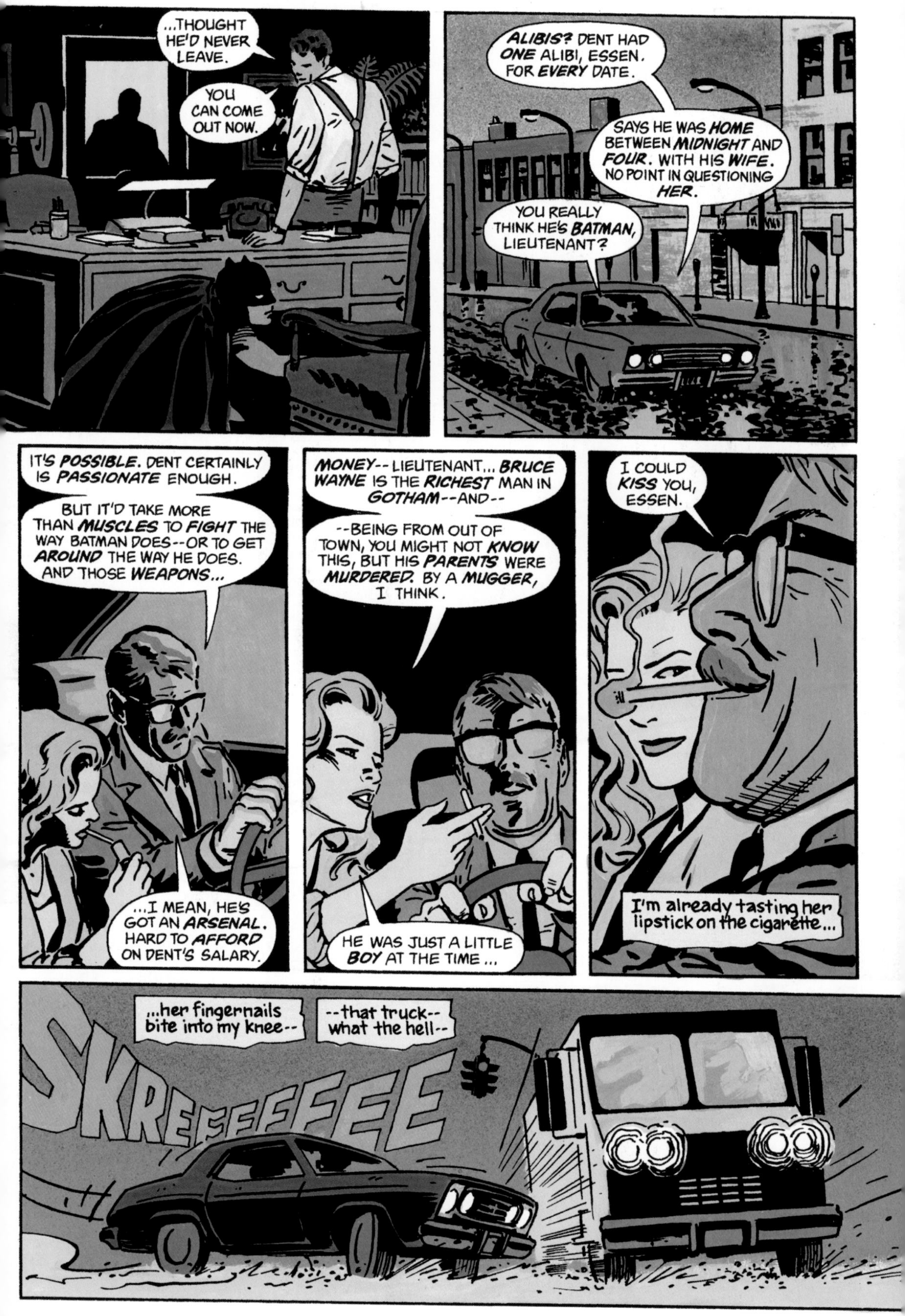

...THOUGHT HE'D NEVER LEAVE.
YOU CAN COME OUT NOW.
ALIBIS? DENT HAD ONE ALIBI, ESSEN. FOR EVERY DATE.
SAYS HE WAS HOME BETWEEN MIDNIGHT AND FOUR. WITH HIS WIFE. NO POINT IN QUESTIONING HER.
YOU REALLY THINK HE'S BATMAN, LIEUTENANT?
IT'S POSSIBLE. DENT CERTAINLY IS PASSIONATE ENOUGH.
BUT IT'D TAKE MORE THAN MUSCLES TO FIGHT THE WAY BATMAN DOES--OR TO GET AROUND THE WAY HE DOES. AND THOSE WEAPONS...
...I MEAN, HE'S GOT AN ARSENAL. HARD TO AFFORD ON DENT'S SALARY.
MONEY-- LIEUTENANT... BRUCE WAYNE IS THE RICHEST MAN IN GOTHAM--AND--
--BEING FROM OUT OF TOWN, YOU MIGHT NOT KNOW THIS, BUT HIS PARENTS WERE MURDERED. BY A MUGGER, I THINK.
HE WAS JUST A LITTLE BOY AT THE TIME ...
I COULD KISS YOU, ESSEN.
I'm already tasting her lipstick on the cigarette...
...her fingernails bite into my knee--
--that truck-- what the hell--
SKREEEEEEE

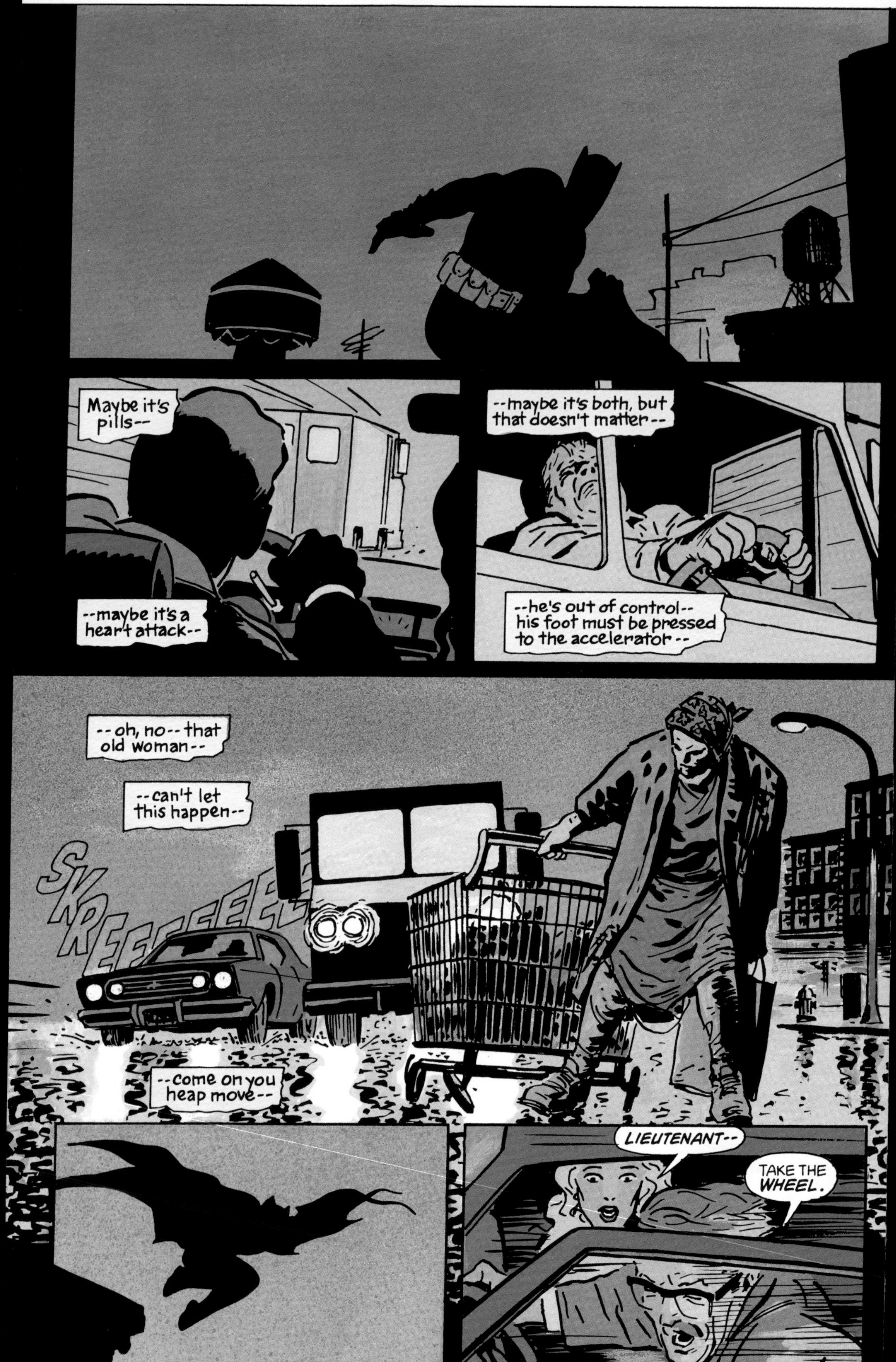

Maybe it's pills--
--maybe it's a heart attack--
--maybe it's both, but that doesn't matter--
--he's out of control-- his foot must be pressed to the accelerator--
--oh, no--that old woman--
--can't let this happen--
SKREEEEEEEE
--come on you heap move--
LIEUTENANT--
TAKE THE WHEEL.

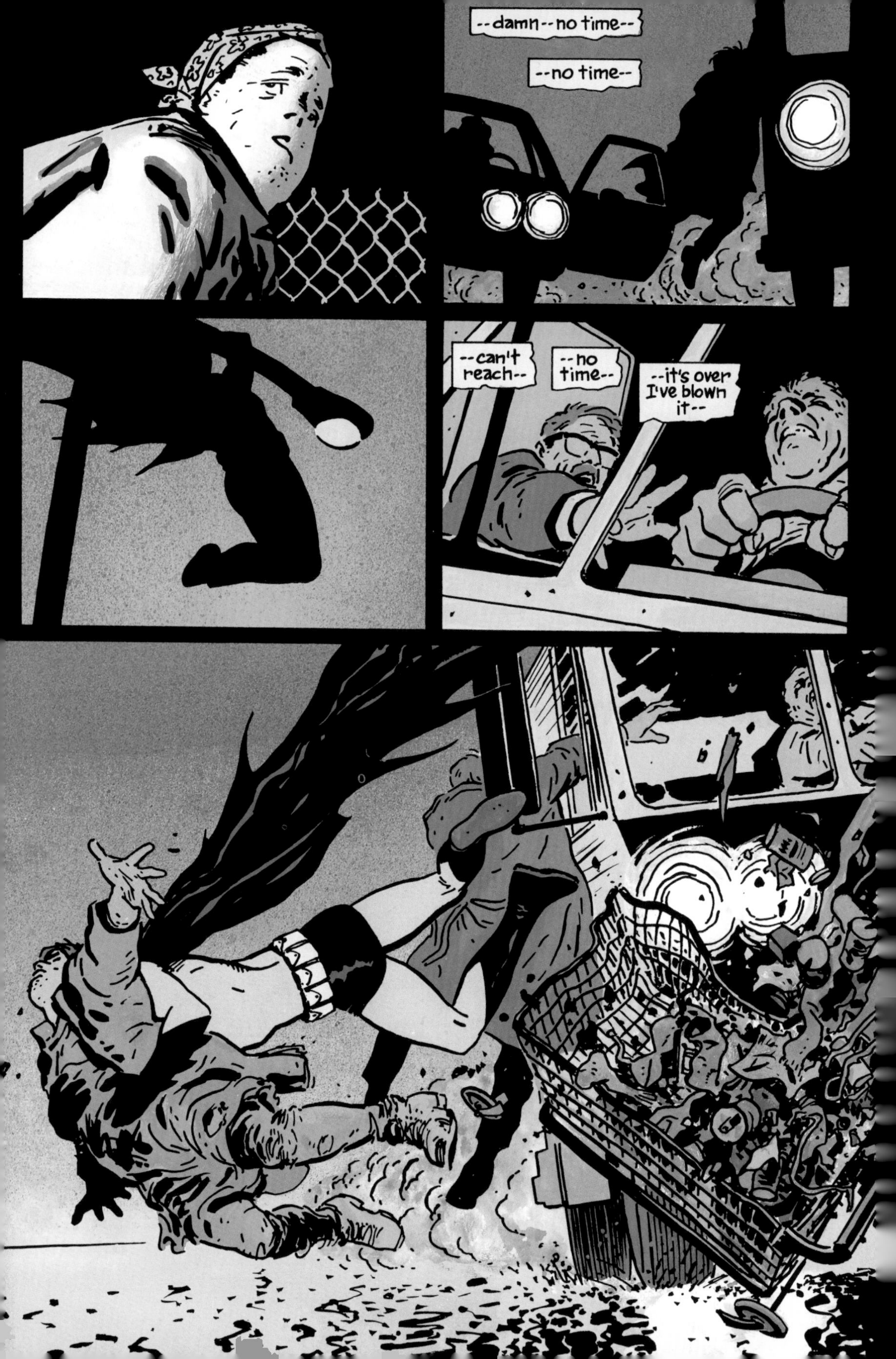
--damn--no time--
--no time--
--can't reach--
--no time--
--it's over I've blown it--

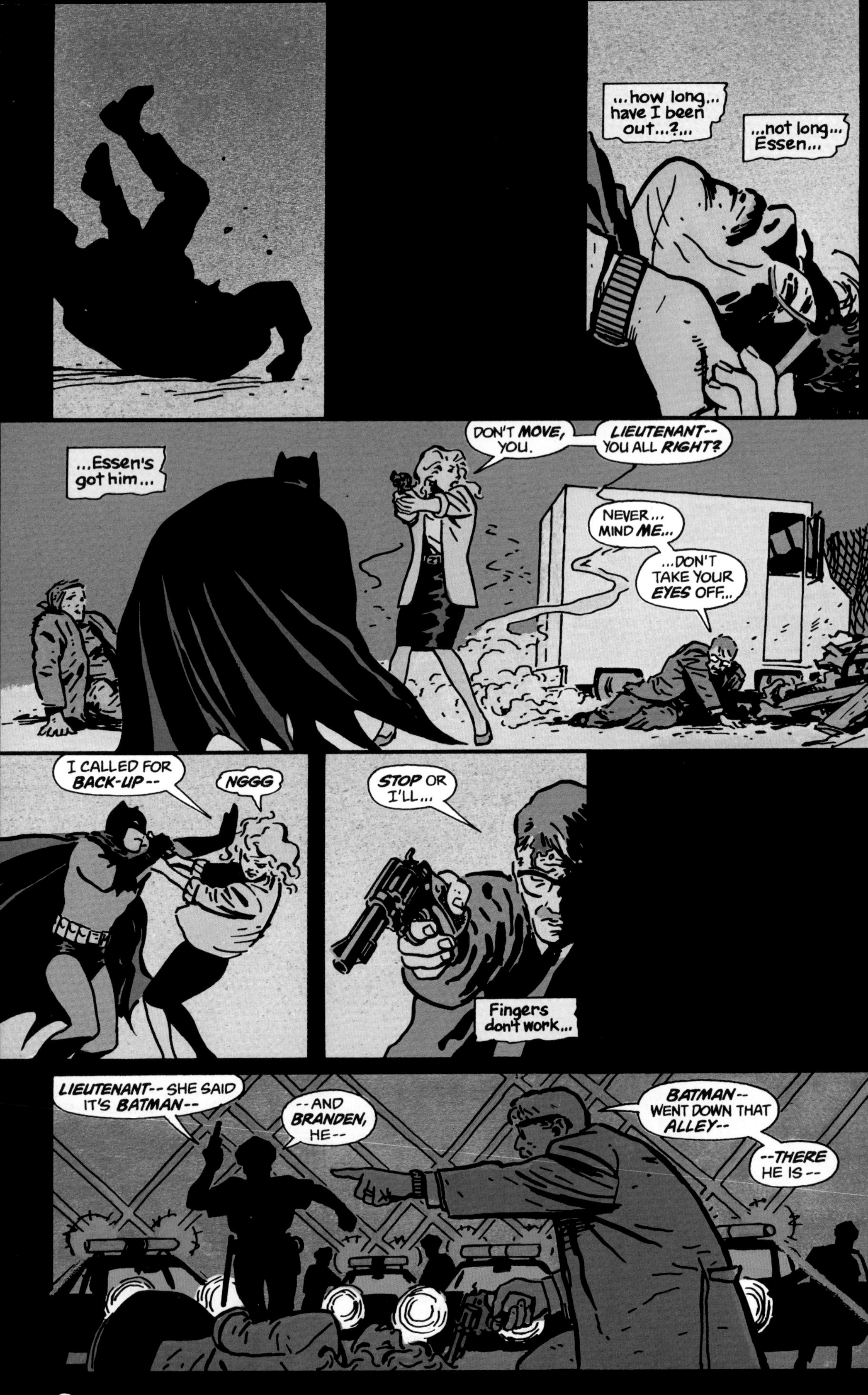

...how long... have I been out...?...
...not long... Essen...
...Essen's got him...
DON'T MOVE, YOU.
LIEUTENANT-- YOU ALL RIGHT?
NEVER... MIND ME...
...DON'T TAKE YOUR EYES OFF...
I CALLED FOR BACK-UP--
NGGG
STOP OR I'LL...
Fingers don't work...
LIEUTENANT-- SHE SAID IT'S BATMAN--
--AND BRANDEN, HE--
BATMAN-- WENT DOWN THAT ALLEY--
--THERE HE IS--

KBLAMM
KBLAMM

--SAVED THAT OLD **WOMAN**... HE...

They think-- I attacked those cops- opening up--

--catch a bullet in my leg--

--ignore it--

Blind alley-- no way out--

--except that window--

--only chance--

--buy me a moment--

NO ONE **FIRES** WITHOUT MY **ORDER**--

--GET THE **FRONT** OF THAT PLACE COVERED--

--**MERKEL**-- TAKE A SQUAD TO THE **ROOF**--

LIEUTENANT--IT'S THE **COMMISSIONER**--

--the roof--if I can reach it before they do--

--before they get air support--

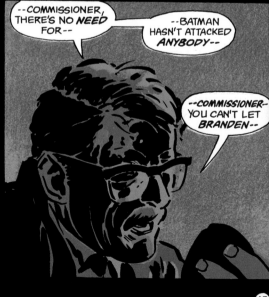

--COMMISSIONER, THERE'S NO **NEED** FOR--

--**BATMAN** HASN'T ATTACKED **ANYBODY**--

--**COMMISSIONER**-- YOU CAN'T LET **BRANDEN**--

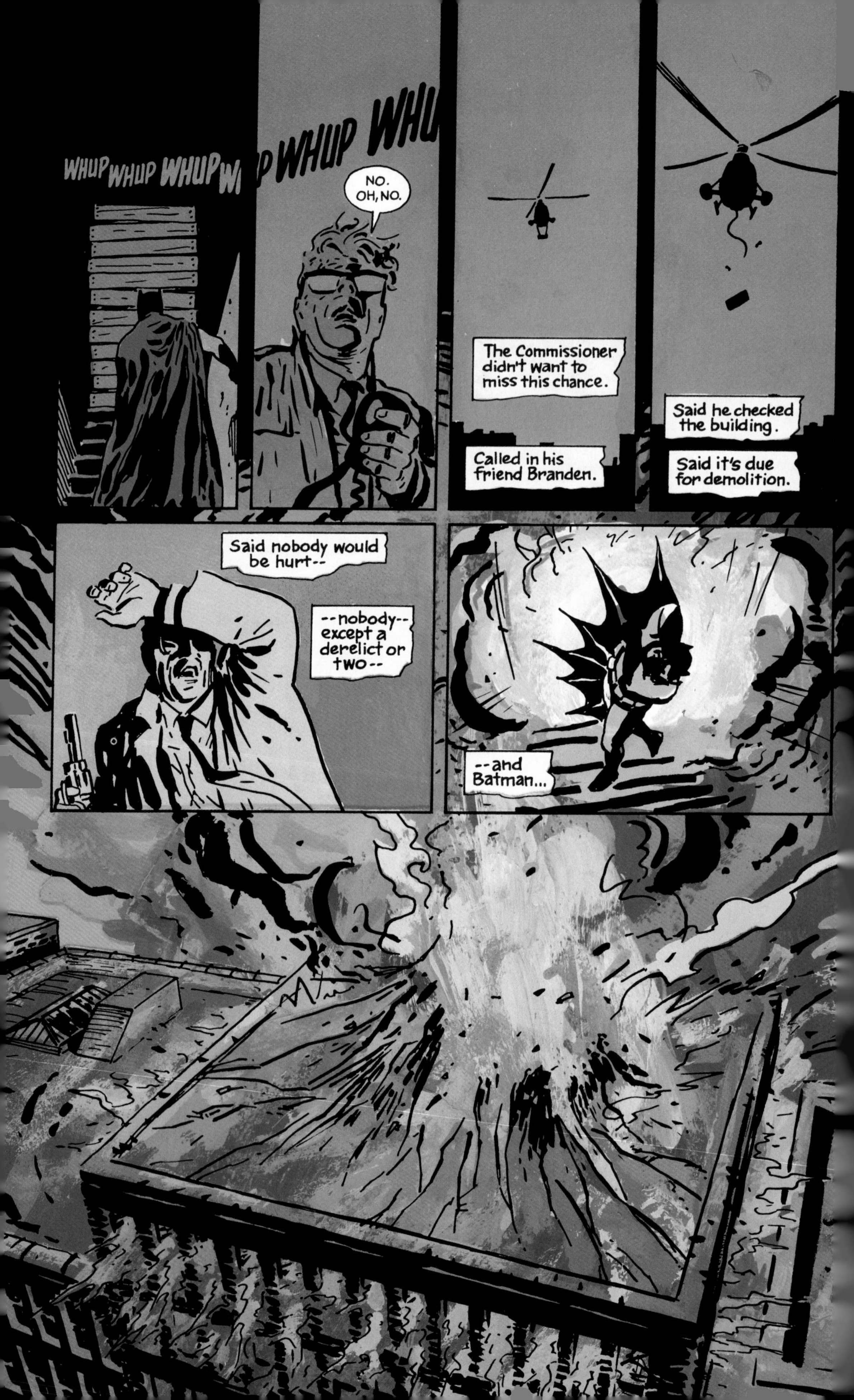
WHUP WHUP WHUP WHUP WHUP WHU
NO. OH, NO.
The Commissioner didn't want to miss this chance.
Called in his friend Branden.
Said he checked the building.
Said it's due for demolition.
Said nobody would be hurt--
--nobody--except a derelict or two--
--and Batman...

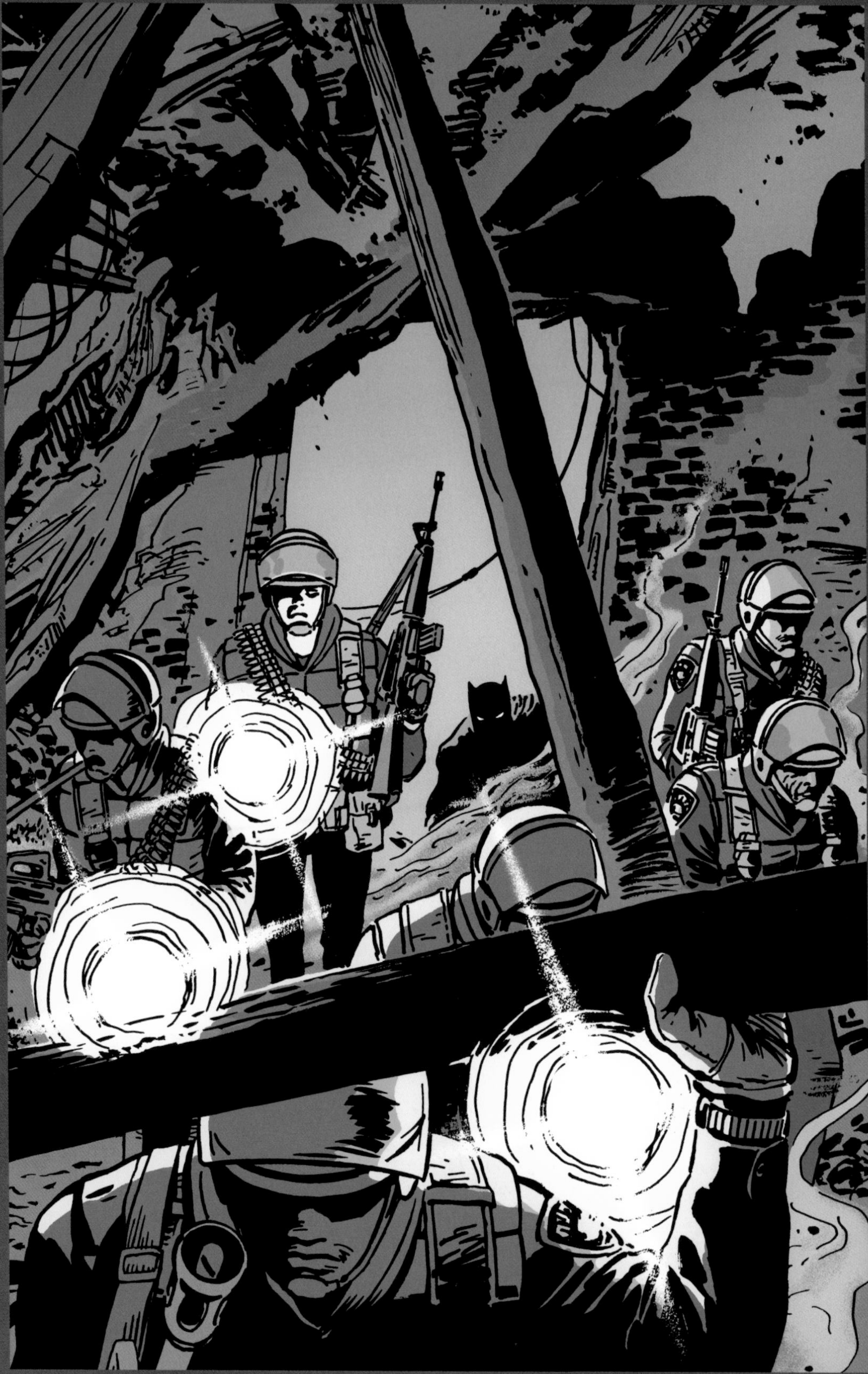

They've got him CORNERED.
They've got him OUTNUMBERED.
They've got him TRAPPED.

They're in TROUBLE...

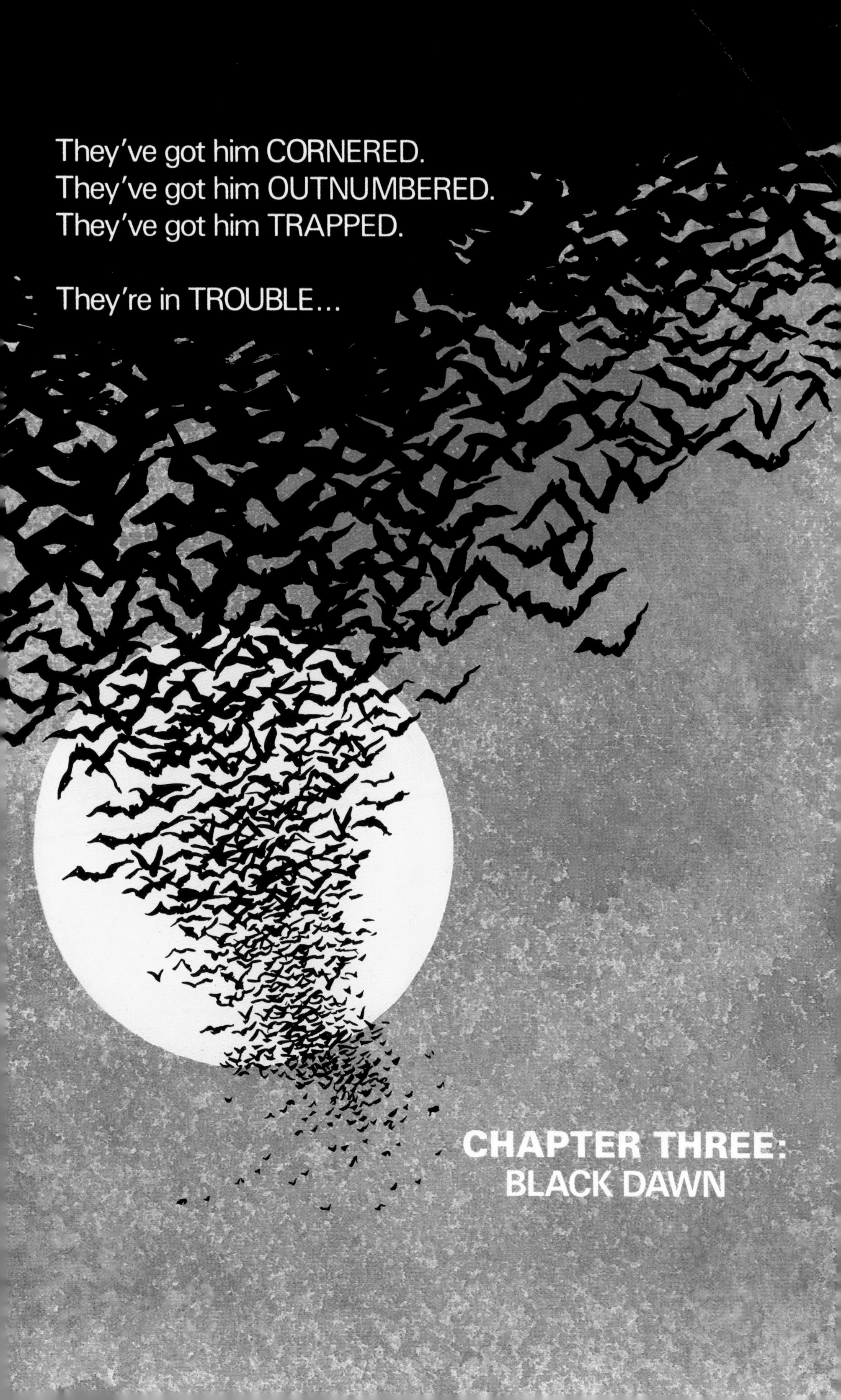

CHAPTER THREE: BLACK DAWN

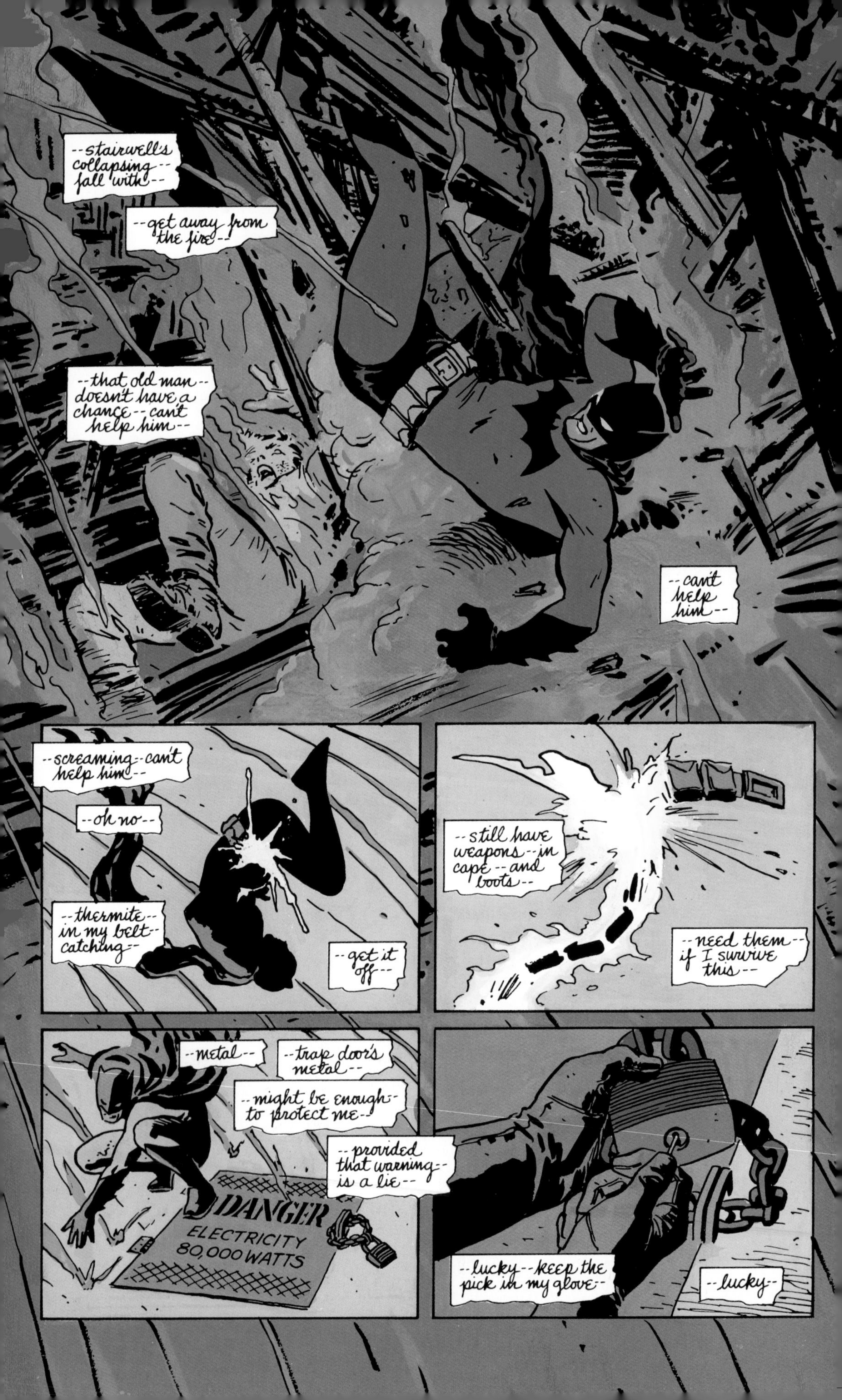
--stairwell's collapsing-- fall with--
--get away from the fire--
--that old man doesn't have a chance--can't help him--
--can't help him--
--screaming--can't help him--
--oh no--
--thermite--in my belt--catching--
--get it off--
--still have weapons--in cape--and boots--
--need them--if I survive this--
--metal--
--trap door's metal--
--might be enough--to protect me--
--provided that warning--is a lie--
DANGER
ELECTRICITY
80,000 WATTS
--lucky--keep the pick in my glove--
--lucky--

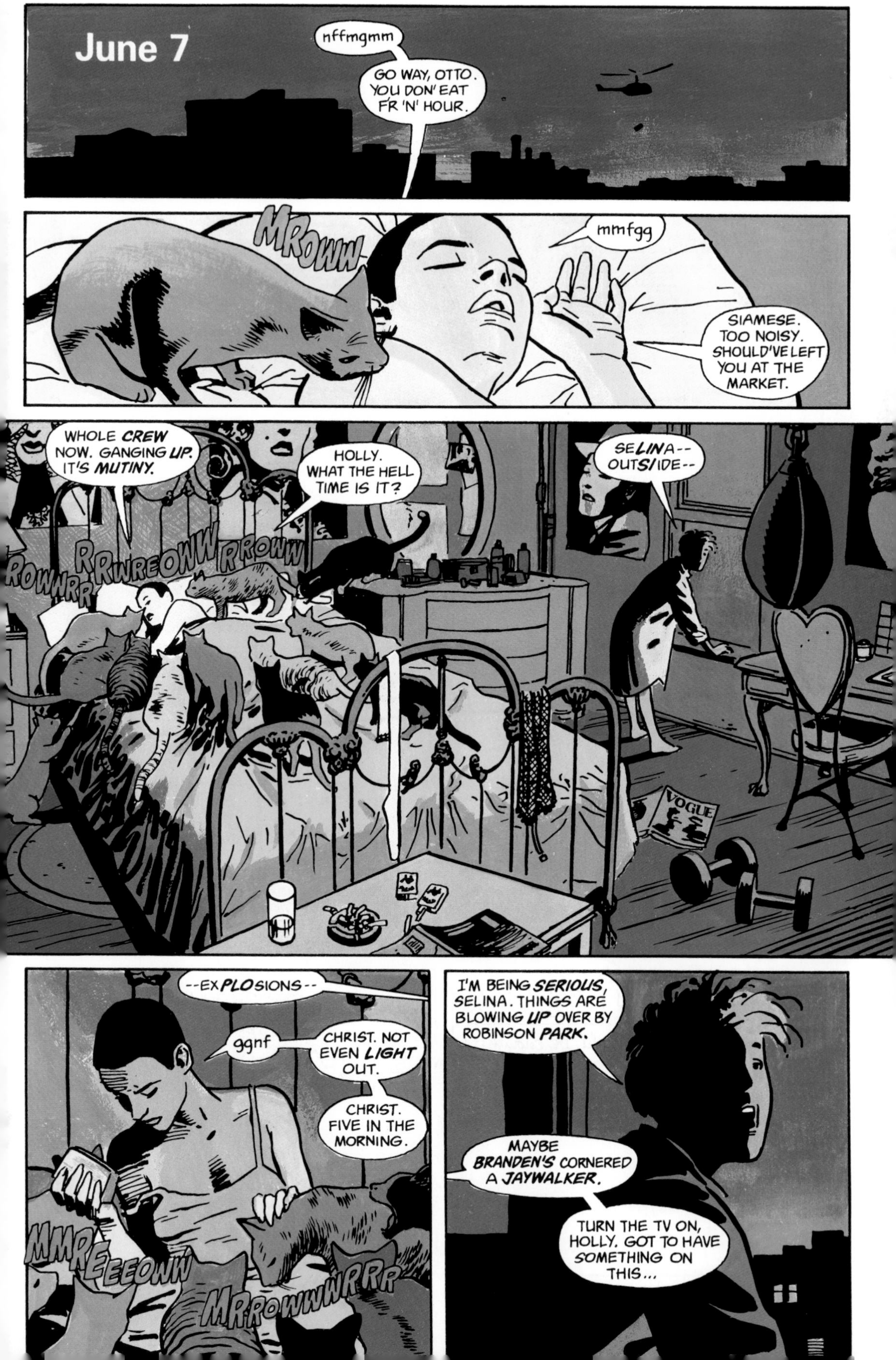
June 7
nffmgmm
GO WAY, OTTO. YOU DON' EAT FR 'N' HOUR.
MROWW
mmfgg
SIAMESE. TOO NOISY. SHOULD'VE LEFT YOU AT THE MARKET.
WHOLE CREW NOW. GANGING UP. IT'S MUTINY.
ROWWRR RRWREOWW RROWW
HOLLY. WHAT THE HELL TIME IS IT?
SELINA-- OUTSIDE--
VOGUE
--EXPLOSIONS--
ggnf
CHRIST. NOT EVEN LIGHT OUT.
CHRIST. FIVE IN THE MORNING.
MMREEEOWW
MRROWWWRRR
I'M BEING SERIOUS, SELINA. THINGS ARE BLOWING UP OVER BY ROBINSON PARK.
MAYBE BRANDEN'S CORNERED A JAYWALKER.
TURN THE TV ON, HOLLY. GOT TO HAVE SOMETHING ON THIS...

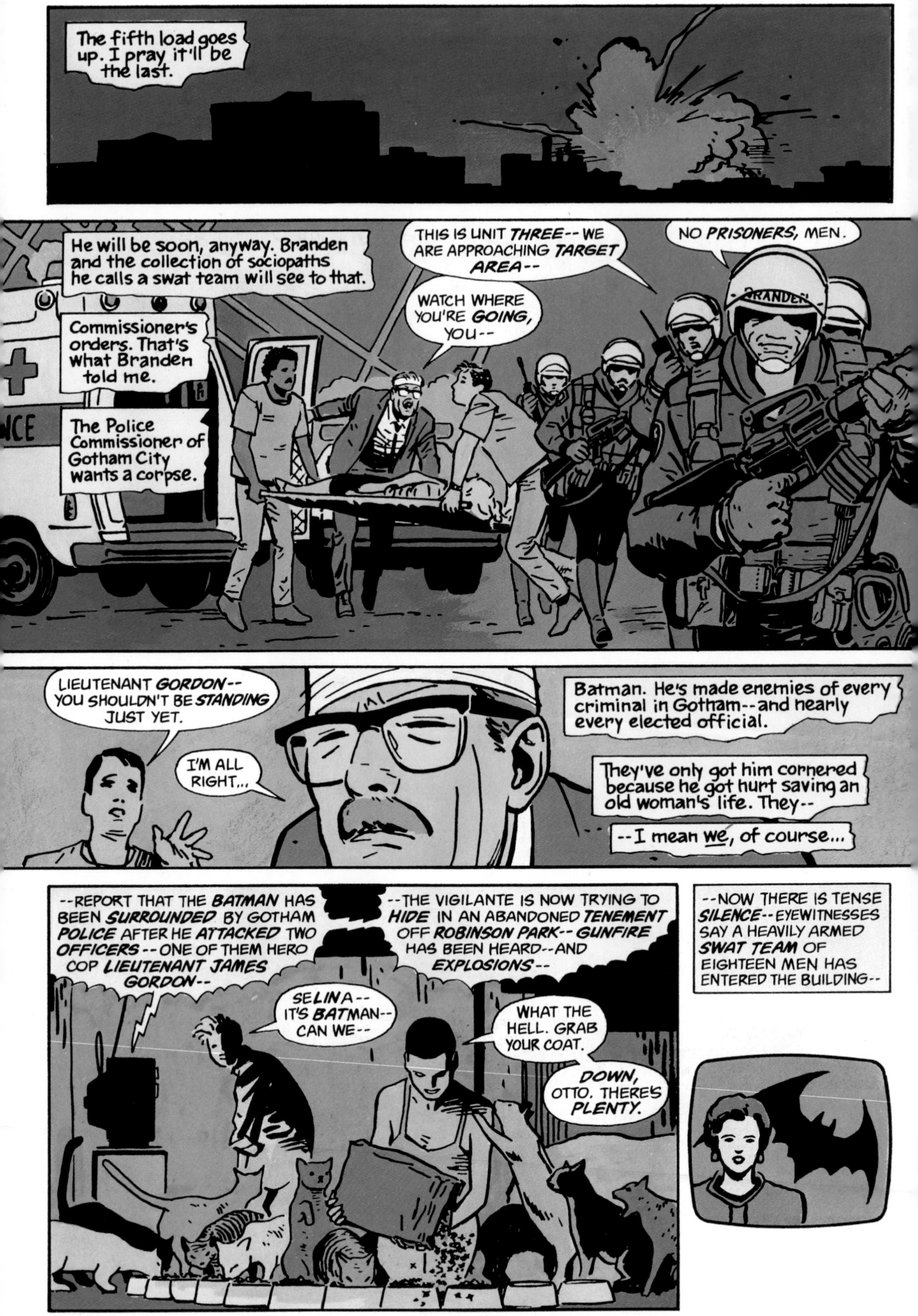

The fifth load goes up. I pray it'll be the last.
He will be soon, anyway. Branden and the collection of sociopaths he calls a swat team will see to that.
THIS IS UNIT THREE-- WE ARE APPROACHING TARGET AREA--
NO PRISONERS, MEN.
BRANDEN
Commissioner's orders. That's what Branden told me.
WATCH WHERE YOU'RE GOING, YOU--
The Police Commissioner of Gotham City wants a corpse.
LIEUTENANT GORDON-- YOU SHOULDN'T BE STANDING JUST YET.
I'M ALL RIGHT...
Batman. He's made enemies of every criminal in Gotham--and nearly every elected official.
They've only got him cornered because he got hurt saving an old woman's life. They--
--I mean we, of course...
--REPORT THAT THE BATMAN HAS BEEN SURROUNDED BY GOTHAM POLICE AFTER HE ATTACKED TWO OFFICERS--ONE OF THEM HERO COP LIEUTENANT JAMES GORDON--
--THE VIGILANTE IS NOW TRYING TO HIDE IN AN ABANDONED TENEMENT OFF ROBINSON PARK-- GUNFIRE HAS BEEN HEARD--AND EXPLOSIONS--
--NOW THERE IS TENSE SILENCE--EYEWITNESSES SAY A HEAVILY ARMED SWAT TEAM OF EIGHTEEN MEN HAS ENTERED THE BUILDING--
SELINA-- IT'S BATMAN-- CAN WE--
WHAT THE HELL. GRAB YOUR COAT.
DOWN, OTTO. THERE'S PLENTY.

—WE HAVE ENTERED THE *LOBBY*—NO *SIGN* OF HIM YET—

UNIT *ONE*, REPORTING— SECOND FLOOR'S A *MESS*— NOTHING *LIVING*—

UNIT *TWO*, REPORTING— FOUND A *BODY* UNDER THE *WATER HEATER*—JUST AN OLD *WINO*—

KEEP IT *TIGHT*—KEEP IT *TIGHT*—

OVER *HERE*—GIVE ME SOME *LIGHT*—

JUST A *CHIMNEY*—

—NO— DOWN *THERE*— OVER *THERE*— THE *FLOOR*—

—IF HE GOT DOWN *THERE*—TRAPDOOR'S *METAL*—HE MIGHT'VE *SURVIVED*—

—SO *PERFORATE* IT, SOLDIER—

DANGER ELECTRICITY 80,000 WATTS

UNITS *ONE* AND *TWO*—STAY WHERE YOU *ARE*—THIS IS ONLY *PRECAUTIONARY* FIRE—

IF HE'S *DOWN* THERE—HE *TRAPPED* HIMSELF—

BRAKABRAKABRA

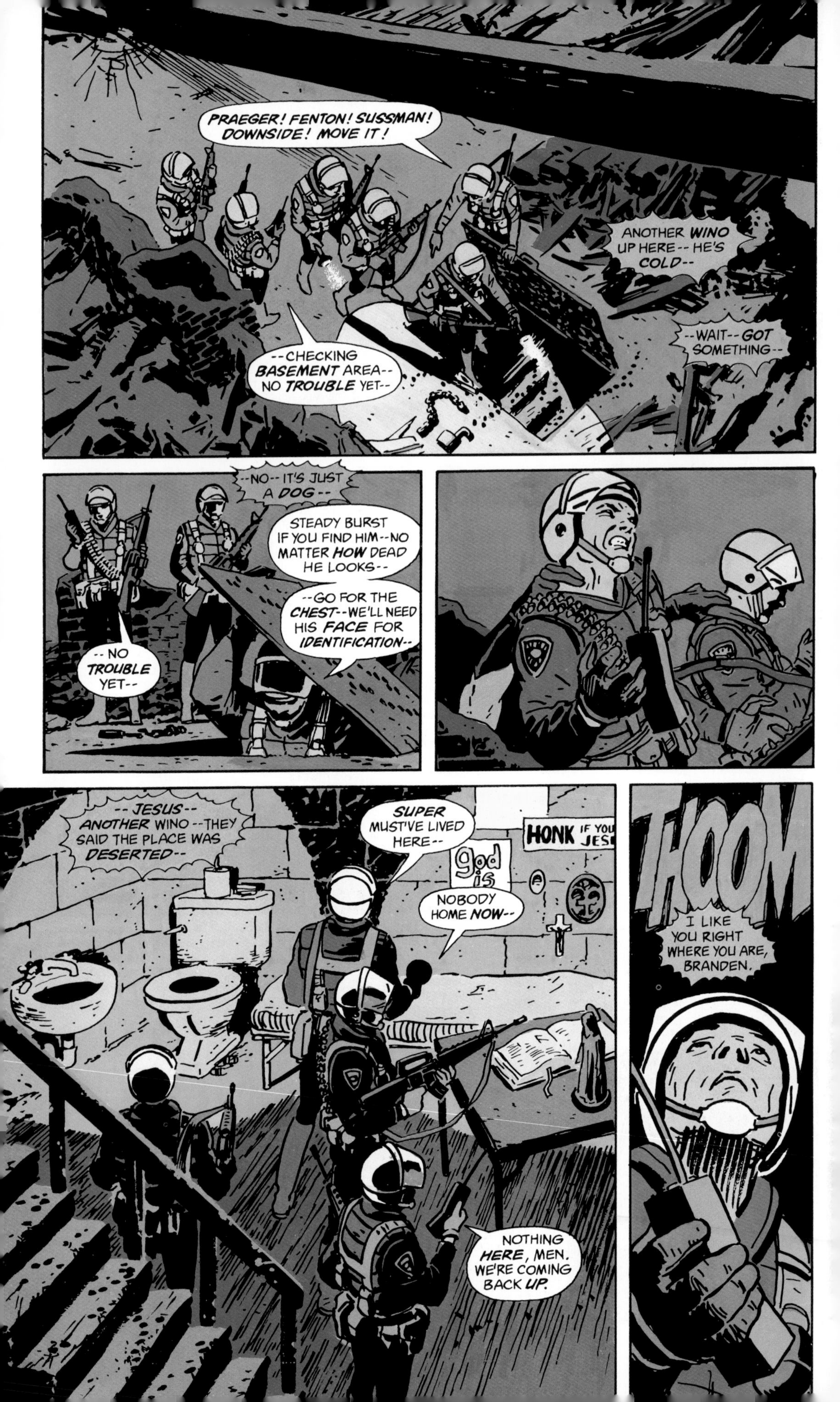
PRAEGER! FENTON! SUSSMAN! DOWNSIDE! MOVE IT!
ANOTHER WINO UP HERE-- HE'S COLD--
--WAIT-- GOT SOMETHING--
--CHECKING BASEMENT AREA-- NO TROUBLE YET--
--NO-- IT'S JUST A DOG--
STEADY BURST IF YOU FIND HIM--NO MATTER HOW DEAD HE LOOKS--
--GO FOR THE CHEST--WE'LL NEED HIS FACE FOR IDENTIFICATION--
--NO TROUBLE YET--
--JESUS-- ANOTHER WINO --THEY SAID THE PLACE WAS DESERTED--
SUPER MUST'VE LIVED HERE--
HONK
god is
NOBODY HOME NOW--
NOTHING HERE, MEN. WE'RE COMING BACK UP.
THOOM
I LIKE YOU RIGHT WHERE YOU ARE, BRANDEN.

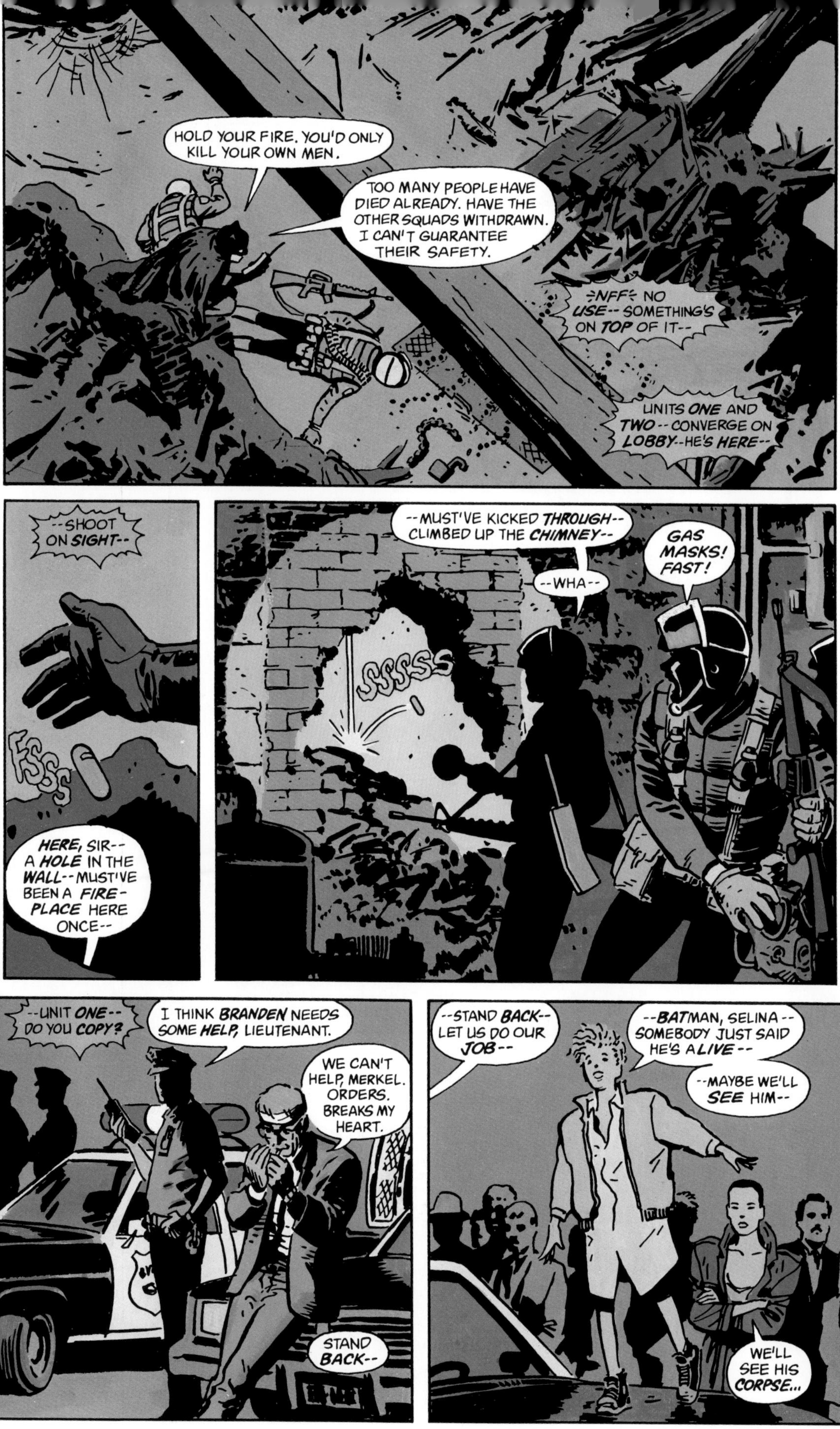
HOLD YOUR FIRE. YOU'D ONLY KILL YOUR OWN MEN.
TOO MANY PEOPLE HAVE DIED ALREADY. HAVE THE OTHER SQUADS WITHDRAWN. I CAN'T GUARANTEE THEIR SAFETY.
NFF NO USE-- SOMETHING'S ON TOP OF IT--
UNITS ONE AND TWO-- CONVERGE ON LOBBY--HE'S HERE--
--SHOOT ON SIGHT--
FSSS
HERE, SIR-- A HOLE IN THE WALL--MUST'VE BEEN A FIRE-PLACE HERE ONCE--
--MUST'VE KICKED THROUGH-- CLIMBED UP THE CHIMNEY--
--WHA--
GAS MASKS! FAST!
SSSSS
--UNIT ONE-- DO YOU COPY?
I THINK BRANDEN NEEDS SOME HELP, LIEUTENANT.
WE CAN'T HELP, MERKEL. ORDERS. BREAKS MY HEART.
STAND BACK--
--STAND BACK-- LET US DO OUR JOB--
--BATMAN, SELINA-- SOMEBODY JUST SAID HE'S ALIVE--
--MAYBE WE'LL SEE HIM--
WE'LL SEE HIS CORPSE...

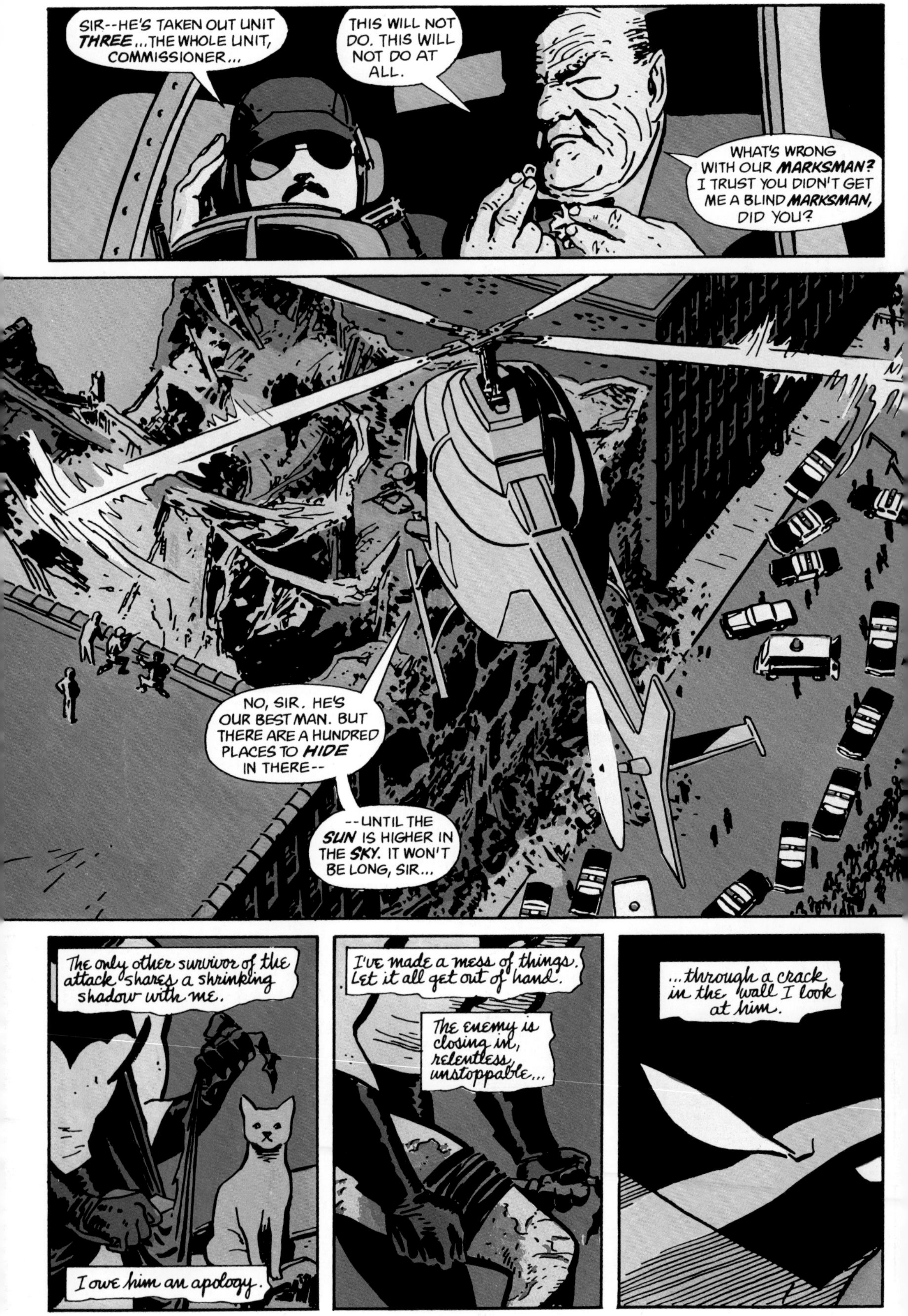
SIR--HE'S TAKEN OUT UNIT THREE...THE WHOLE UNIT, COMMISSIONER...
THIS WILL NOT DO. THIS WILL NOT DO AT ALL.
WHAT'S WRONG WITH OUR MARKSMAN? I TRUST YOU DIDN'T GET ME A BLIND MARKSMAN, DID YOU?
NO, SIR. HE'S OUR BEST MAN. BUT THERE ARE A HUNDRED PLACES TO HIDE IN THERE--
--UNTIL THE SUN IS HIGHER IN THE SKY. IT WON'T BE LONG, SIR...
The only other survivor of the attack shares a shrinking shadow with me.
I owe him an apology.
I've made a mess of things. Let it all get out of hand.
The enemy is closing in, relentless, unstoppable...
...through a crack in the wall I look at him.

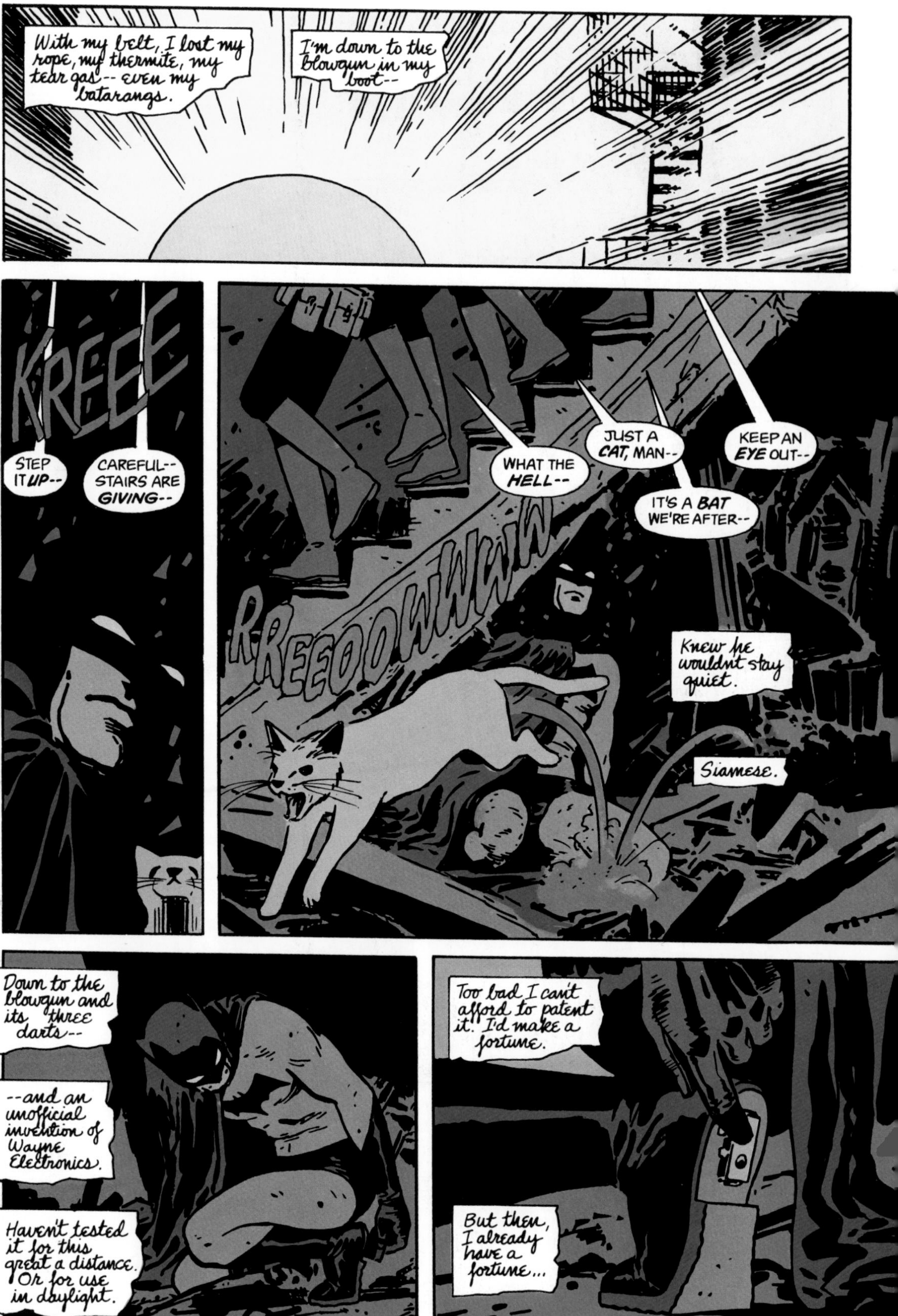
With my belt, I lost my rope, my thermite, my tear gas -- even my batarangs.
I'm down to the blowgun in my boot--
KREEE
STEP IT UP--
CAREFUL-- STAIRS ARE GIVING--
WHAT THE HELL--
JUST A CAT, MAN--
KEEP AN EYE OUT--
IT'S A BAT WE'RE AFTER--
RREEOOWWWW
Knew he wouldn't stay quiet.
Siamese.
Down to the blowgun and its three darts--
--and an unofficial invention of Wayne Electronics.
Haven't tested it for this great a distance. Or for use in daylight.
Too bad I can't afford to patent it. I'd make a fortune.
But then, I already have a fortune...

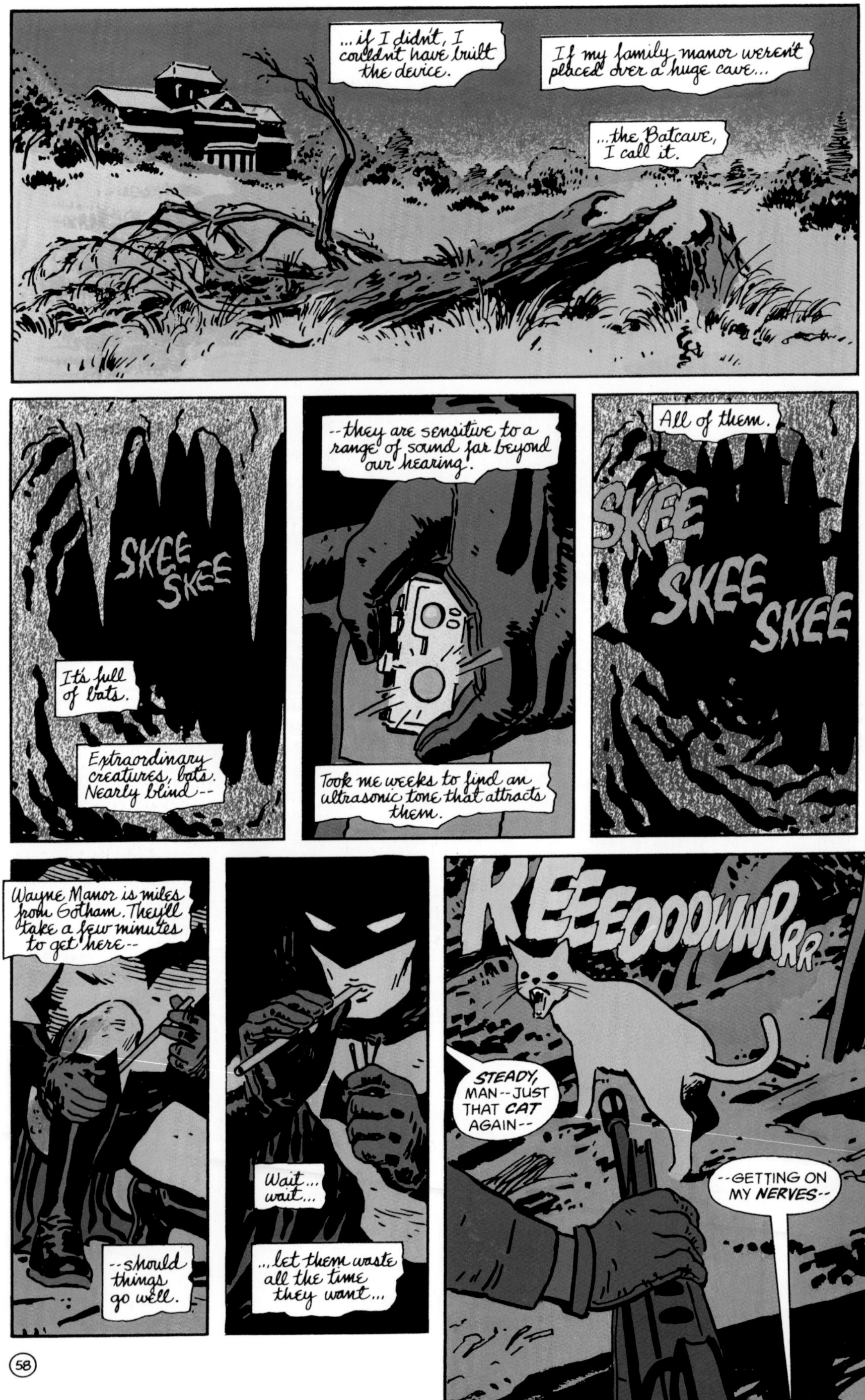

If my family manor weren't placed over a huge cave...
...if I didn't, I couldn't have built the device.
...the Batcave, I call it.
SKEE SKEE
It's full of bats.
Extraordinary creatures, bats. Nearly blind--
--they are sensitive to a range of sound far beyond our hearing.
Took me weeks to find an ultrasonic tone that attracts them.
All of them.
SKEE SKEE SKEE
Wayne Manor is miles from Gotham. They'll take a few minutes to get here--
--should things go well.
Wait... wait...
...let them waste all the time they want...
REEEEOOOWWRRR
STEADY, MAN--JUST THAT CAT AGAIN--
--GETTING ON MY NERVES--

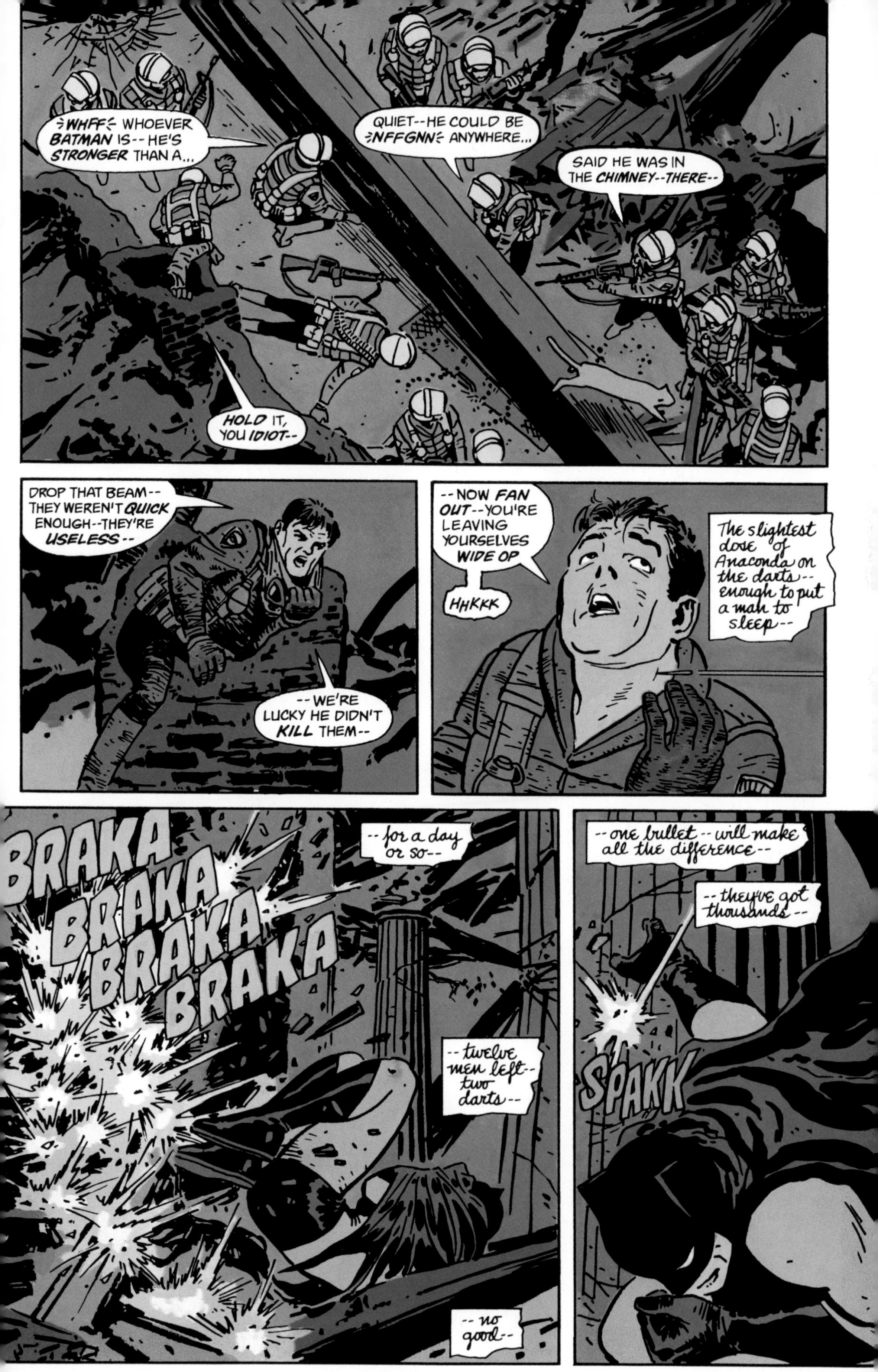

WHFF WHOEVER BATMAN IS--HE'S STRONGER THAN A...
QUIET--HE COULD BE NFFGNN ANYWHERE...
SAID HE WAS IN THE CHIMNEY--THERE--
HOLD IT, YOU IDIOT--
DROP THAT BEAM--THEY WEREN'T QUICK ENOUGH--THEY'RE USELESS--
--WE'RE LUCKY HE DIDN'T KILL THEM--
--NOW FAN OUT--YOU'RE LEAVING YOURSELVES WIDE OP
HHKKK
The slightest dose of Anaconda on the darts--enough to put a man to sleep--
BRAKA BRAKA BRAKA BRAKA
--for a day or so--
--twelve men left--two darts--
--no good--
--one bullet--will make all the difference--
--they've got thousands--
SPAKK

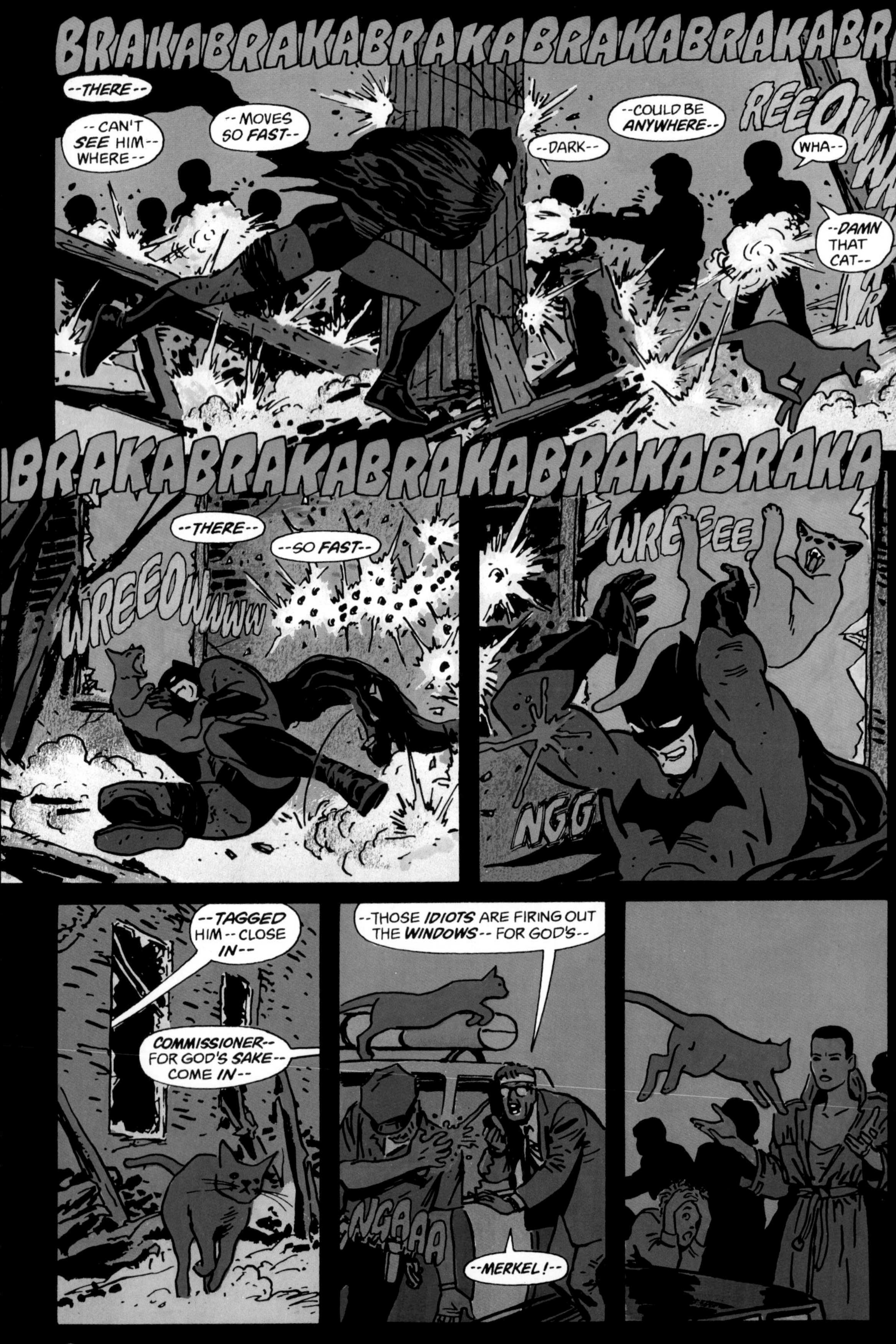
BRAKABRAKABRAKABRAKABRAKABR
--THERE--
--CAN'T SEE HIM--WHERE--
--MOVES SO FAST--
--DARK--
--COULD BE ANYWHERE--
REEOWW
WHA--
--DAMN THAT CAT--
BRAKABRAKABRAKABRAKABRAKA
--THERE--
--SO FAST--
WREEOWwww
WREEEE
NGG
--TAGGED HIM--CLOSE IN--
COMMISSIONER--FOR GOD'S SAKE--COME IN--
--THOSE IDIOTS ARE FIRING OUT THE WINDOWS--FOR GOD'S--
NGAAA
--MERKEL!--

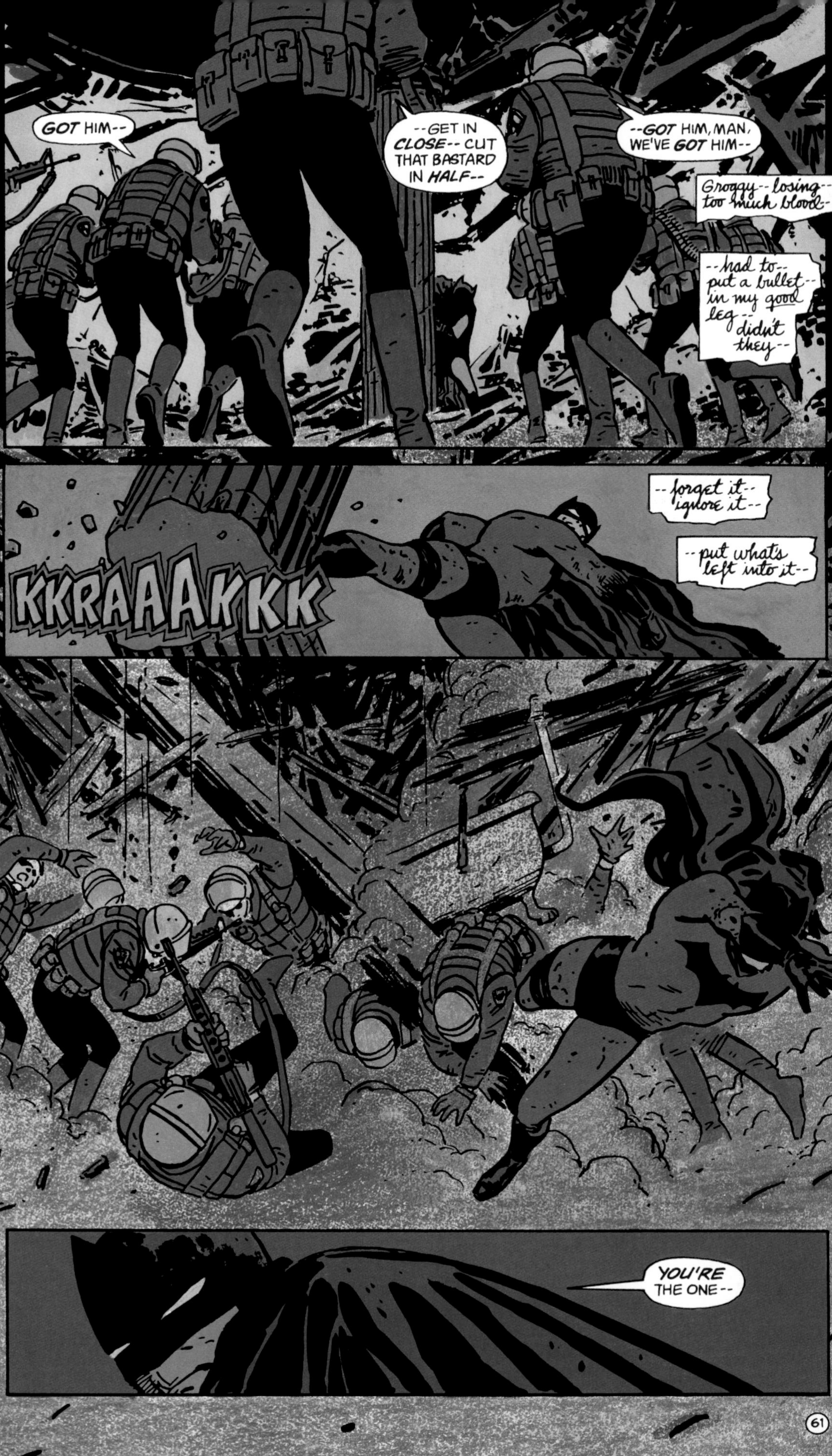
GOT HIM--
--GET IN CLOSE-- CUT THAT BASTARD IN HALF--
--GOT HIM, MAN, WE'VE GOT HIM--
Groggy-- losing-- too much blood--
--had to-- put a bullet-- in my good leg-- didn't they--
--forget it-- ignore it--
--put what's left into it--
KKRAAAKKK
YOU'RE THE ONE--

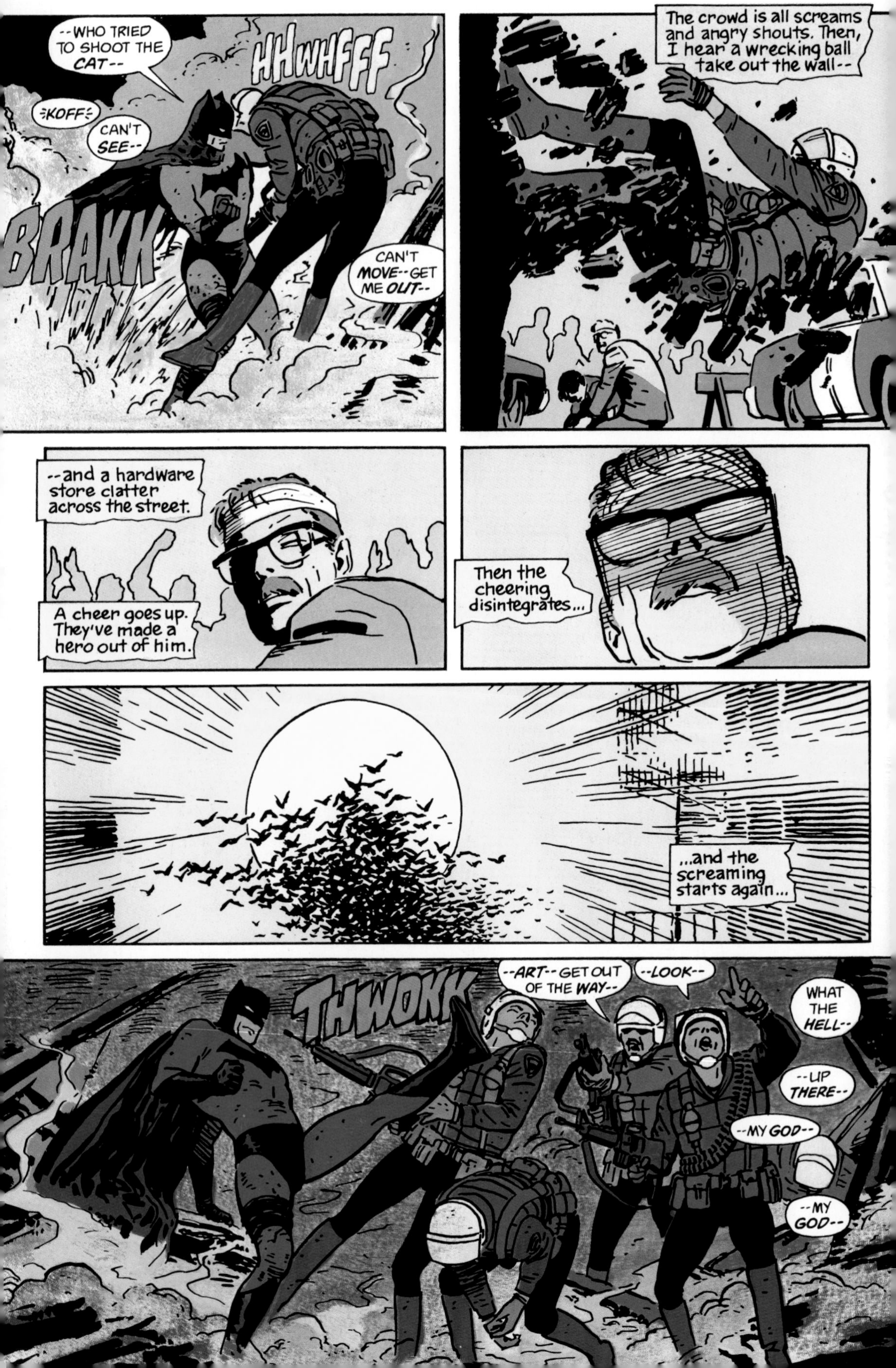
--WHO TRIED TO SHOOT THE CAT--
HHWHFFF
KOFF
CAN'T SEE--
BRAKK
CAN'T MOVE--GET ME OUT--
The crowd is all screams and angry shouts. Then, I hear a wrecking ball take out the wall--
--and a hardware store clatter across the street.
A cheer goes up. They've made a hero out of him.
Then the cheering disintegrates...
...and the screaming starts again...
THWOKK
--ART--GET OUT OF THE WAY--
--LOOK--
WHAT THE HELL--
--UP THERE--
--MY GOD--
--MY GOD--

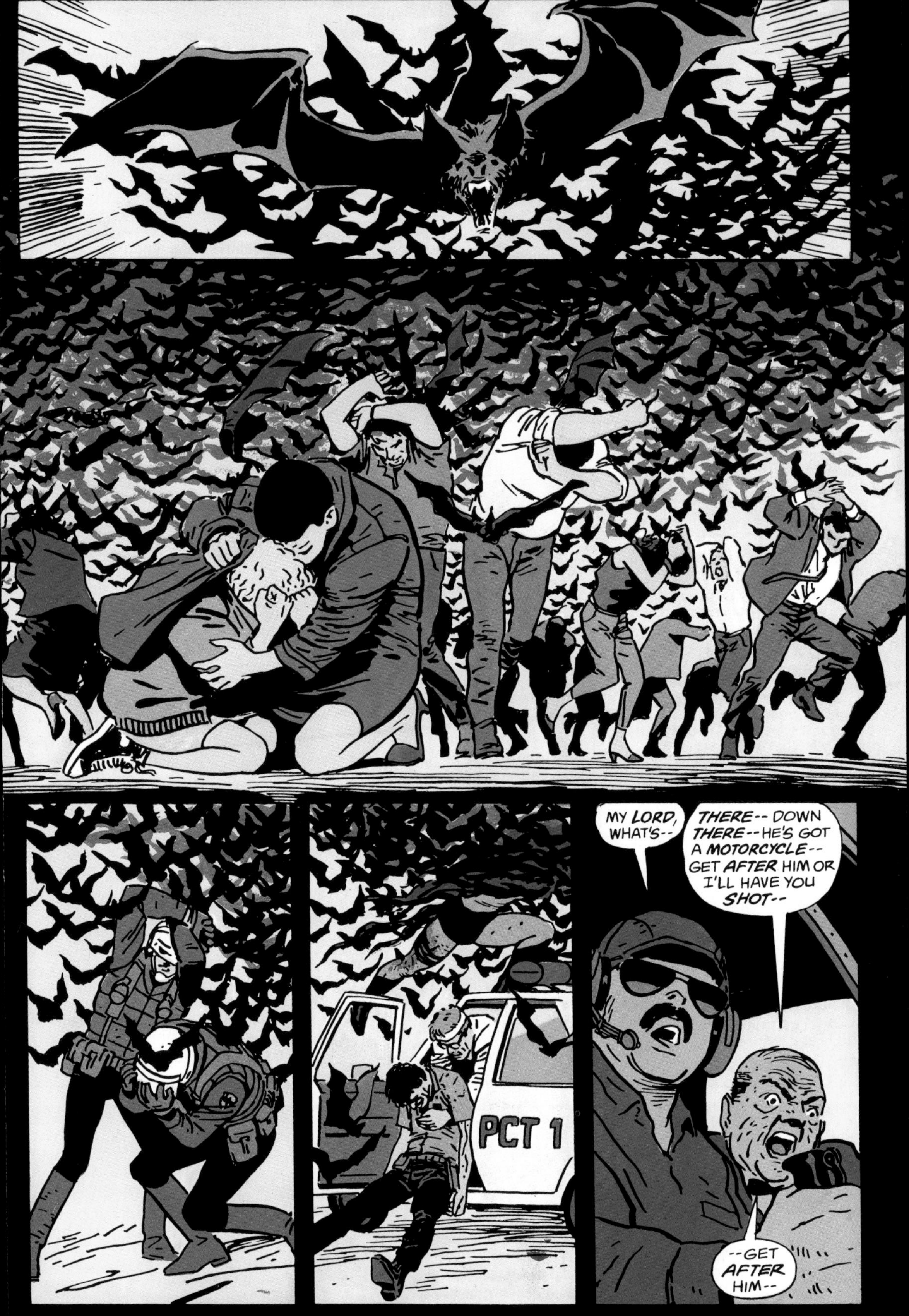
MY LORD, WHAT'S--
THERE-- DOWN THERE-- HE'S GOT A MOTORCYCLE-- GET AFTER HIM OR I'LL HAVE YOU SHOT--
--GET AFTER HIM--

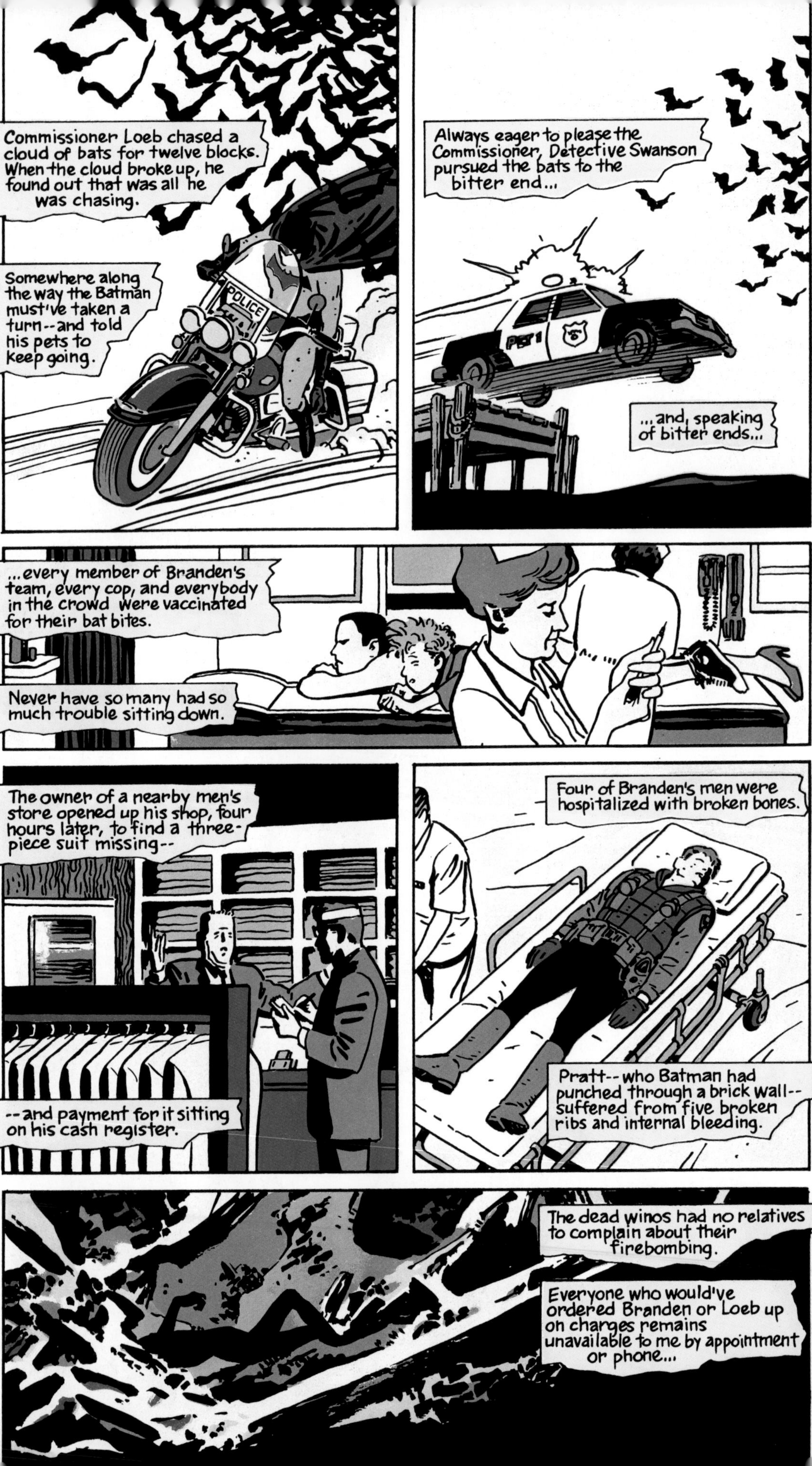
Commissioner Loeb chased a cloud of bats for twelve blocks. When the cloud broke up, he found out that was all he was chasing.
Somewhere along the way the Batman must've taken a turn--and told his pets to keep going.
POLICE
Always eager to please the Commissioner, Detective Swanson pursued the bats to the bitter end...
...and, speaking of bitter ends...
...every member of Branden's team, every cop, and everybody in the crowd were vaccinated for their bat bites.
Never have so many had so much trouble sitting down.
The owner of a nearby men's store opened up his shop, four hours later, to find a three-piece suit missing--
--and payment for it sitting on his cash register.
Four of Branden's men were hospitalized with broken bones.
Pratt--who Batman had punched through a brick wall--suffered from five broken ribs and internal bleeding.
The dead winos had no relatives to complain about their firebombing.
Everyone who would've ordered Branden or Loeb up on charges remains unavailable to me by appointment or phone...

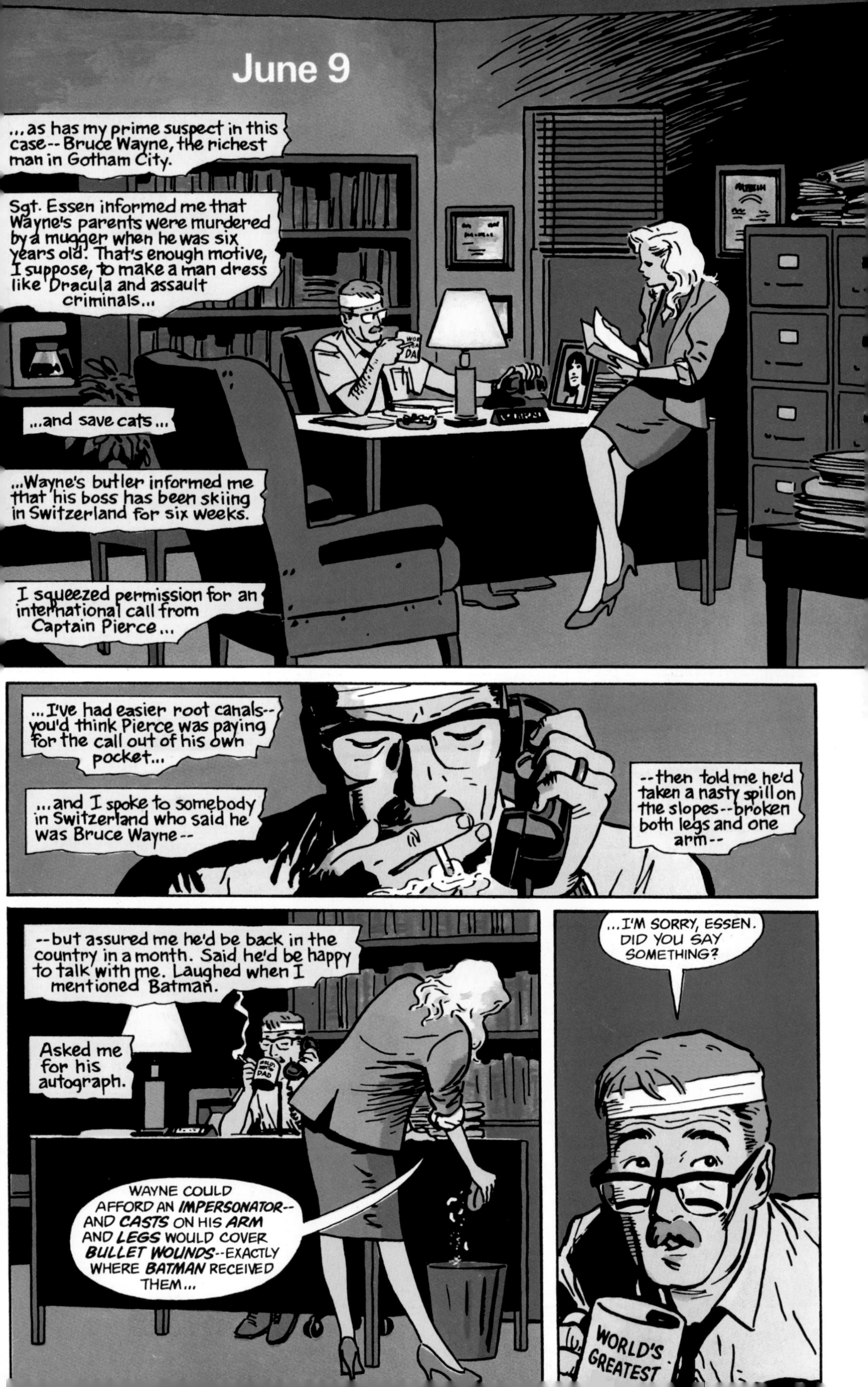
June 9
...as has my prime suspect in this case--Bruce Wayne, the richest man in Gotham City.
Sgt. Essen informed me that Wayne's parents were murdered by a mugger when he was six years old. That's enough motive, I suppose, to make a man dress like Dracula and assault criminals...
...and save cats...
...Wayne's butler informed me that his boss has been skiing in Switzerland for six weeks.
I squeezed permission for an international call from Captain Pierce...
...I've had easier root canals--you'd think Pierce was paying for the call out of his own pocket...
...and I spoke to somebody in Switzerland who said he was Bruce Wayne--
--then told me he'd taken a nasty spill on the slopes--broken both legs and one arm--
--but assured me he'd be back in the country in a month. Said he'd be happy to talk with me. Laughed when I mentioned Batman.
Asked me for his autograph.
WAYNE COULD AFFORD AN IMPERSONATOR--AND CASTS ON HIS ARM AND LEGS WOULD COVER BULLET WOUNDS--EXACTLY WHERE BATMAN RECEIVED THEM...
...I'M SORRY, ESSEN. DID YOU SAY SOMETHING?
WORLD'S GREATEST

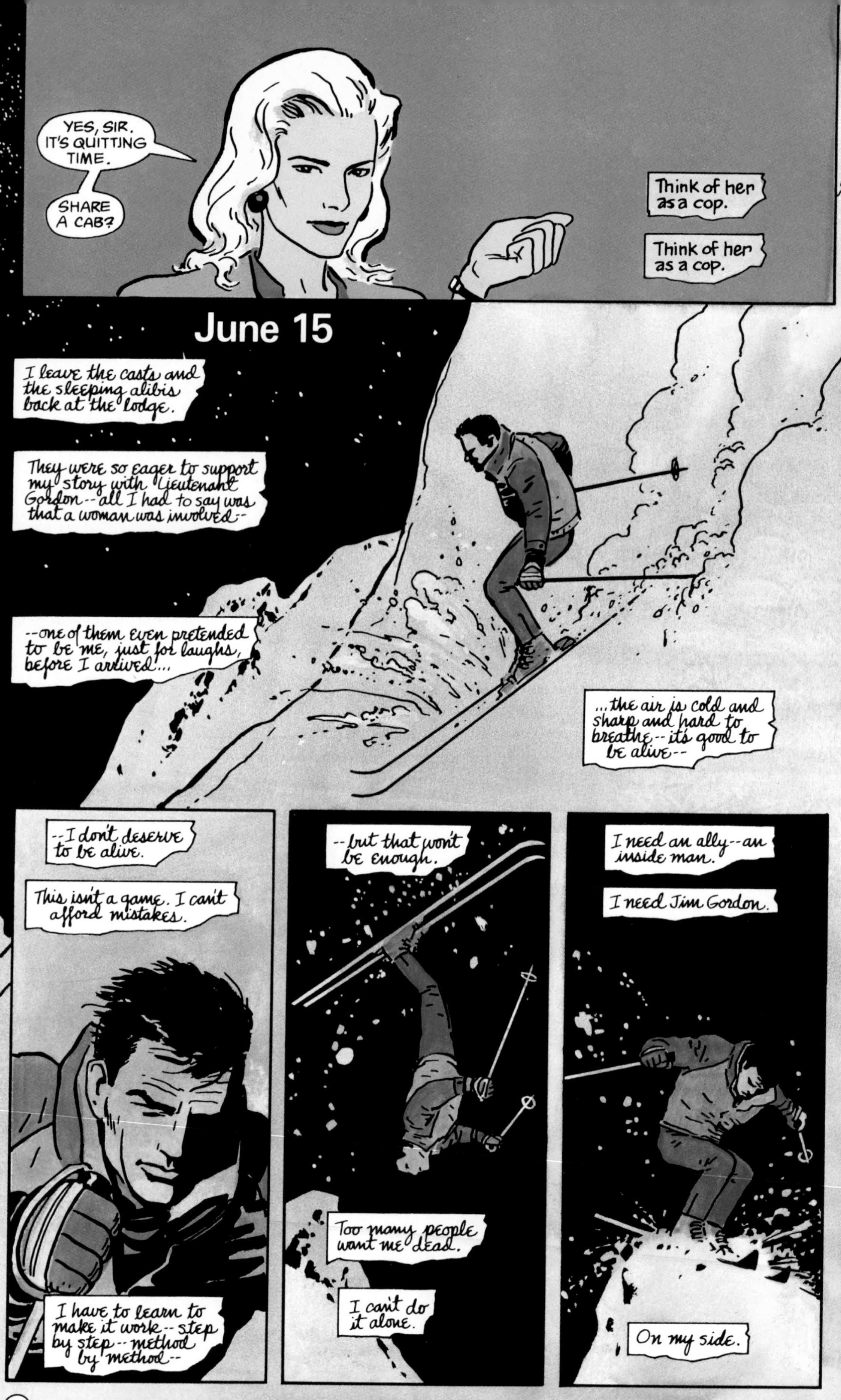

YES, SIR. IT'S QUITTING TIME.
SHARE A CAB?
Think of her as a cop.
Think of her as a cop.
June 15
I leave the casts and the sleeping alibis back at the lodge.
They were so eager to support my story with Lieutenant Gordon--all I had to say was that a woman was involved--
--one of them even pretended to be me, just for laughs, before I arrived...
...the air is cold and sharp and hard to breathe--it's good to be alive--
--I don't deserve to be alive.
This isn't a game. I can't afford mistakes.
I have to learn to make it work--step by step--method by method--
--but that won't be enough.
Too many people want me dead.
I can't do it alone.
I need an ally--an inside man.
I need Jim Gordon.
On my side.

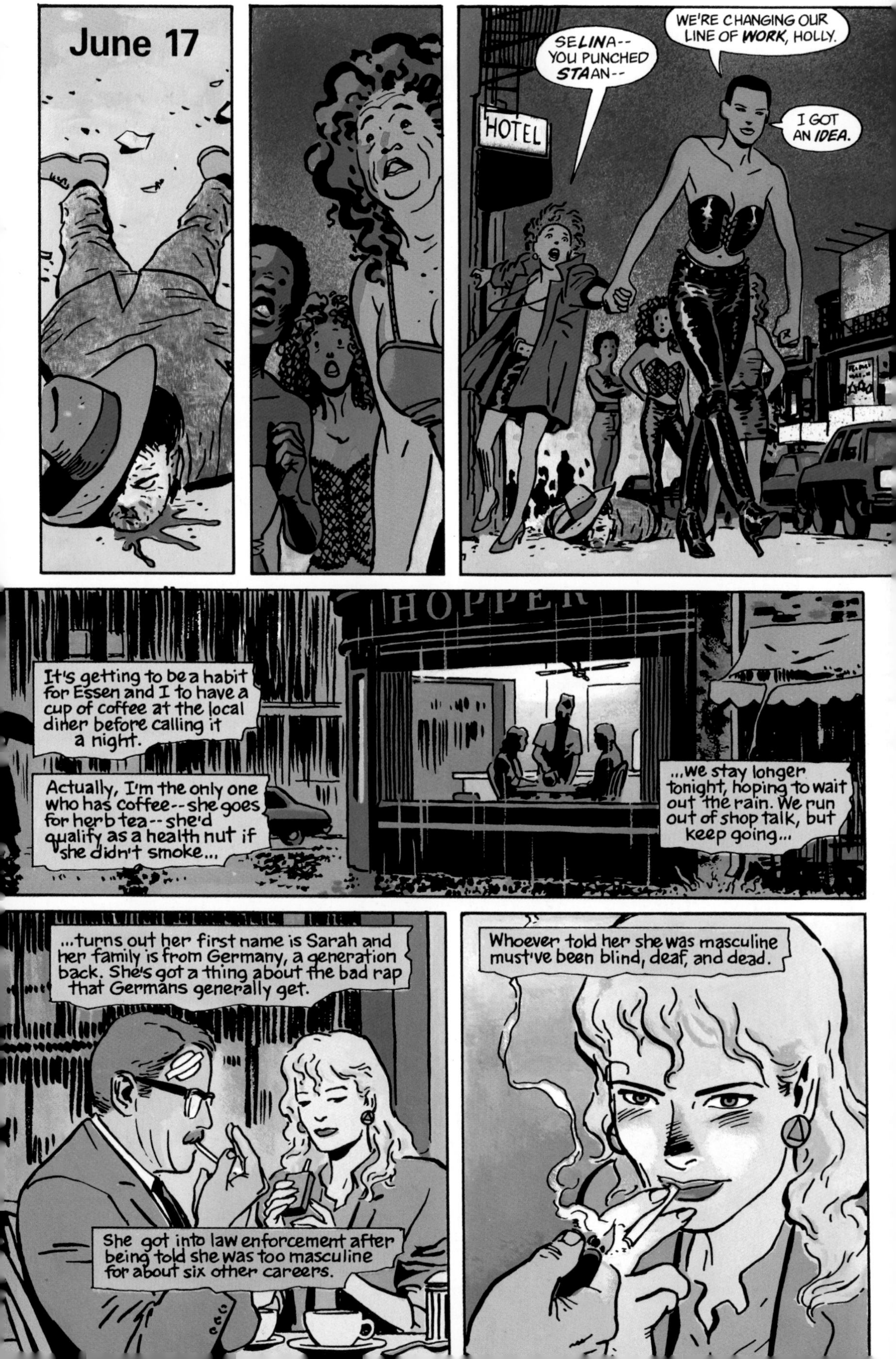
June 17
SELINA--
YOU PUNCHED
STAAN--
WE'RE CHANGING OUR
LINE OF WORK, HOLLY.
I GOT
AN IDEA.
HOTEL
HOPPER
It's getting to be a habit for Essen and I to have a cup of coffee at the local diner before calling it a night.
Actually, I'm the only one who has coffee--she goes for herb tea--she'd qualify as a health nut if she didn't smoke...
...we stay longer tonight, hoping to wait out the rain. We run out of shop talk, but keep going...
...turns out her first name is Sarah and her family is from Germany, a generation back. She's got a thing about the bad rap that Germans generally get.
She got into law enforcement after being told she was too masculine for about six other careers.
Whoever told her she was masculine must've been blind, deaf, and dead.

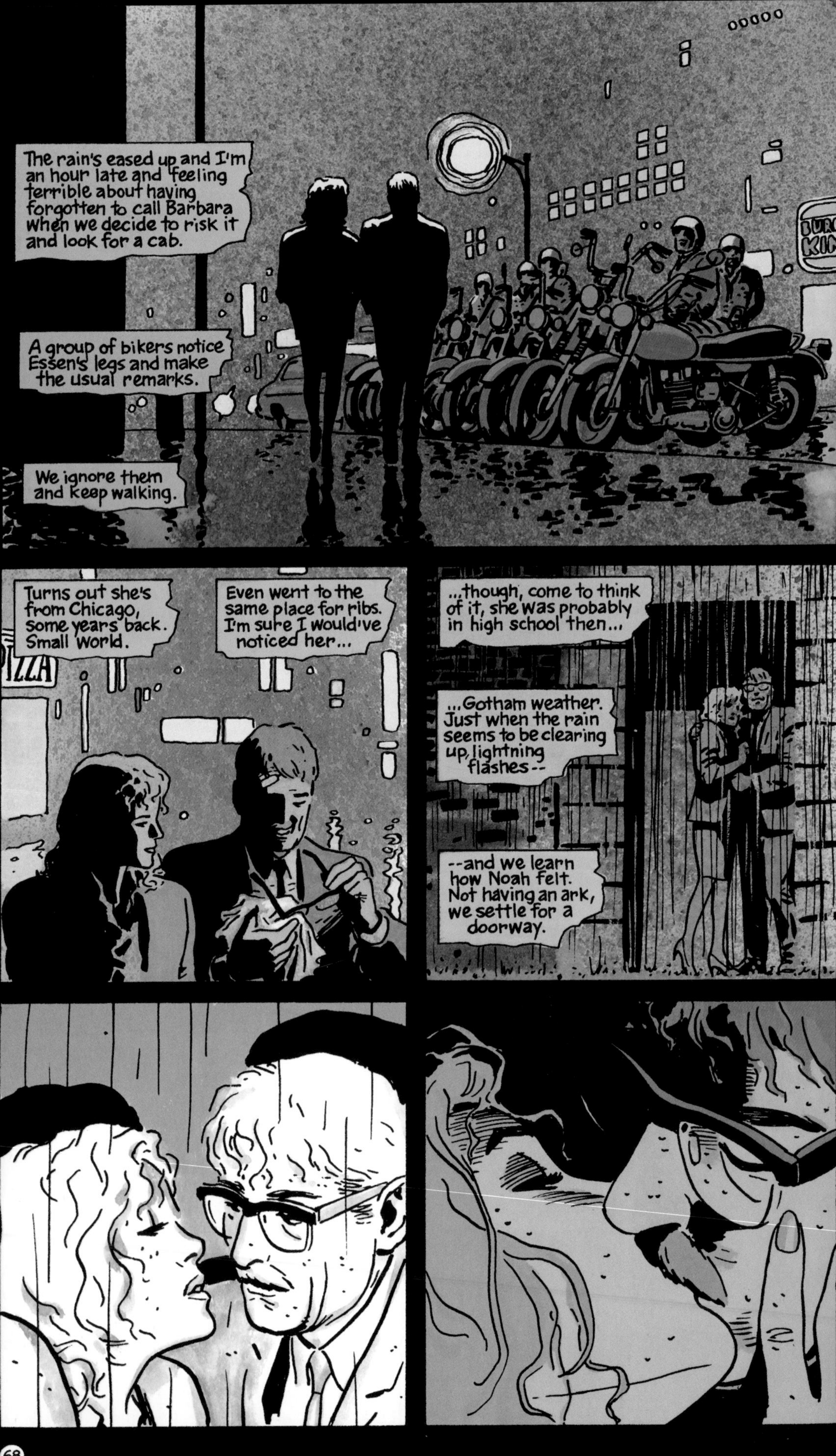
The rain's eased up and I'm an hour late and feeling terrible about having forgotten to call Barbara when we decide to risk it and look for a cab.
A group of bikers notice Essen's legs and make the usual remarks.
We ignore them and keep walking.
BURG KIN
Turns out she's from Chicago, some years back. Small world.
Even went to the same place for ribs. I'm sure I would've noticed her...
PIZZA
...though, come to think of it, she was probably in high school then...
...Gotham weather. Just when the rain seems to be clearing up, lightning flashes--
--and we learn how Noah felt. Not having an ark, we settle for a doorway.

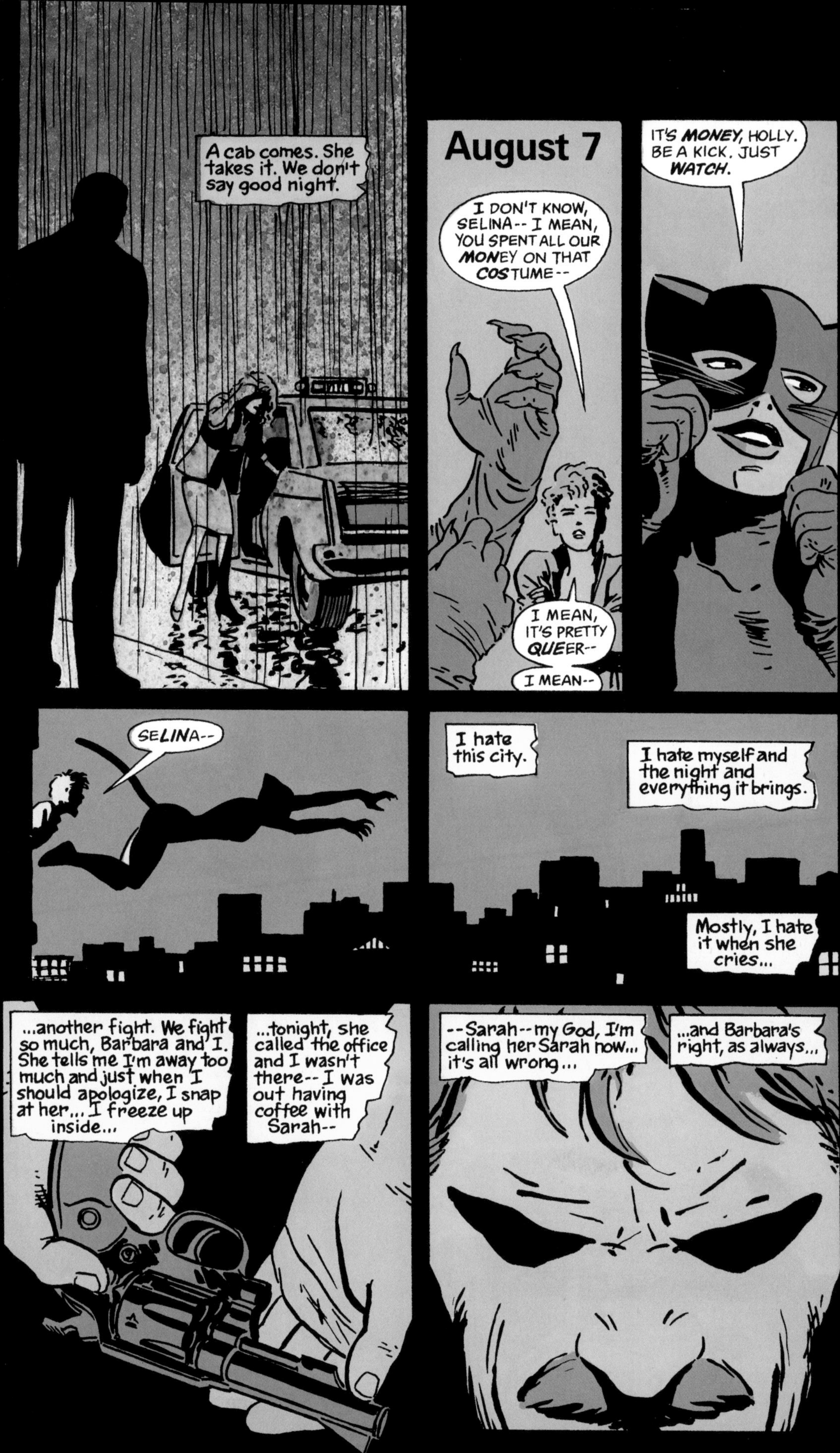
A cab comes. She takes it. We don't say good night.
August 7
I DON'T KNOW, SELINA-- I MEAN, YOU SPENT ALL OUR MONEY ON THAT COSTUME--
I MEAN, IT'S PRETTY QUEER--
I MEAN--
IT'S MONEY, HOLLY. BE A KICK. JUST WATCH.
SELINA--
I hate this city.
I hate myself and the night and everything it brings.
Mostly, I hate it when she cries...
...another fight. We fight so much, Barbara and I. She tells me I'm away too much and just when I should apologize, I snap at her... I freeze up inside...
...tonight, she called the office and I wasn't there-- I was out having coffee with Sarah--
--Sarah--my God, I'm calling her Sarah now... it's all wrong...
...and Barbara's right, as always...

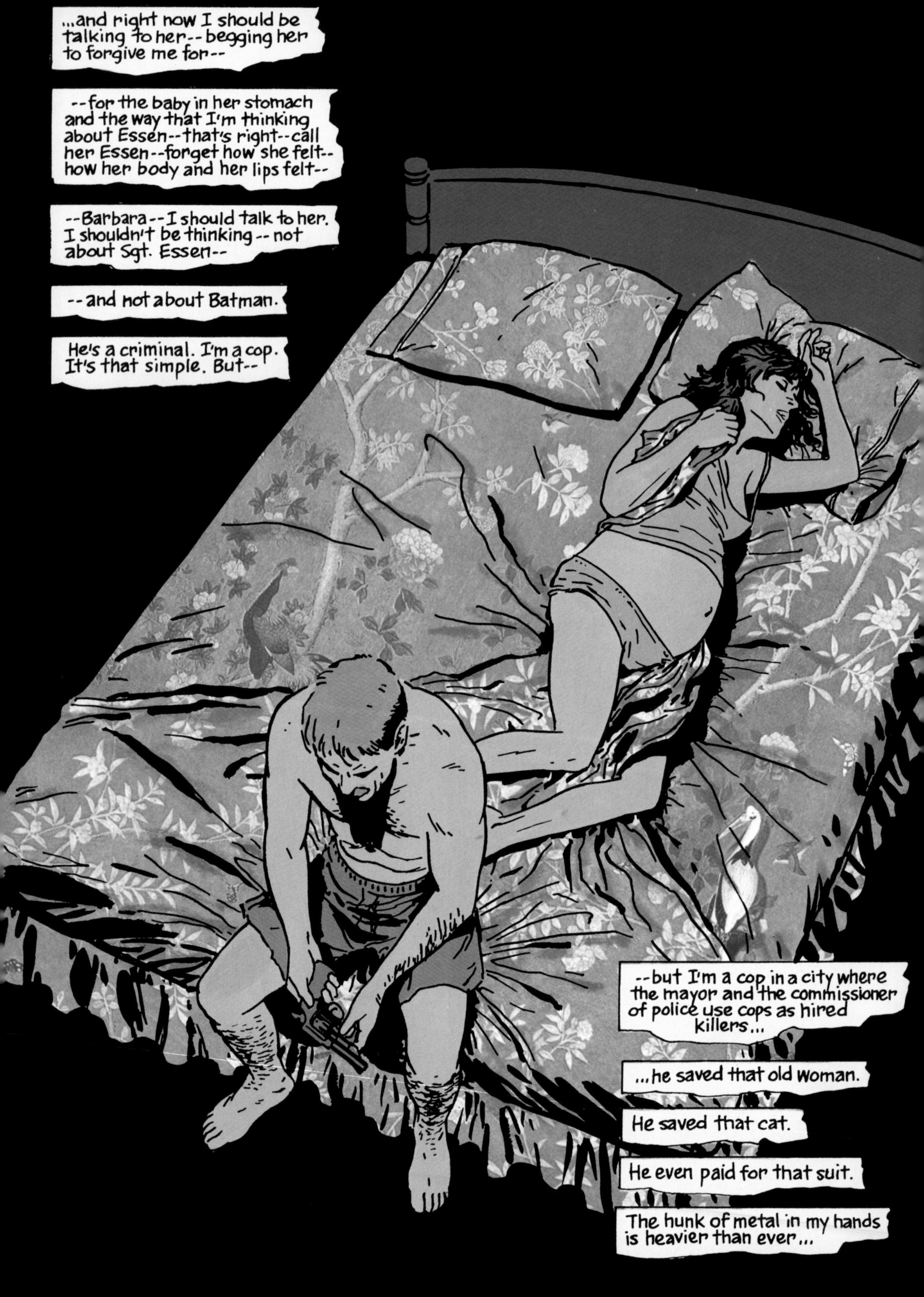
...and right now I should be talking to her-- begging her to forgive me for--
--for the baby in her stomach and the way that I'm thinking about Essen--that's right--call her Essen--forget how she felt--how her body and her lips felt--
--Barbara--I should talk to her. I shouldn't be thinking--not about Sgt. Essen--
--and not about Batman.
He's a criminal. I'm a cop. It's that simple. But--
--but I'm a cop in a city where the mayor and the commissioner of police use cops as hired killers...
...he saved that old woman.
He saved that cat.
He even paid for that suit.
The hunk of metal in my hands is heavier than ever...

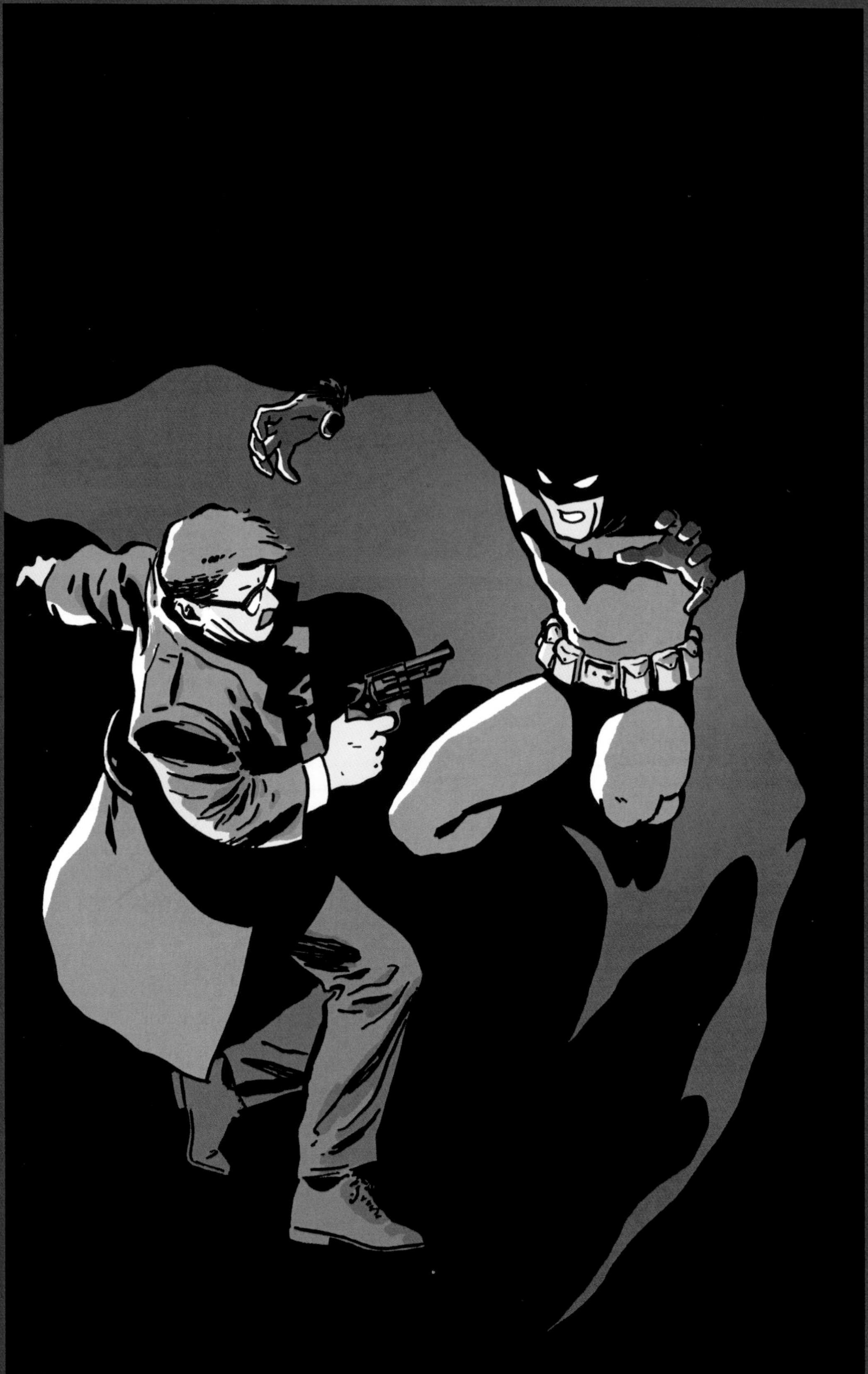

He's out to clean
up a city that
likes being dirty.

He can't do it alone.

CHAPTER FOUR:
FRIEND IN NEED

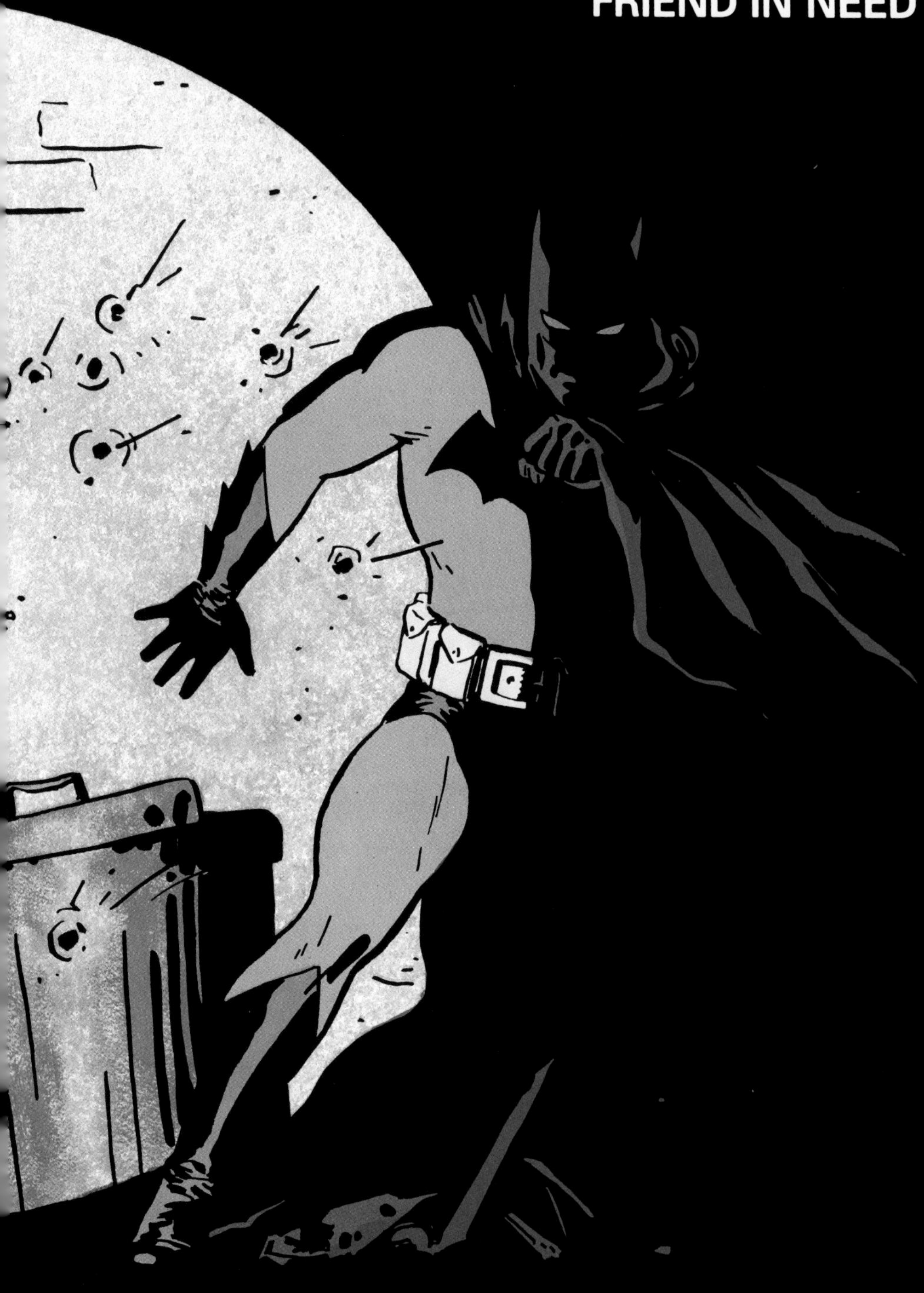

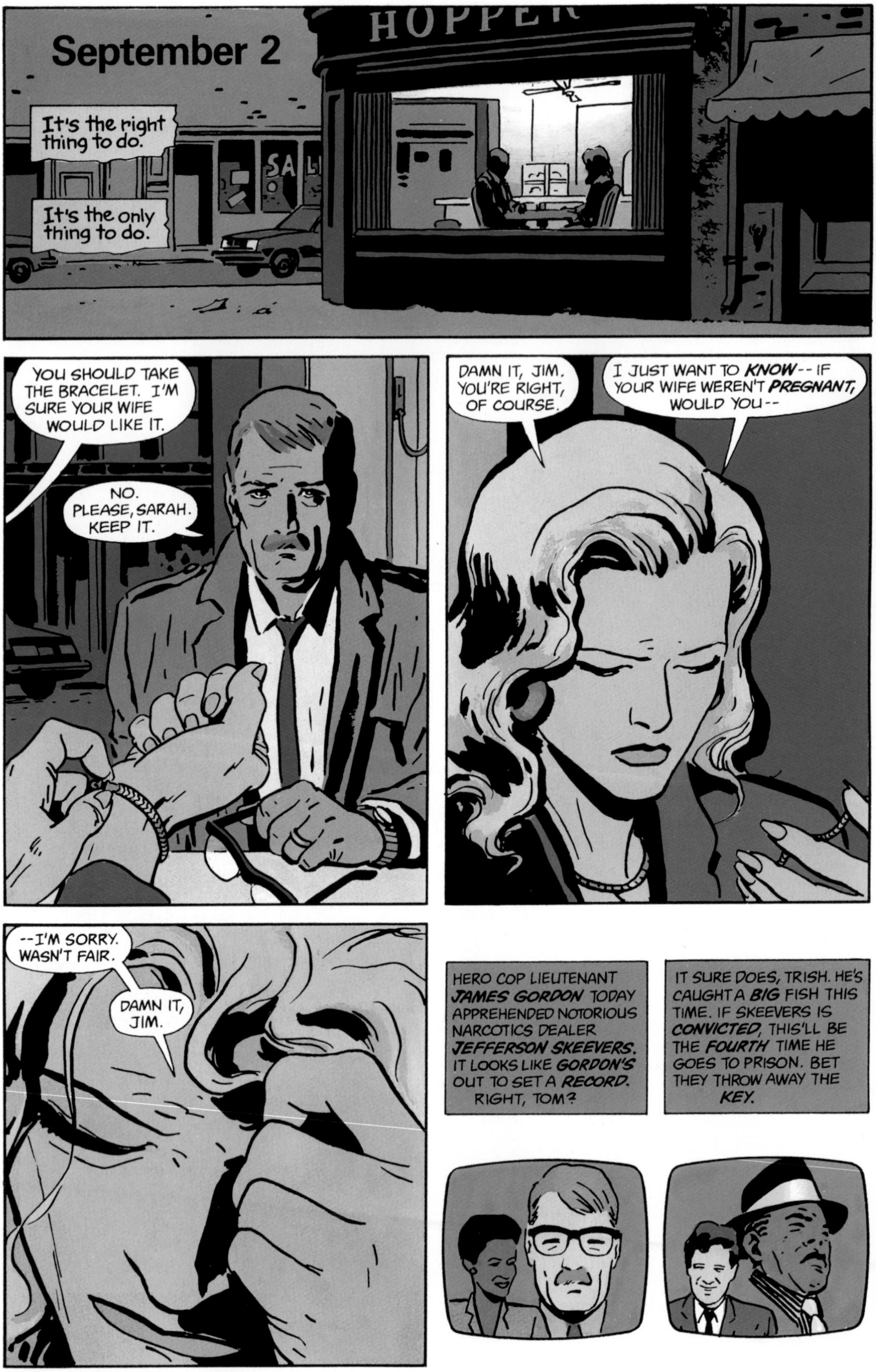
September 2
It's the right thing to do.
It's the only thing to do.
HOPPER
YOU SHOULD TAKE THE BRACELET. I'M SURE YOUR WIFE WOULD LIKE IT.
NO. PLEASE, SARAH. KEEP IT.
DAMN IT, JIM. YOU'RE RIGHT, OF COURSE.
I JUST WANT TO KNOW-- IF YOUR WIFE WEREN'T PREGNANT, WOULD YOU--
--I'M SORRY. WASN'T FAIR.
DAMN IT, JIM.
HERO COP LIEUTENANT JAMES GORDON TODAY APPREHENDED NOTORIOUS NARCOTICS DEALER JEFFERSON SKEEVERS. IT LOOKS LIKE GORDON'S OUT TO SET A RECORD. RIGHT, TOM?
IT SURE DOES, TRISH. HE'S CAUGHT A BIG FISH THIS TIME. IF SKEEVERS IS CONVICTED, THIS'LL BE THE FOURTH TIME HE GOES TO PRISON. BET THEY THROW AWAY THE KEY.

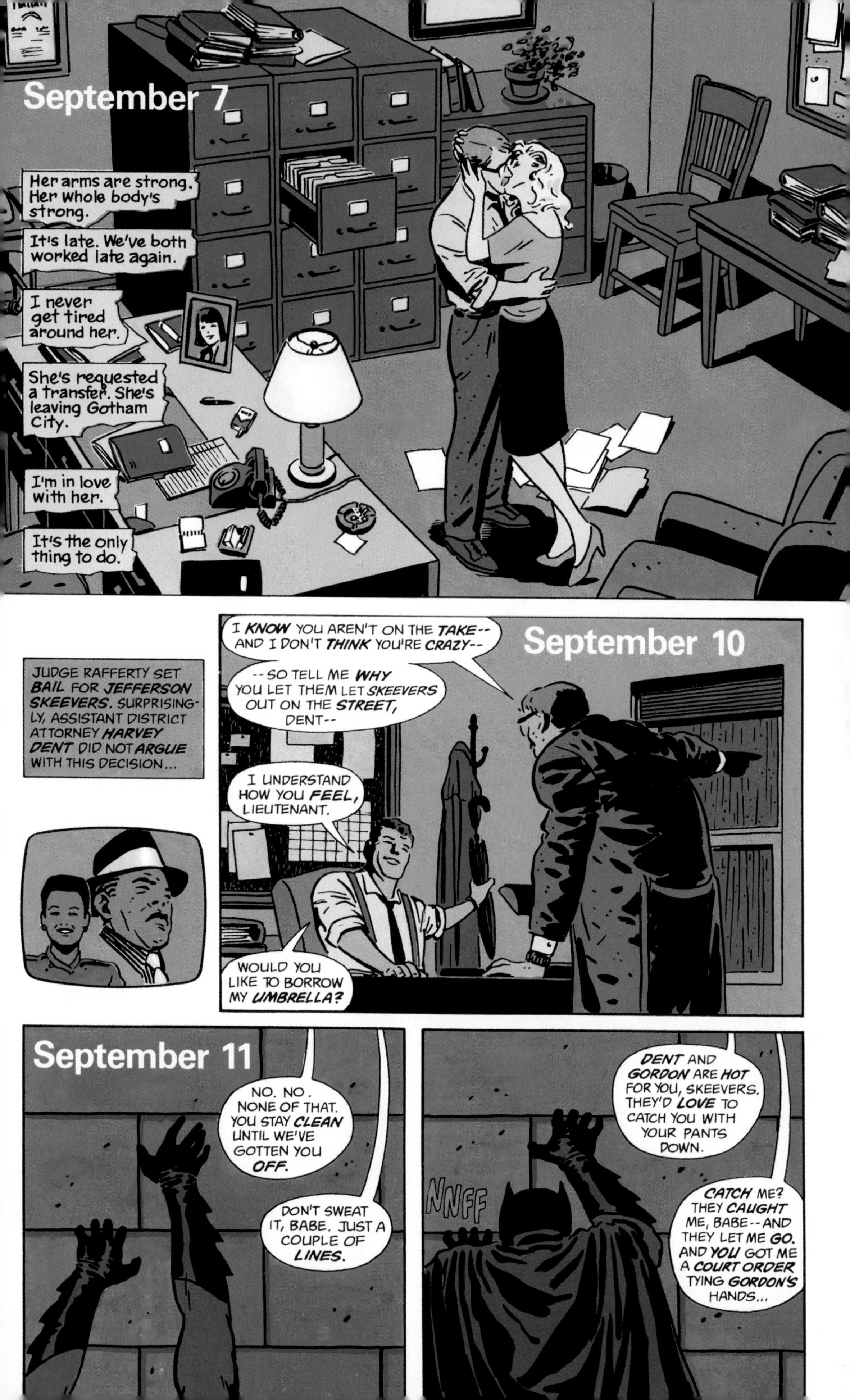
September 7
Her arms are strong. Her whole body's strong.
It's late. We've both worked late again.
I never get tired around her.
She's requested a transfer. She's leaving Gotham City.
I'm in love with her.
It's the only thing to do.
JUDGE RAFFERTY SET BAIL FOR JEFFERSON SKEEVERS. SURPRISINGLY, ASSISTANT DISTRICT ATTORNEY HARVEY DENT DID NOT ARGUE WITH THIS DECISION...
September 10
I KNOW YOU AREN'T ON THE TAKE-- AND I DON'T THINK YOU'RE CRAZY--
--SO TELL ME WHY YOU LET THEM LET SKEEVERS OUT ON THE STREET, DENT--
I UNDERSTAND HOW YOU FEEL, LIEUTENANT.
WOULD YOU LIKE TO BORROW MY UMBRELLA?
September 11
NO. NO. NONE OF THAT. YOU STAY CLEAN UNTIL WE'VE GOTTEN YOU OFF.
DON'T SWEAT IT, BABE. JUST A COUPLE OF LINES.
DENT AND GORDON ARE HOT FOR YOU, SKEEVERS. THEY'D LOVE TO CATCH YOU WITH YOUR PANTS DOWN.
NNFF
CATCH ME? THEY CAUGHT ME, BABE--AND THEY LET ME GO. AND YOU GOT ME A COURT ORDER TYING GORDON'S HANDS...

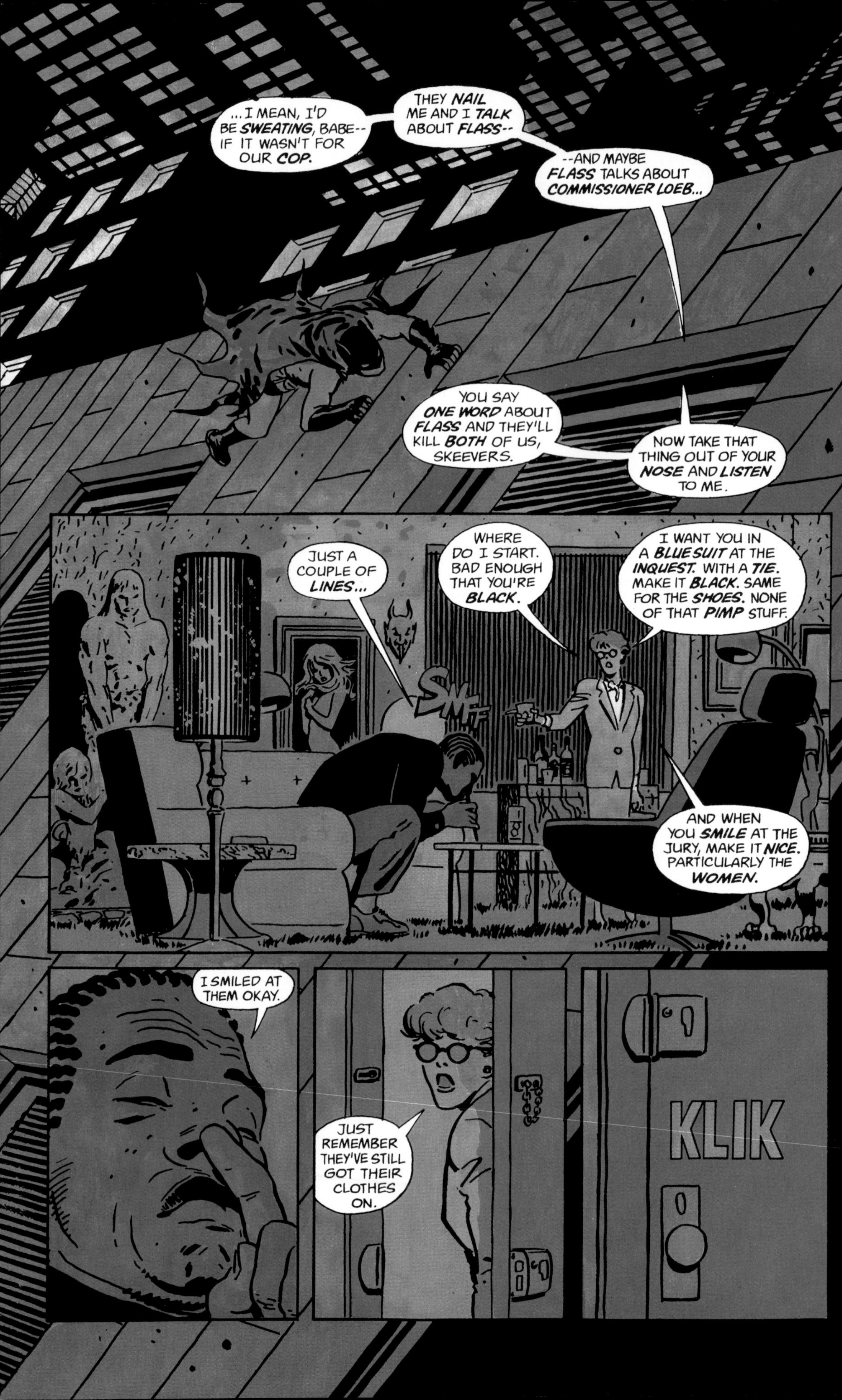
...I MEAN, I'D BE SWEATING, BABE-- IF IT WASN'T FOR OUR COP.
THEY NAIL ME AND I TALK ABOUT FLASS--
--AND MAYBE FLASS TALKS ABOUT COMMISSIONER LOEB...
YOU SAY ONE WORD ABOUT FLASS AND THEY'LL KILL BOTH OF US, SKEEVERS.
NOW TAKE THAT THING OUT OF YOUR NOSE AND LISTEN TO ME.
JUST A COUPLE OF LINES...
WHERE DO I START. BAD ENOUGH THAT YOU'RE BLACK.
I WANT YOU IN A BLUE SUIT AT THE INQUEST. WITH A TIE. MAKE IT BLACK. SAME FOR THE SHOES. NONE OF THAT PIMP STUFF.
SNF
AND WHEN YOU SMILE AT THE JURY, MAKE IT NICE. PARTICULARLY THE WOMEN.
I SMILED AT THEM OKAY.
JUST REMEMBER THEY'VE STILL GOT THEIR CLOTHES ON.
KLIK

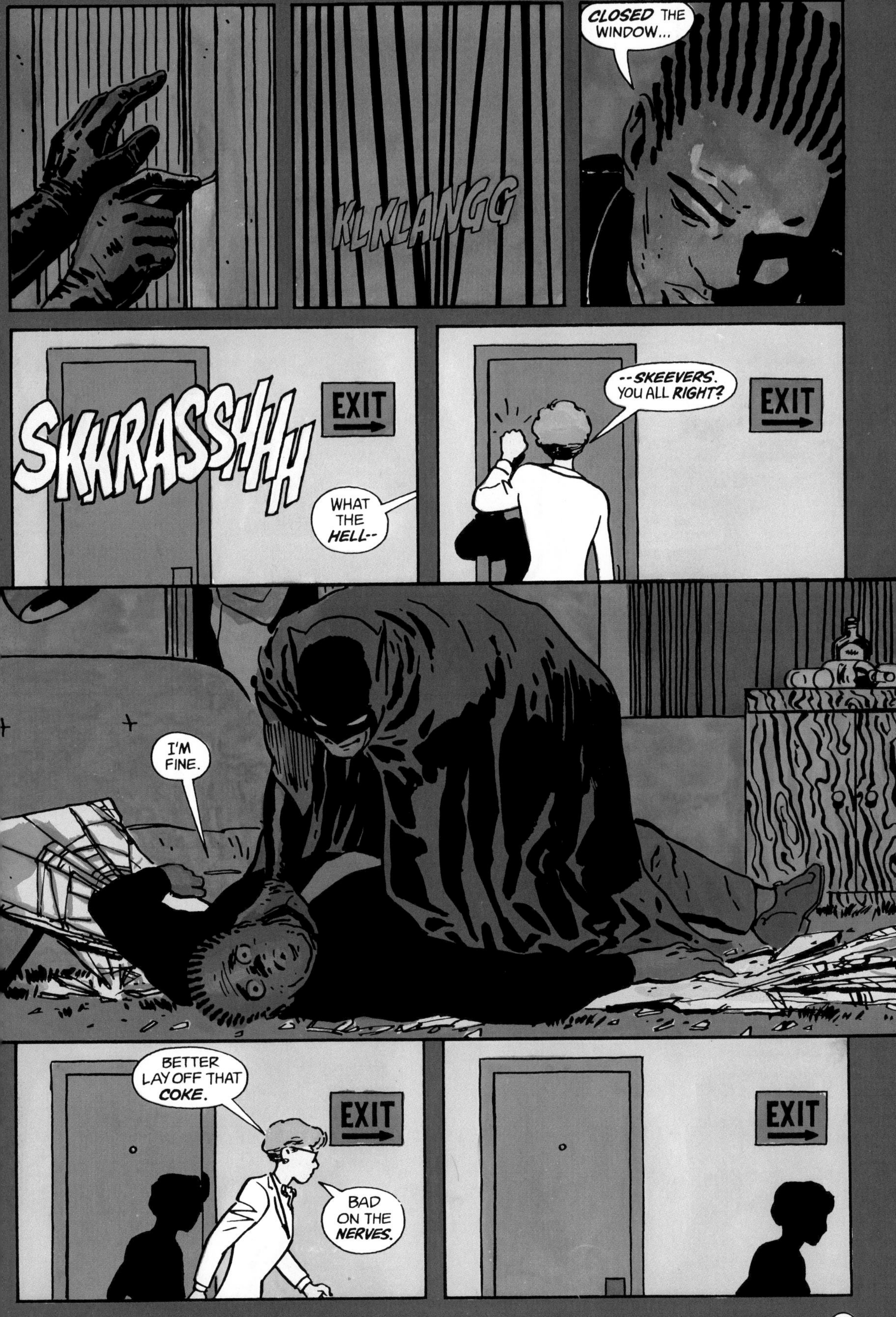
KLKLANGG
CLOSED THE WINDOW...
SKKRASSHHH
WHAT THE HELL--
--SKEEVERS. YOU ALL RIGHT?
I'M FINE.
BETTER LAY OFF THAT COKE.
BAD ON THE NERVES.

YOU CAN NEVER ESCAPE ME.

NNGG

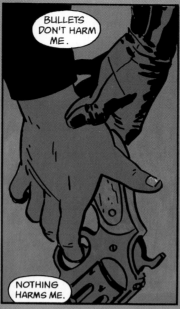

BULLETS DON'T HARM ME.

NOTHING HARMS ME.

BUT I KNOW PAIN.

I KNOW PAIN.

SOMETIMES I SHARE IT.

WITH SOMEONE LIKE YOU.

WANT TO TALK TO *DENT*. COP A *PLEA*. WANT TO *TALK*. ABOUT *FLASS*.

September 12

MERKEL. GET *DENT*.

FORGET TO TELL THE *COMMISSIONER*.

I'M GONE...

SOURCES INSIDE THE POLICE DEPARTMENT REVEALED THAT GOTHAM POLICE DETECTIVE *ARNOLD FLASS* HAS BEEN IMPLICATED IN SKEEVERS' DRUG OPERATION...

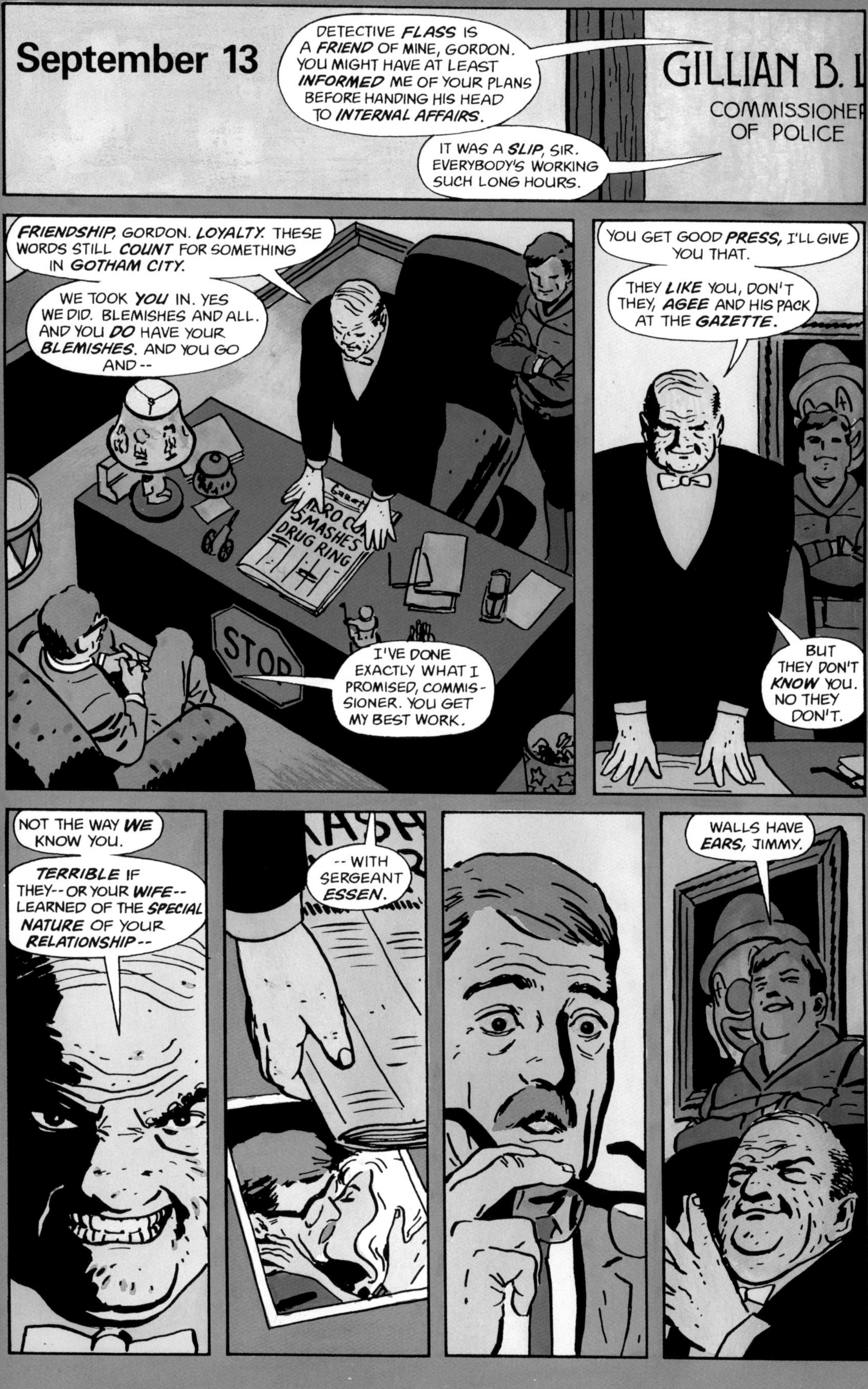
September 13
DETECTIVE FLASS IS A FRIEND OF MINE, GORDON. YOU MIGHT HAVE AT LEAST INFORMED ME OF YOUR PLANS BEFORE HANDING HIS HEAD TO INTERNAL AFFAIRS.
IT WAS A SLIP, SIR. EVERYBODY'S WORKING SUCH LONG HOURS.
GILLIAN B. L
COMMISSIONER
OF POLICE
FRIENDSHIP, GORDON. LOYALTY. THESE WORDS STILL COUNT FOR SOMETHING IN GOTHAM CITY.
WE TOOK YOU IN. YES WE DID. BLEMISHES AND ALL. AND YOU DO HAVE YOUR BLEMISHES. AND YOU GO AND --
SMASHES DRUG RING
STOP
I'VE DONE EXACTLY WHAT I PROMISED, COMMISSIONER. YOU GET MY BEST WORK.
YOU GET GOOD PRESS, I'LL GIVE YOU THAT.
THEY LIKE YOU, DON'T THEY, AGEE AND HIS PACK AT THE GAZETTE.
BUT THEY DON'T KNOW YOU. NO THEY DON'T.
NOT THE WAY WE KNOW YOU.
TERRIBLE IF THEY-- OR YOUR WIFE-- LEARNED OF THE SPECIAL NATURE OF YOUR RELATIONSHIP --
-- WITH SERGEANT ESSEN.
WALLS HAVE EARS, JIMMY.

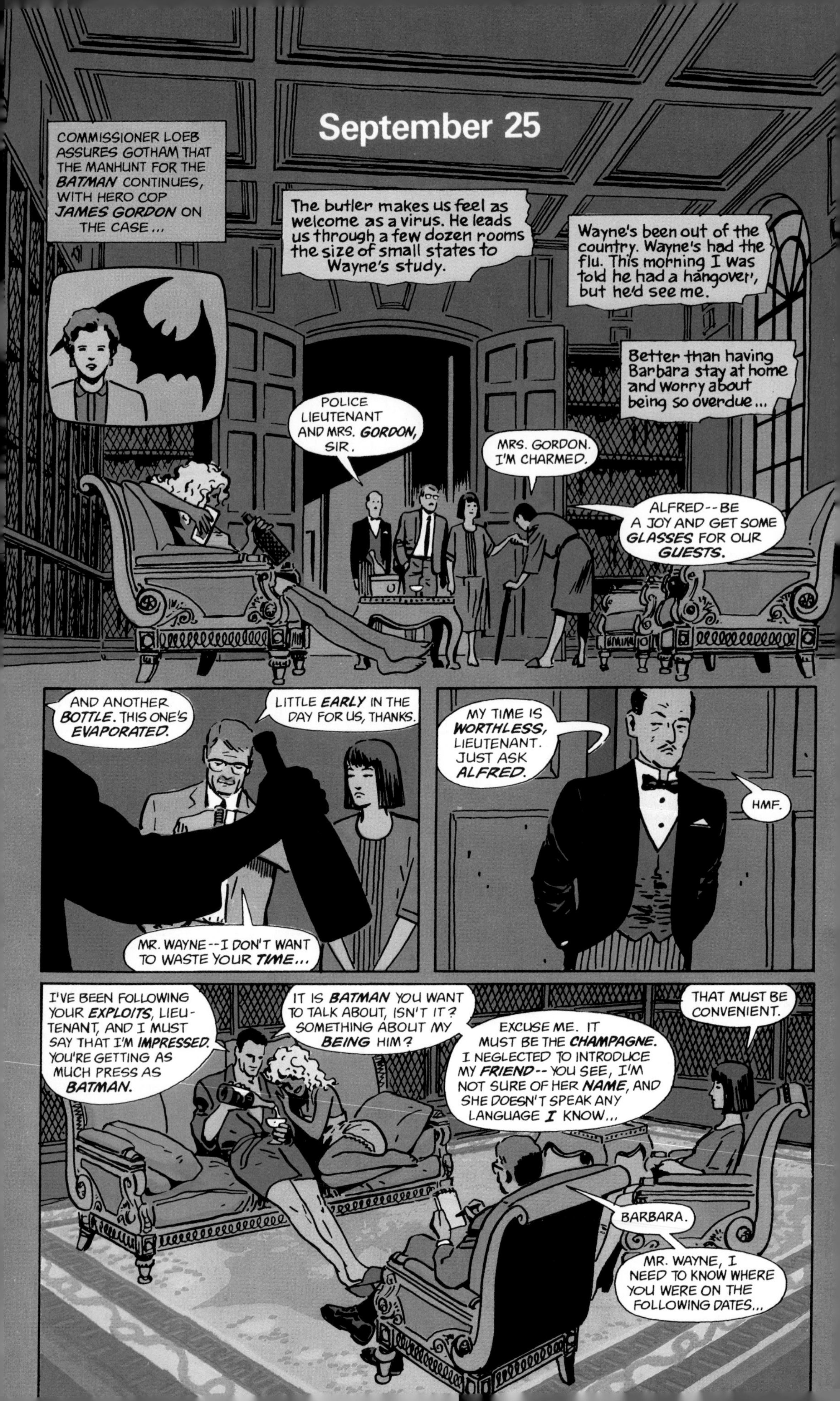

September 25
COMMISSIONER LOEB ASSURES GOTHAM THAT THE MANHUNT FOR THE BATMAN CONTINUES, WITH HERO COP JAMES GORDON ON THE CASE...
The butler makes us feel as welcome as a virus. He leads us through a few dozen rooms the size of small states to Wayne's study.
Wayne's been out of the country. Wayne's had the flu. This morning I was told he had a hangover, but he'd see me.
Better than having Barbara stay at home and worry about being so overdue...
POLICE LIEUTENANT AND MRS. GORDON, SIR.
MRS. GORDON. I'M CHARMED.
ALFRED--BE A JOY AND GET SOME GLASSES FOR OUR GUESTS.
AND ANOTHER BOTTLE. THIS ONE'S EVAPORATED.
LITTLE EARLY IN THE DAY FOR US, THANKS.
MR. WAYNE--I DON'T WANT TO WASTE YOUR TIME...
MY TIME IS WORTHLESS, LIEUTENANT. JUST ASK ALFRED.
HMF.
I'VE BEEN FOLLOWING YOUR EXPLOITS, LIEU-TENANT, AND I MUST SAY THAT I'M IMPRESSED. YOU'RE GETTING AS MUCH PRESS AS BATMAN.
IT IS BATMAN YOU WANT TO TALK ABOUT, ISN'T IT? SOMETHING ABOUT MY BEING HIM?
EXCUSE ME. IT MUST BE THE CHAMPAGNE. I NEGLECTED TO INTRODUCE MY FRIEND--YOU SEE, I'M NOT SURE OF HER NAME, AND SHE DOESN'T SPEAK ANY LANGUAGE I KNOW...
THAT MUST BE CONVENIENT.
BARBARA.
MR. WAYNE, I NEED TO KNOW WHERE YOU WERE ON THE FOLLOWING DATES...

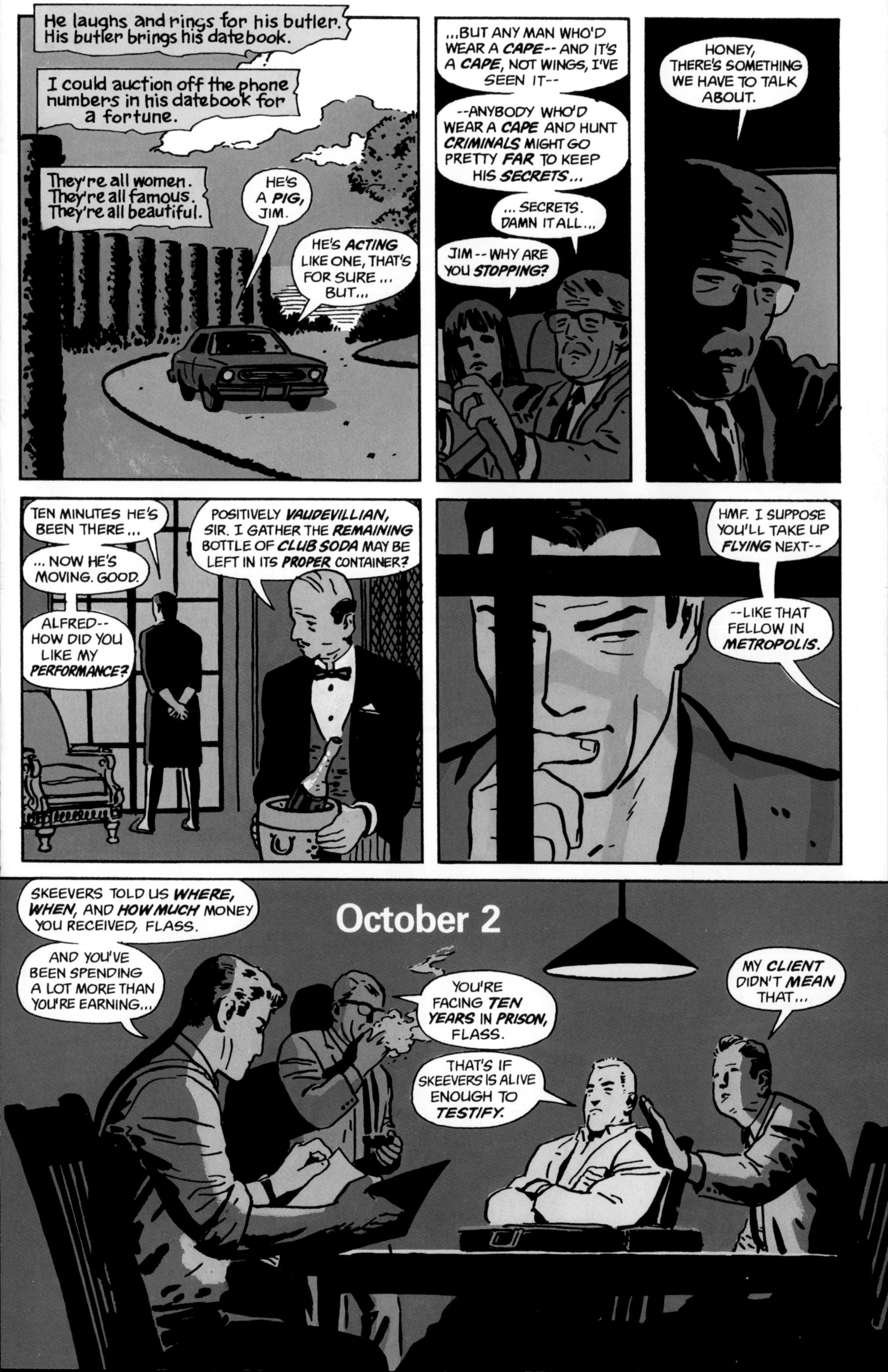
He laughs and rings for his butler. His butler brings his datebook.
I could auction off the phone numbers in his datebook for a fortune.
They're all women. They're all famous. They're all beautiful.
HE'S A PIG, JIM.
HE'S ACTING LIKE ONE, THAT'S FOR SURE ... BUT...
...BUT ANY MAN WHO'D WEAR A CAPE-- AND IT'S A CAPE, NOT WINGS, I'VE SEEN IT--
--ANYBODY WHO'D WEAR A CAPE AND HUNT CRIMINALS MIGHT GO PRETTY FAR TO KEEP HIS SECRETS...
... SECRETS. DAMN IT ALL...
JIM -- WHY ARE YOU STOPPING?
HONEY, THERE'S SOMETHING WE HAVE TO TALK ABOUT.
TEN MINUTES HE'S BEEN THERE...
... NOW HE'S MOVING. GOOD.
ALFRED-- HOW DID YOU LIKE MY PERFORMANCE?
POSITIVELY VAUDEVILLIAN, SIR. I GATHER THE REMAINING BOTTLE OF CLUB SODA MAY BE LEFT IN ITS PROPER CONTAINER?
HMF. I SUPPOSE YOU'LL TAKE UP FLYING NEXT--
--LIKE THAT FELLOW IN METROPOLIS.
October 2
SKEEVERS TOLD US WHERE, WHEN, AND HOW MUCH MONEY YOU RECEIVED, FLASS.
AND YOU'VE BEEN SPENDING A LOT MORE THAN YOU'RE EARNING...
YOU'RE FACING TEN YEARS IN PRISON, FLASS.
THAT'S IF SKEEVERS IS ALIVE ENOUGH TO TESTIFY.
MY CLIENT DIDN'T MEAN THAT...

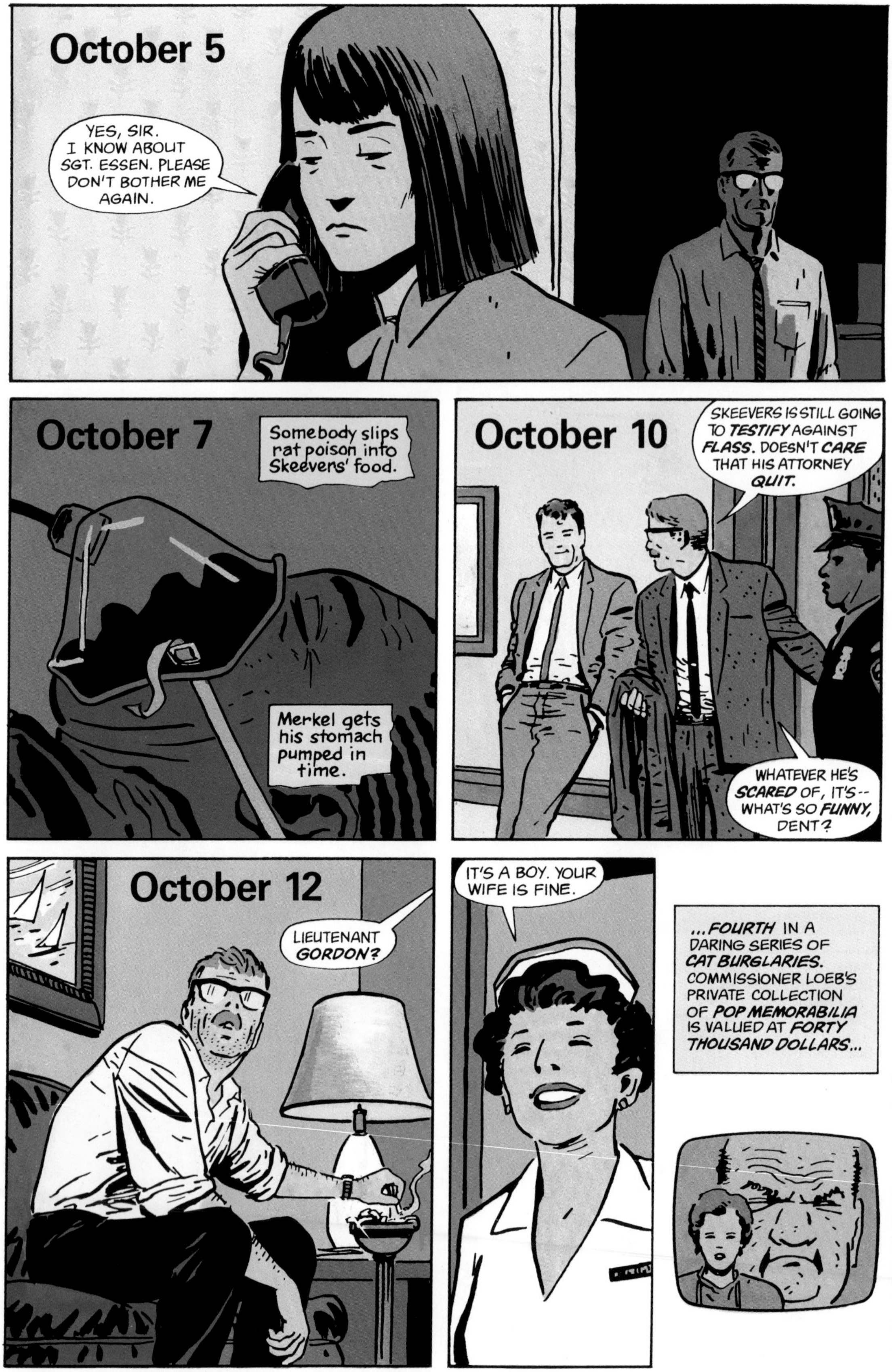
October 5
YES, SIR. I KNOW ABOUT SGT. ESSEN. PLEASE DON'T BOTHER ME AGAIN.
October 7
Somebody slips rat poison into Skeevers' food.
Merkel gets his stomach pumped in time.
October 10
SKEEVERS IS STILL GOING TO TESTIFY AGAINST FLASS. DOESN'T CARE THAT HIS ATTORNEY QUIT.
WHATEVER HE'S SCARED OF, IT'S-- WHAT'S SO FUNNY, DENT?
October 12
LIEUTENANT GORDON?
IT'S A BOY. YOUR WIFE IS FINE.
...FOURTH IN A DARING SERIES OF CAT BURGLARIES. COMMISSIONER LOEB'S PRIVATE COLLECTION OF POP MEMORABILIA IS VALUED AT FORTY THOUSAND DOLLARS...

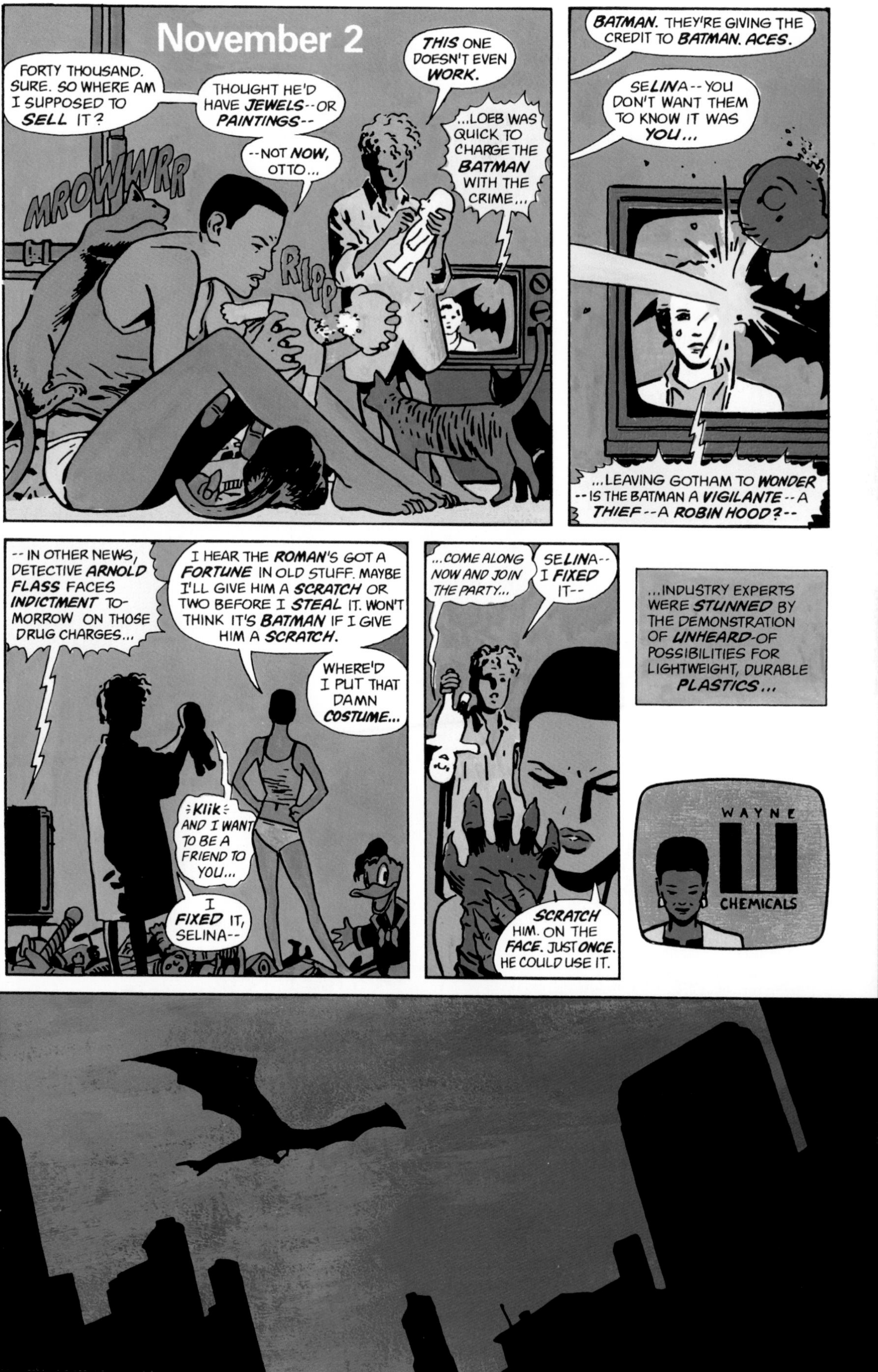
November 2
FORTY THOUSAND. SURE. SO WHERE AM I SUPPOSED TO SELL IT?
THOUGHT HE'D HAVE JEWELS--OR PAINTINGS--
--NOT NOW, OTTO...
THIS ONE DOESN'T EVEN WORK.
...LOEB WAS QUICK TO CHARGE THE BATMAN WITH THE CRIME...
MROWWRR
RIPP
BATMAN. THEY'RE GIVING THE CREDIT TO BATMAN. ACES.
SELINA--YOU DON'T WANT THEM TO KNOW IT WAS YOU...
...LEAVING GOTHAM TO WONDER--IS THE BATMAN A VIGILANTE--A THIEF--A ROBIN HOOD?--
--IN OTHER NEWS, DETECTIVE ARNOLD FLASS FACES INDICTMENT TOMORROW ON THOSE DRUG CHARGES...
I HEAR THE ROMAN'S GOT A FORTUNE IN OLD STUFF. MAYBE I'LL GIVE HIM A SCRATCH OR TWO BEFORE I STEAL IT. WON'T THINK IT'S BATMAN IF I GIVE HIM A SCRATCH.
WHERE'D I PUT THAT DAMN COSTUME...
Klik AND I WANT TO BE A FRIEND TO YOU...
I FIXED IT, SELINA--
...COME ALONG NOW AND JOIN THE PARTY...
SELINA--I FIXED IT--
SCRATCH HIM. ON THE FACE. JUST ONCE. HE COULD USE IT.
...INDUSTRY EXPERTS WERE STUNNED BY THE DEMONSTRATION OF UNHEARD-OF POSSIBILITIES FOR LIGHTWEIGHT, DURABLE PLASTICS...
WAYNE
CHEMICALS

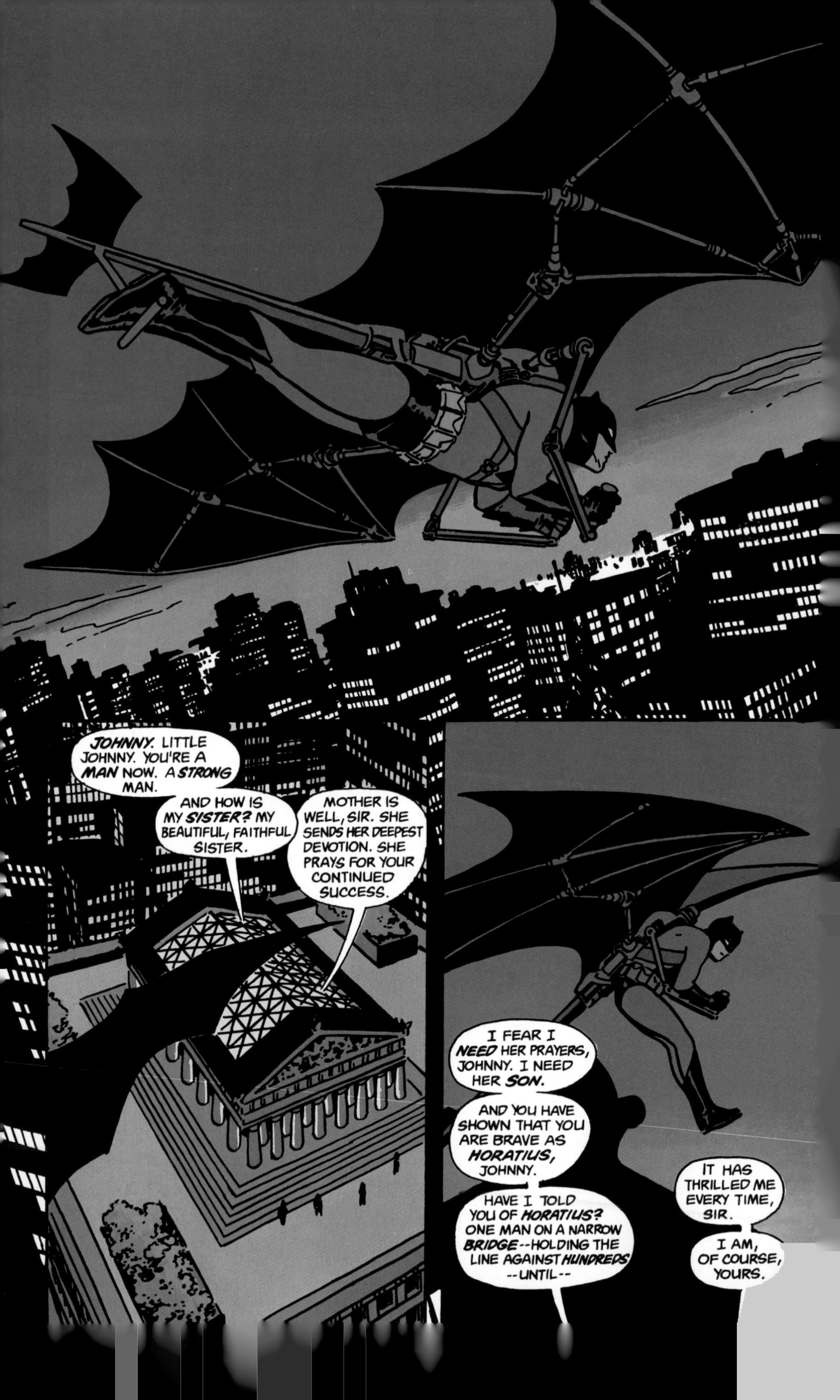

JOHNNY. LITTLE JOHNNY. YOU'RE A MAN NOW. A STRONG MAN.
AND HOW IS MY SISTER? MY BEAUTIFUL, FAITHFUL SISTER.
MOTHER IS WELL, SIR. SHE SENDS HER DEEPEST DEVOTION. SHE PRAYS FOR YOUR CONTINUED SUCCESS.
I FEAR I NEED HER PRAYERS, JOHNNY. I NEED HER SON.
AND YOU HAVE SHOWN THAT YOU ARE BRAVE AS HORATIUS, JOHNNY.
HAVE I TOLD YOU OF HORATIUS? ONE MAN ON A NARROW BRIDGE--HOLDING THE LINE AGAINST HUNDREDS --UNTIL--
IT HAS THRILLED ME EVERY TIME, SIR.
I AM, OF COURSE, YOURS.

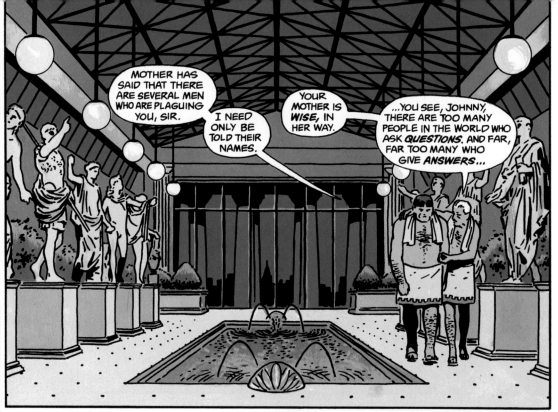

MOTHER HAS SAID THAT THERE ARE SEVERAL MEN WHO ARE PLAGUING YOU, SIR.

I NEED ONLY BE TOLD THEIR NAMES.

YOUR MOTHER IS *WISE*, IN HER WAY.

...YOU SEE, JOHNNY, THERE ARE TOO MANY PEOPLE IN THE WORLD WHO ASK *QUESTIONS*. AND FAR, FAR TOO MANY WHO GIVE *ANSWERS*...

MOTHER SAID--

...WE MUST AVOID MORE BAD *PUBLICITY*, JOHNNY. LISTEN TO ME. I WILL TELL YOU WHAT MUST BE DONE.

WHAPP

OVER THERE-- IT'S--

HSSSSSSS

--IT'S A *WOMGGAHHH*

SSSSS

--OVER *HERE*--

--MY *FACE*--

--IT'S A *WOMAN*--

WHAT'S GOING ON OUT--

--LET *GO* OF ME YOU *IDIOT*--

--HOW'D SHE GET *UP* HERE--

--WHO THE *HELL*--

--CLAWS MY *FACE*--

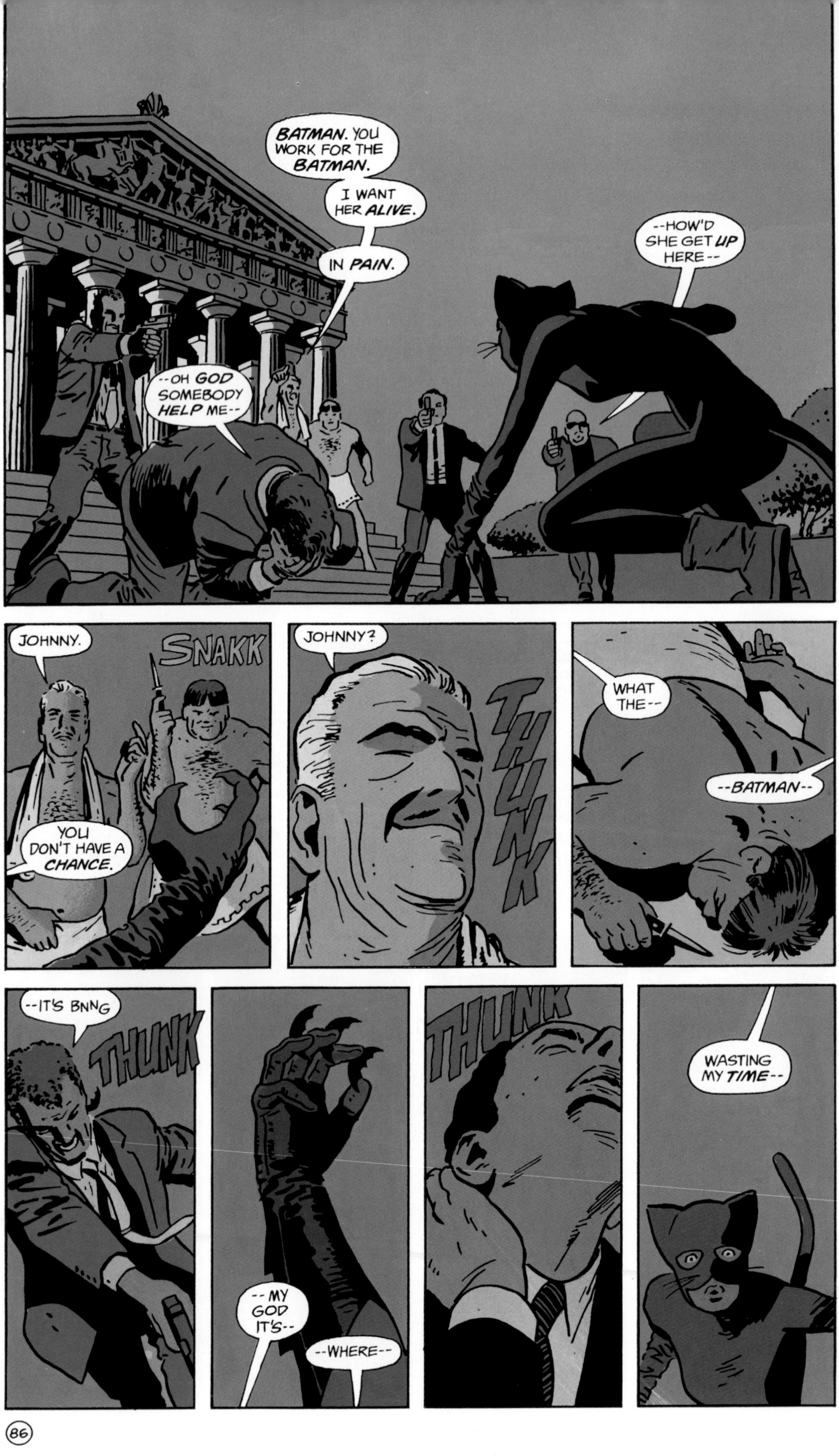
BATMAN. YOU WORK FOR THE BATMAN.
I WANT HER ALIVE.
IN PAIN.
--HOW'D SHE GET UP HERE--
--OH GOD SOMEBODY HELP ME--
JOHNNY.
SNAKK
YOU DON'T HAVE A CHANCE.
JOHNNY?
THUNK
WHAT THE--
--BATMAN--
--IT'S BNNG
THUNK
--MY GOD IT'S--
--WHERE--
THUNK
WASTING MY TIME--

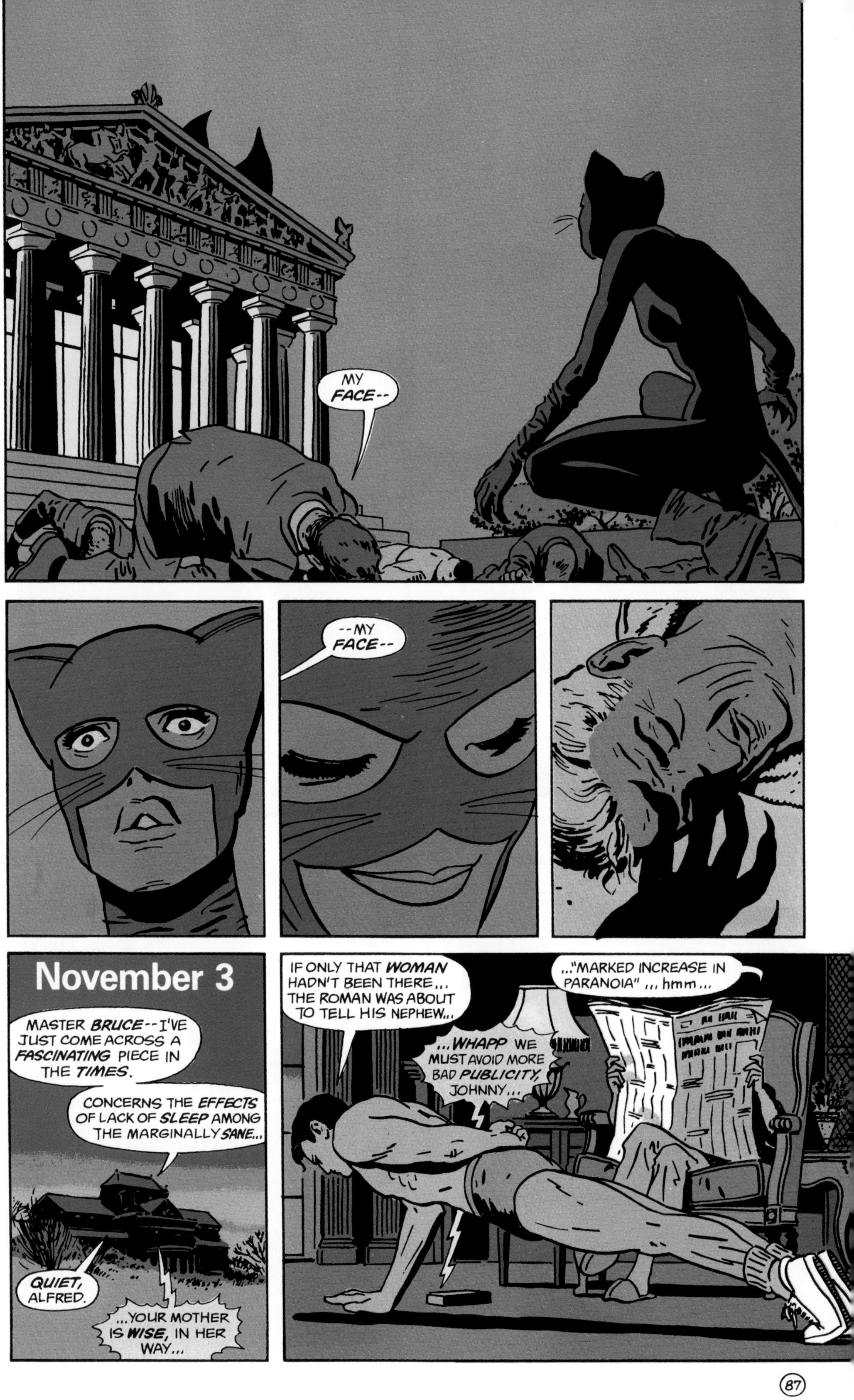
MY FACE--
--MY FACE--
November 3
MASTER BRUCE--I'VE JUST COME ACROSS A FASCINATING PIECE IN THE TIMES.
CONCERNS THE EFFECTS OF LACK OF SLEEP AMONG THE MARGINALLY SANE...
QUIET, ALFRED.
...YOUR MOTHER IS WISE, IN HER WAY...
IF ONLY THAT WOMAN HADN'T BEEN THERE... THE ROMAN WAS ABOUT TO TELL HIS NEPHEW...
...WHAPP WE MUST AVOID MORE BAD PUBLICITY, JOHNNY...
..."MARKED INCREASE IN PARANOIA" ... hmm...

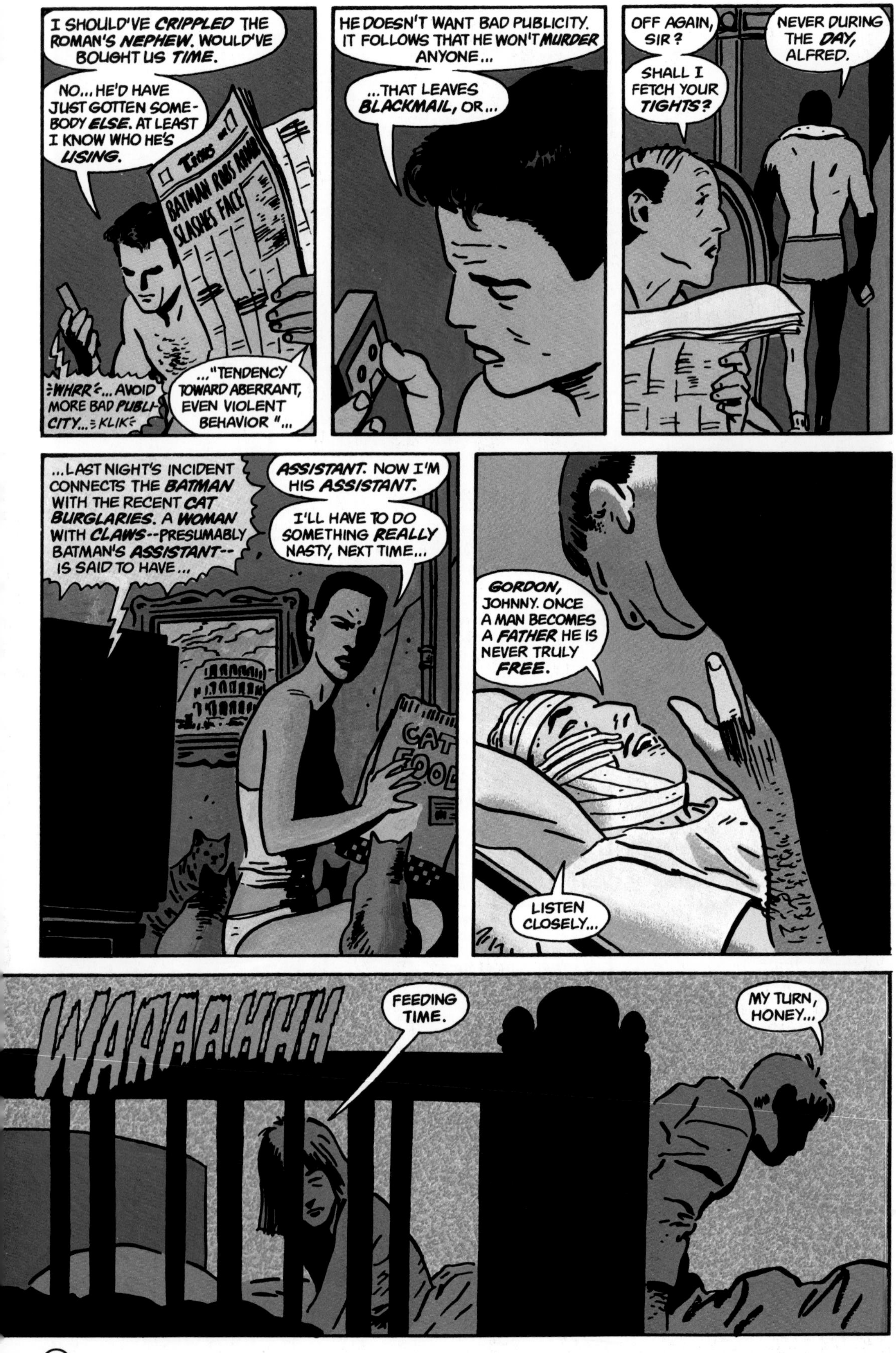
I SHOULD'VE CRIPPLED THE ROMAN'S NEPHEW. WOULD'VE BOUGHT US TIME.
NO... HE'D HAVE JUST GOTTEN SOMEBODY ELSE. AT LEAST I KNOW WHO HE'S USING.
BATMAN ROBS ROMAN SLASHES FACE
WHRR... AVOID MORE BAD PUBLICITY... KLIK
..."TENDENCY TOWARD ABERRANT, EVEN VIOLENT BEHAVIOR"...
HE DOESN'T WANT BAD PUBLICITY. IT FOLLOWS THAT HE WON'T MURDER ANYONE...
...THAT LEAVES BLACKMAIL, OR...
OFF AGAIN, SIR?
SHALL I FETCH YOUR TIGHTS?
NEVER DURING THE DAY, ALFRED.
...LAST NIGHT'S INCIDENT CONNECTS THE BATMAN WITH THE RECENT CAT BURGLARIES. A WOMAN WITH CLAWS--PRESUMABLY BATMAN'S ASSISTANT--IS SAID TO HAVE...
ASSISTANT. NOW I'M HIS ASSISTANT.
I'LL HAVE TO DO SOMETHING REALLY NASTY, NEXT TIME...
CAT FOOD
GORDON, JOHNNY. ONCE A MAN BECOMES A FATHER HE IS NEVER TRULY FREE.
LISTEN CLOSELY...
WAAAAHHH
FEEDING TIME.
MY TURN, HONEY...

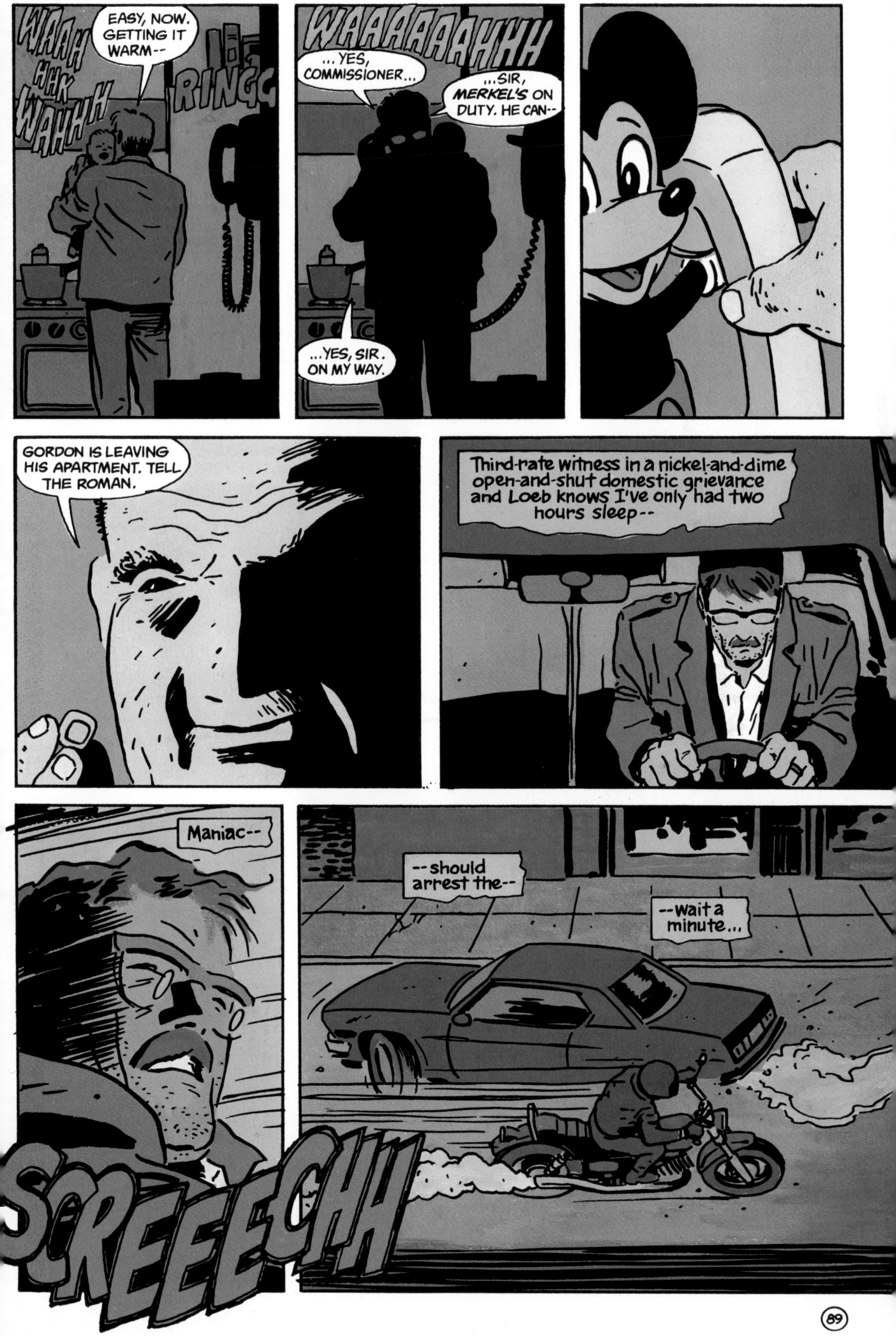
WAAH HHK WAHHH
EASY, NOW. GETTING IT WARM--
RINGG
WAAAAAAAHHH
...YES, COMMISSIONER...
...SIR, MERKEL'S ON DUTY. HE CAN--
...YES, SIR. ON MY WAY.
GORDON IS LEAVING HIS APARTMENT. TELL THE ROMAN.
Third-rate witness in a nickel-and-dime open-and-shut domestic grievance and Loeb knows I've only had two hours sleep--
Maniac--
--should arrest the--
--wait a minute...
SCREEECHH

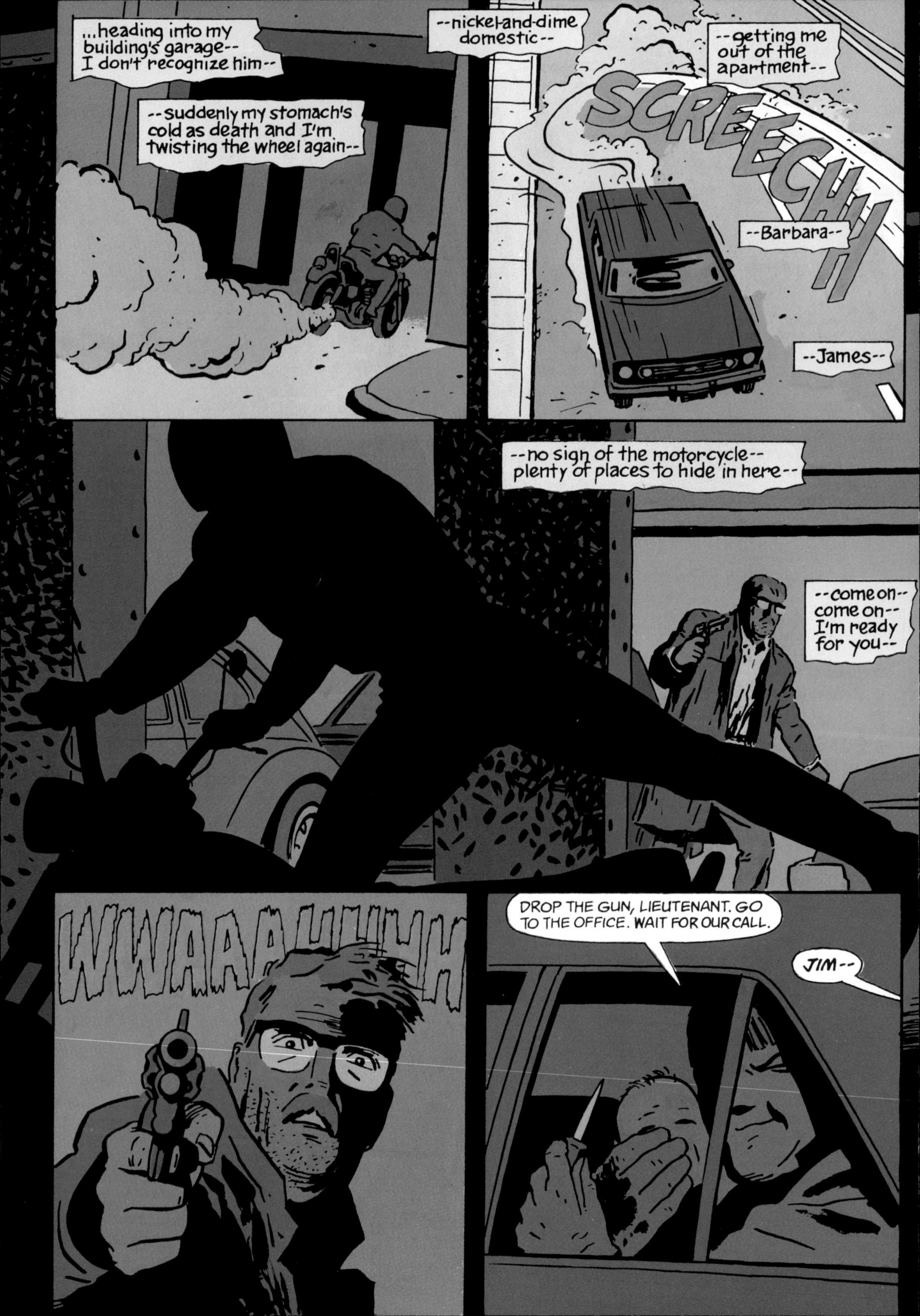
...heading into my building's garage-- I don't recognize him--
--suddenly my stomach's cold as death and I'm twisting the wheel again--
--nickel-and-dime domestic--
--getting me out of the apartment--
SCREECHH
--Barbara--
--James--
--no sign of the motorcycle-- plenty of places to hide in here--
--come on-- come on-- I'm ready for you--
WWAAAUHHH
DROP THE GUN, LIEUTENANT. GO TO THE OFFICE. WAIT FOR OUR CALL.
JIM--

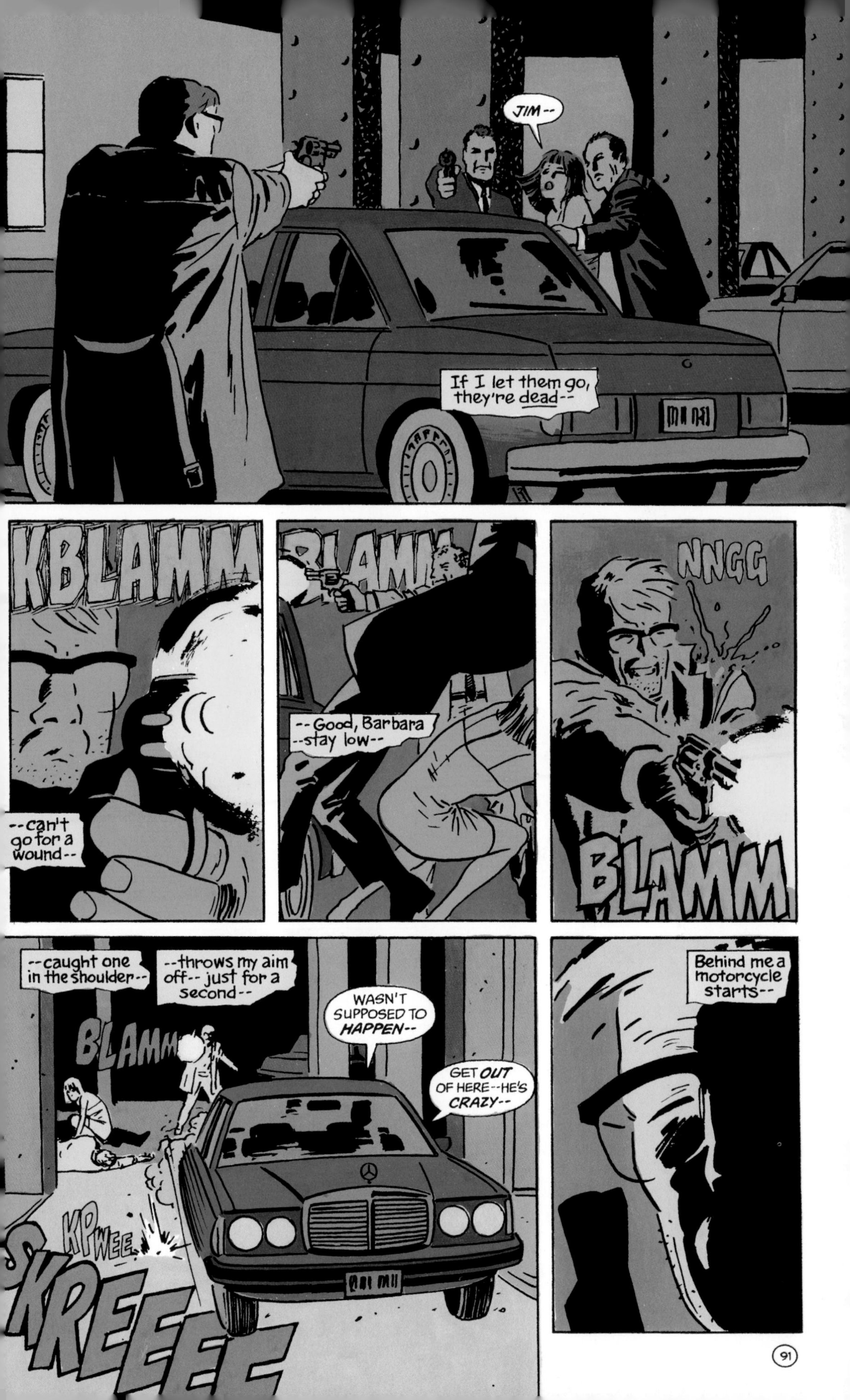
JIM--
If I let them go, they're dead--
KBLAMM
--can't go for a wound--
BLAMM
--Good, Barbara --stay low--
NNGG
BLAMM
--caught one in the shoulder--
--throws my aim off-- just for a second--
BLAMM
WASN'T SUPPOSED TO HAPPEN--
GET OUT OF HERE--HE'S CRAZY--
KPWEE
SKREEEE
Behind me a motorcycle starts--

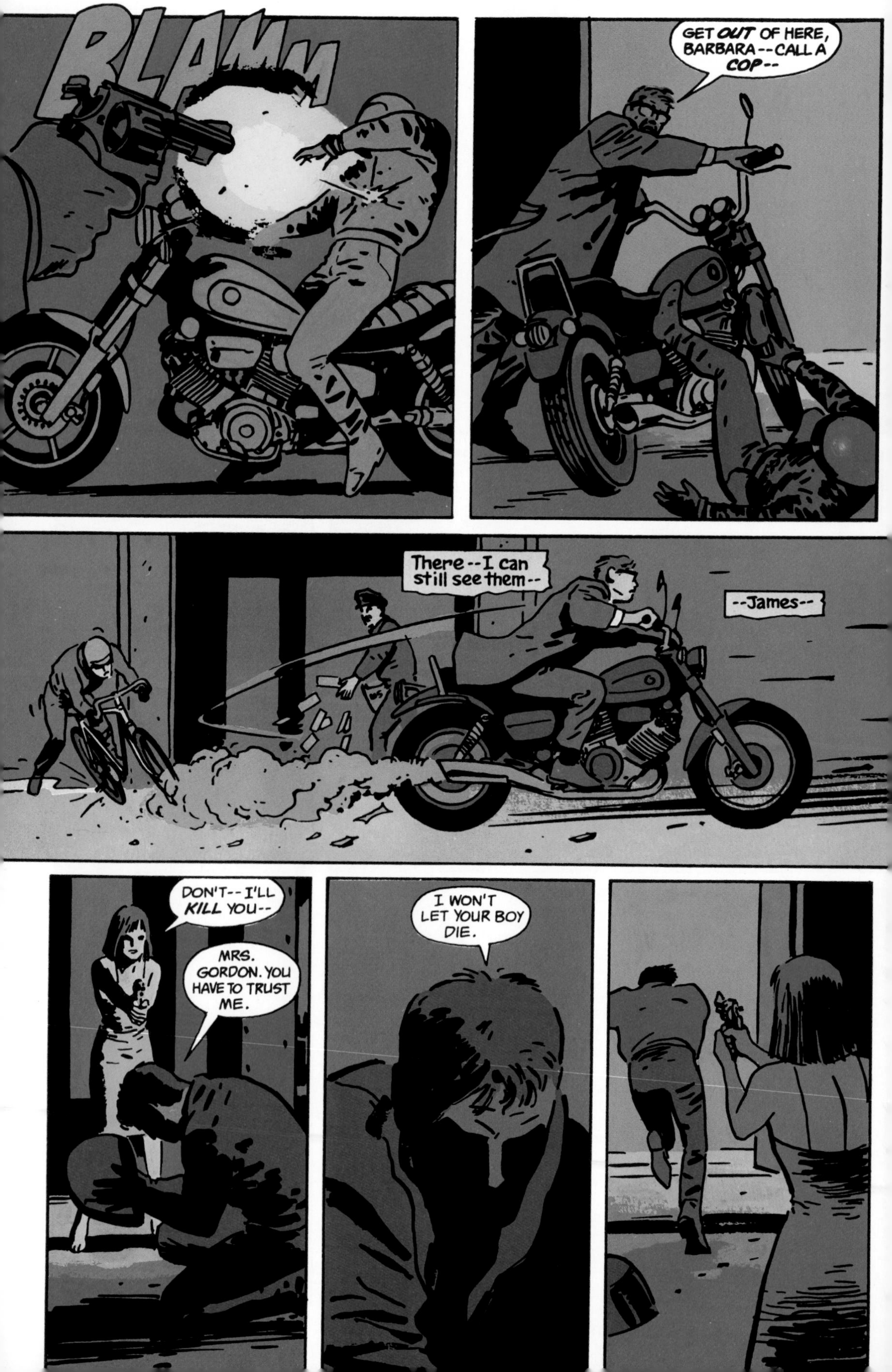
BLAMM
GET OUT OF HERE, BARBARA--CALL A COP--
There--I can still see them--
--James--
DON'T--I'LL KILL YOU--
MRS. GORDON. YOU HAVE TO TRUST ME.
I WON'T LET YOUR BOY DIE.

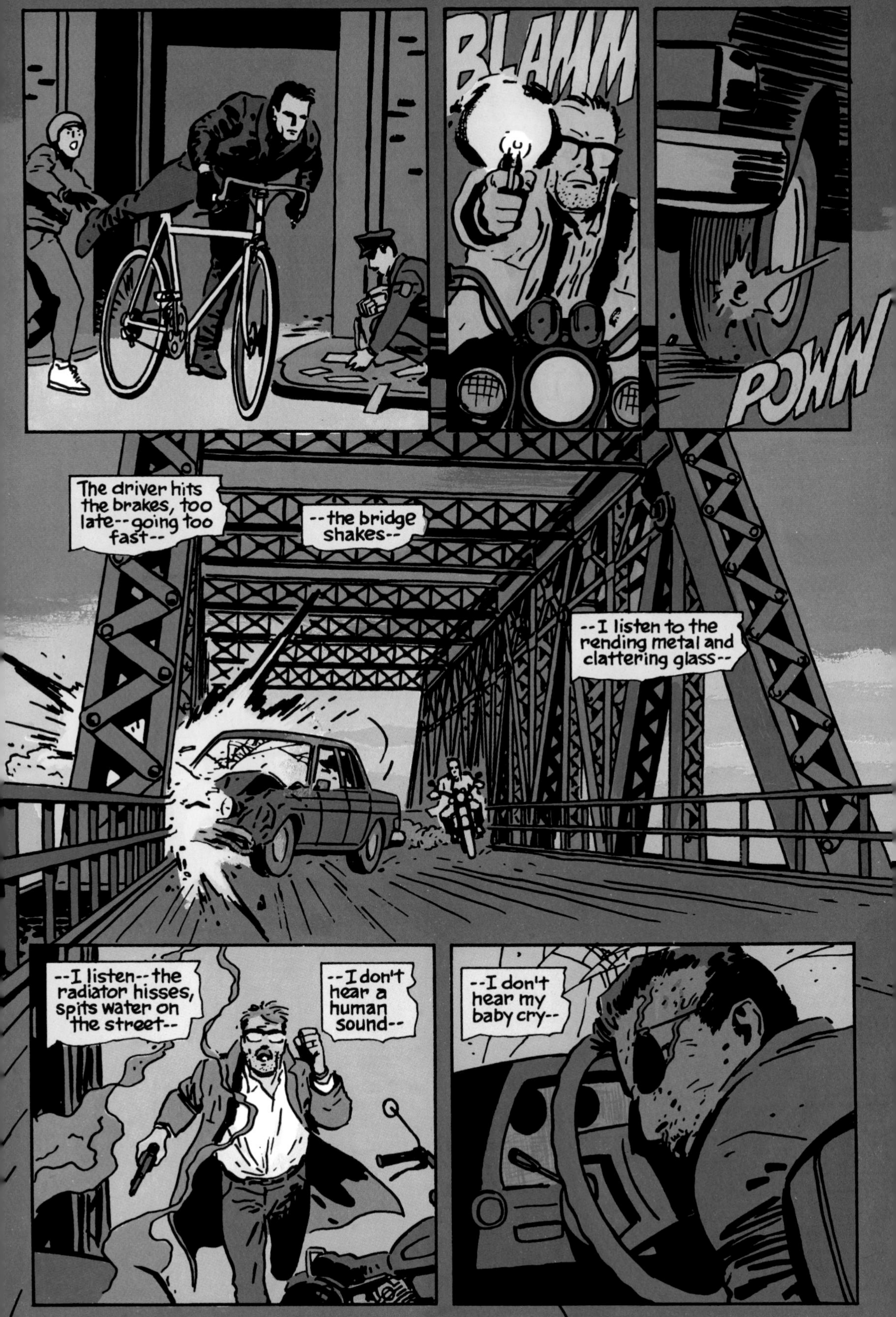
BLAMM
POWW
The driver hits the brakes, too late--going too fast--
--the bridge shakes--
--I listen to the rending metal and clattering glass--
--I listen--the radiator hisses, spits water on the street--
--I don't hear a human sound--
--I don't hear my baby cry--

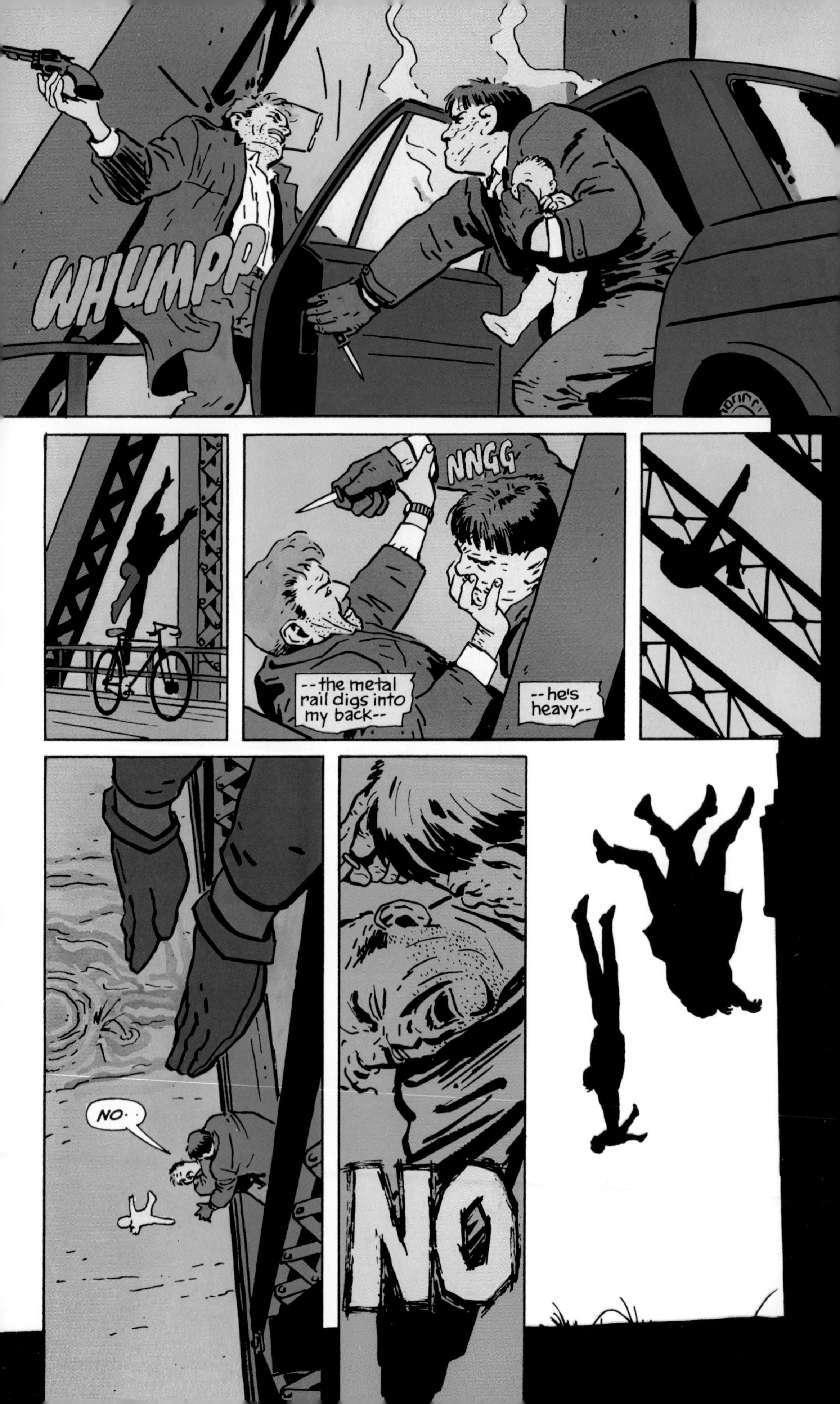
WHUMPP
NNGG
--the metal rail digs into my back--
--he's heavy--
NO..
NO

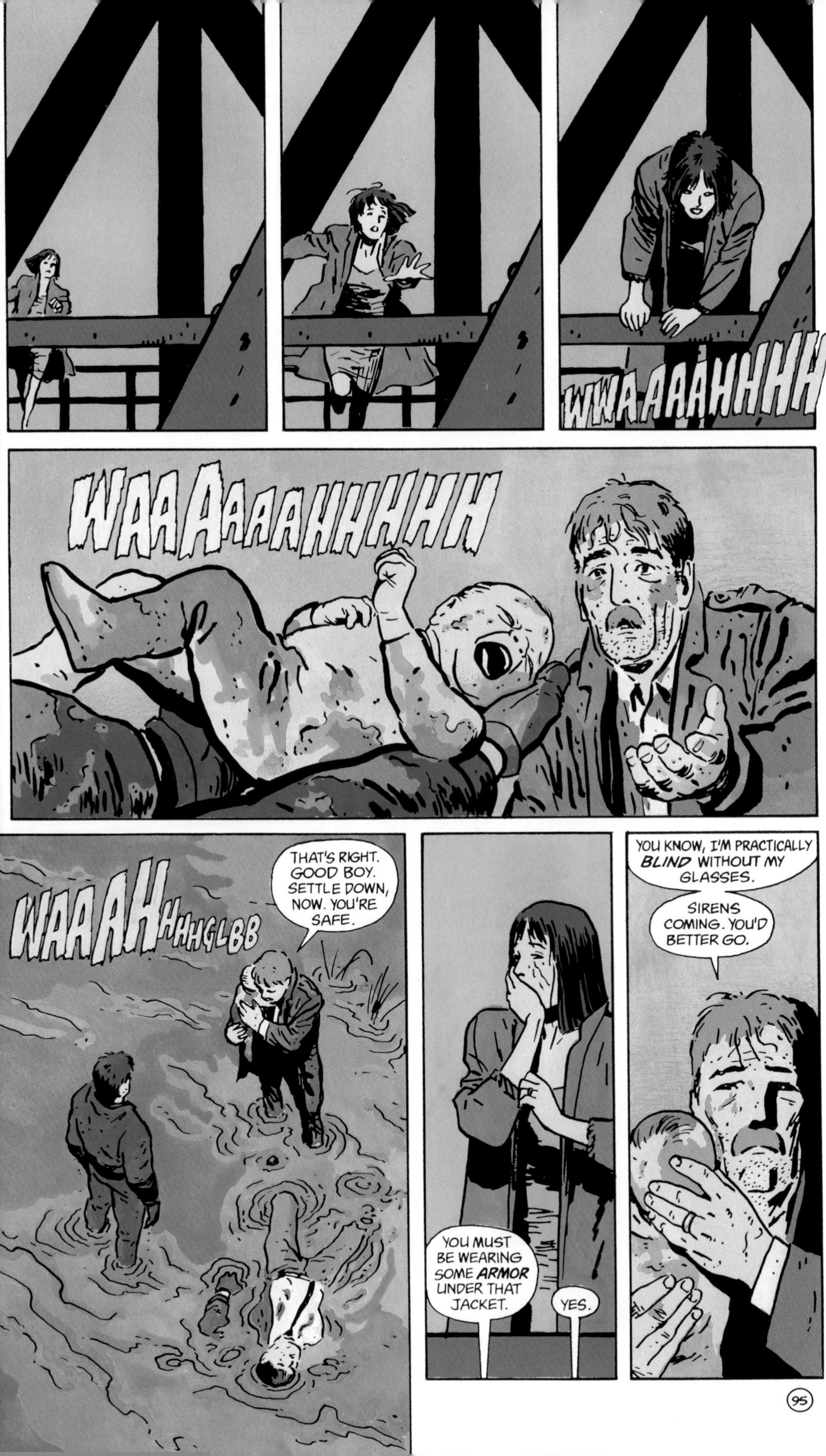
WWAAAAAHHHH
WAAAAAAAHHHHHH
WAAAHHHHGLBB
THAT'S RIGHT. GOOD BOY. SETTLE DOWN, NOW. YOU'RE SAFE.
YOU MUST BE WEARING SOME ARMOR UNDER THAT JACKET.
YES.
YOU KNOW, I'M PRACTICALLY BLIND WITHOUT MY GLASSES.
SIRENS COMING. YOU'D BETTER GO.

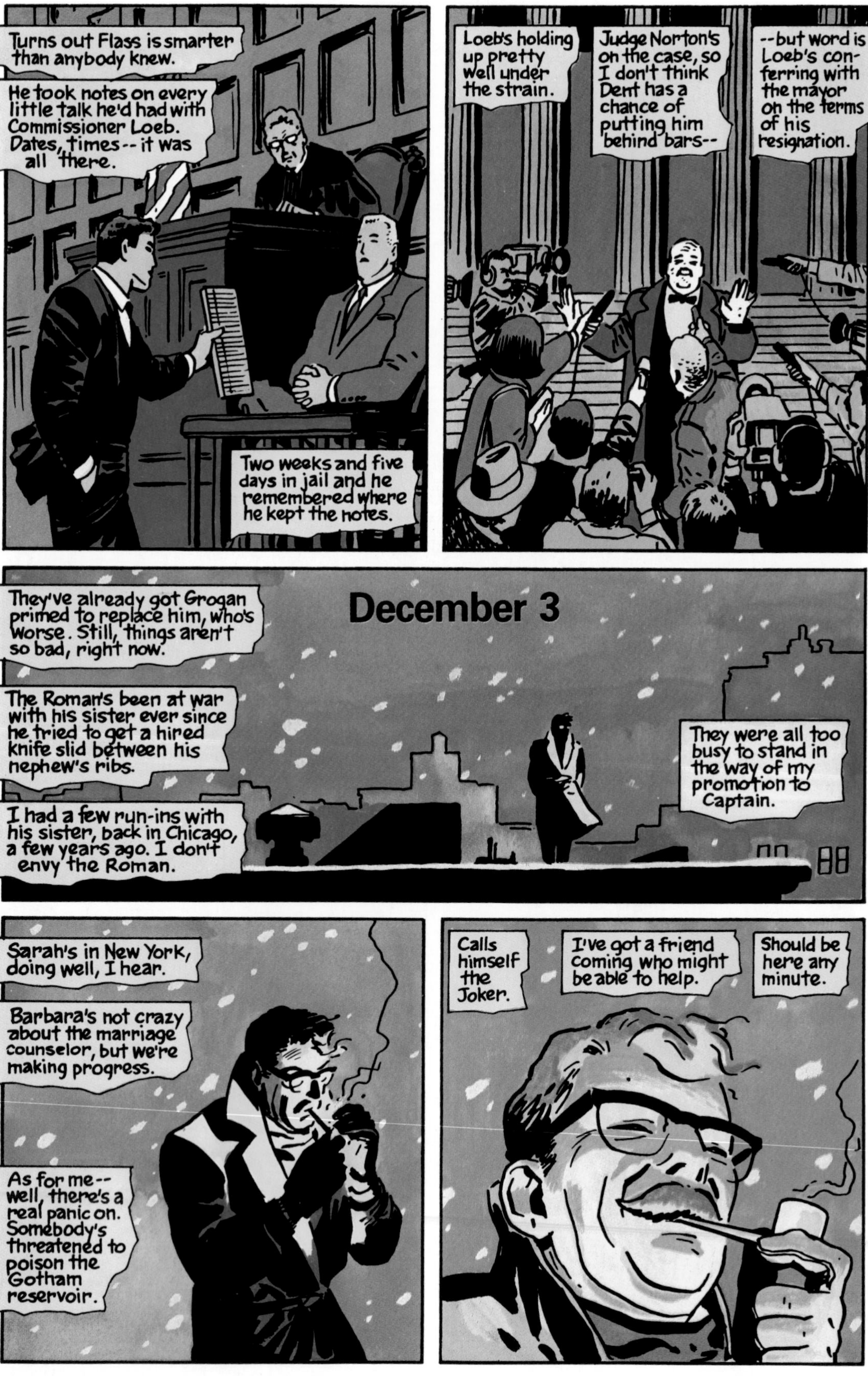
Turns out Flass is smarter than anybody knew.
He took notes on every little talk he'd had with Commissioner Loeb. Dates, times -- it was all there.
Two weeks and five days in jail and he remembered where he kept the notes.
Loeb's holding up pretty well under the strain.
Judge Norton's on the case, so I don't think Dent has a chance of putting him behind bars--
--but word is Loeb's conferring with the mayor on the terms of his resignation.
They've already got Grogan primed to replace him, who's worse. Still, things aren't so bad, right now.
December 3
The Roman's been at war with his sister ever since he tried to get a hired knife slid between his nephew's ribs.
I had a few run-ins with his sister, back in Chicago, a few years ago. I don't envy the Roman.
They were all too busy to stand in the way of my promotion to Captain.
Sarah's in New York, doing well, I hear.
Barbara's not crazy about the marriage counselor, but we're making progress.
As for me-- well, there's a real panic on. Somebody's threatened to poison the Gotham reservoir.
Calls himself the Joker.
I've got a friend coming who might be able to help.
Should be here any minute.

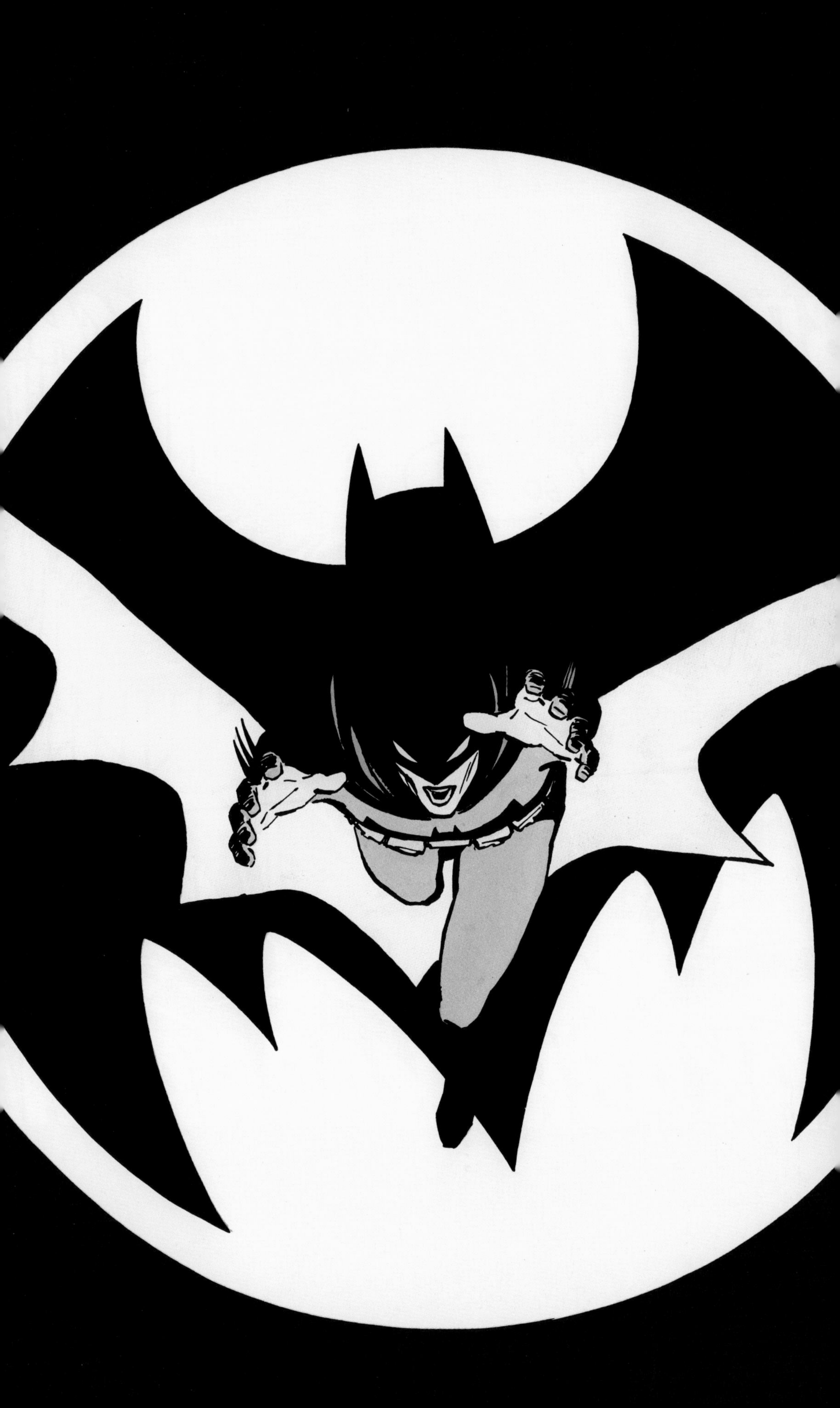

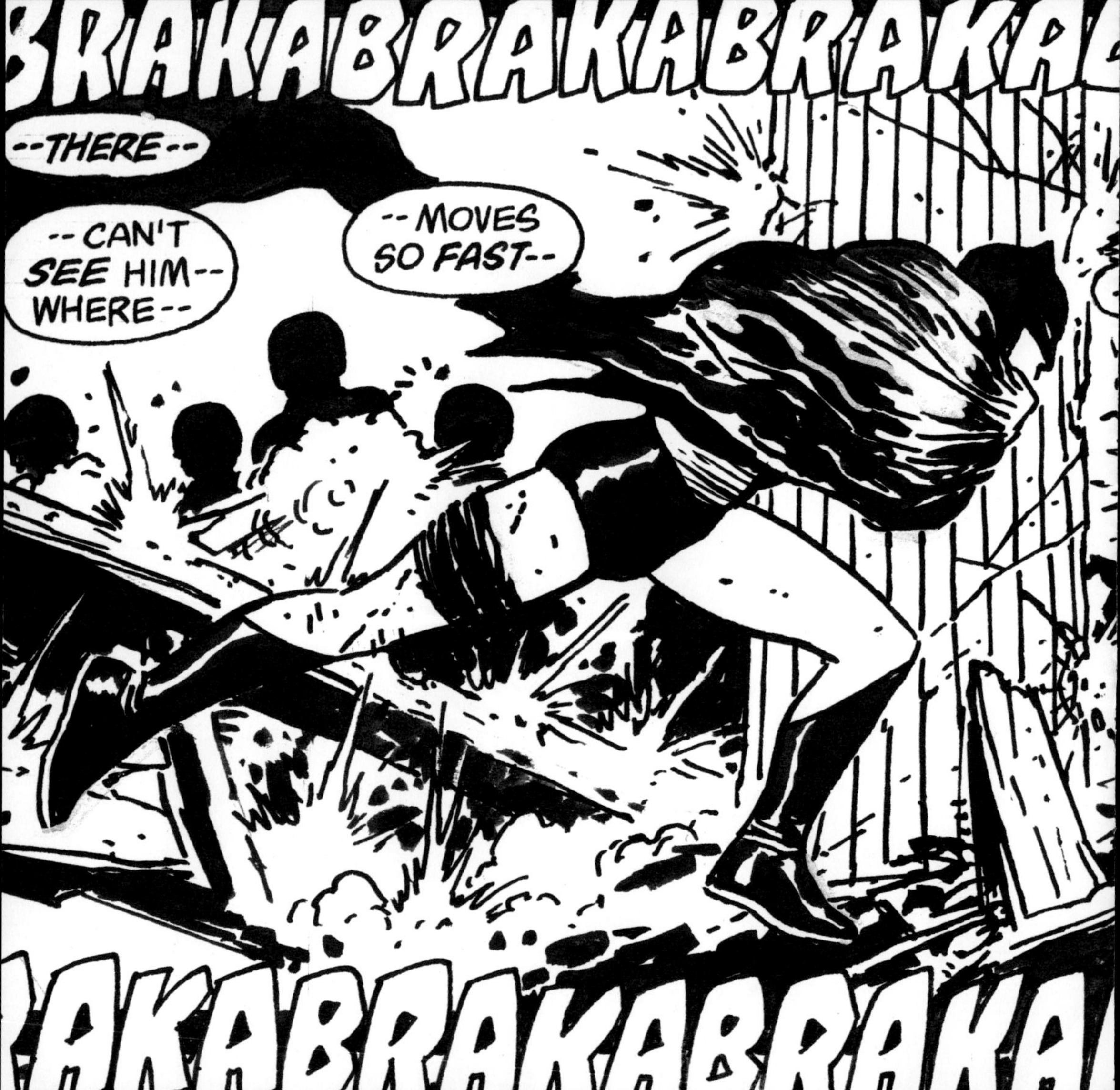
BRAKABRAKABRAKABRAKA
--CAN'T SEE HIM-- WHERE--
--THERE--
--MOVES SO FAST--
AKABRAKABRAKA

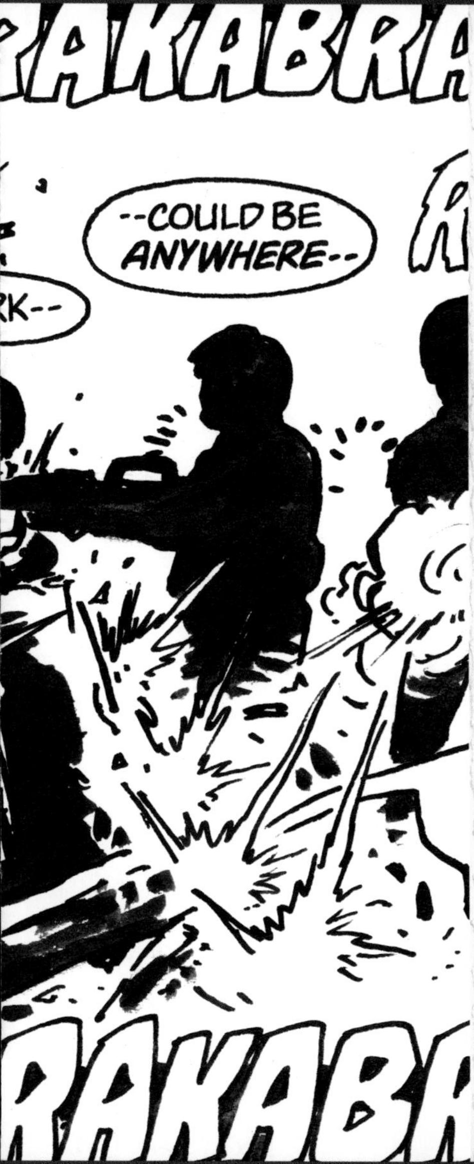
RAKABRA
--COULD BE ANYWHERE--
RK--
RAKABR

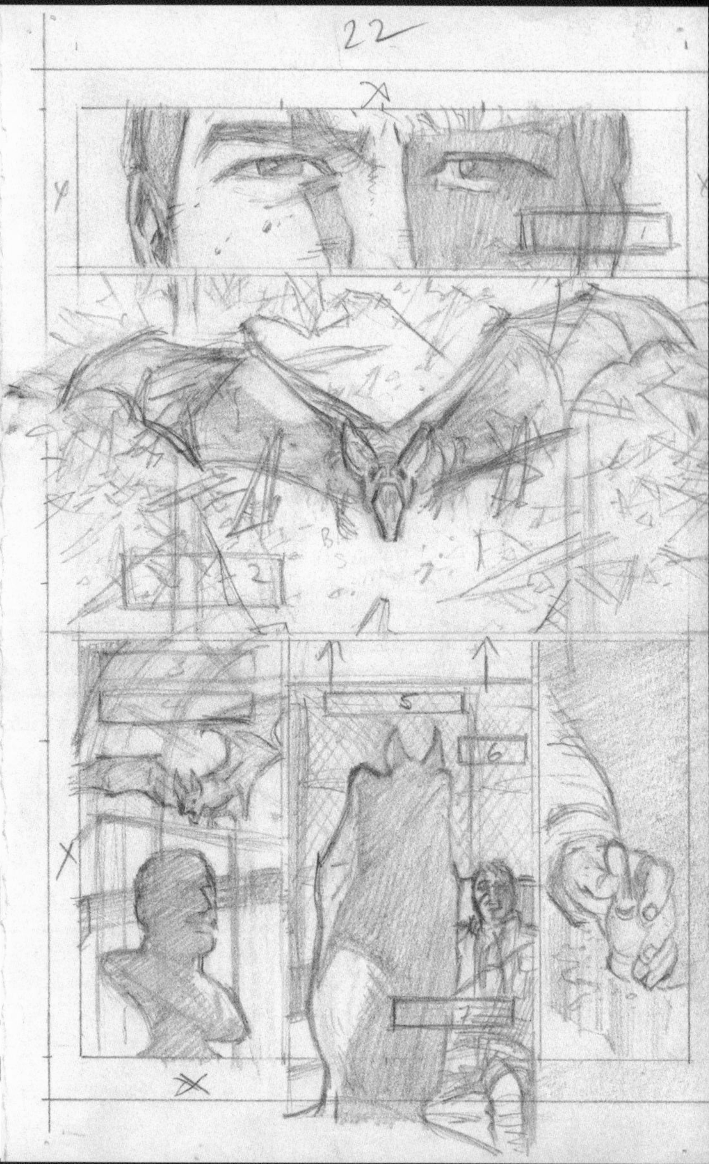

THE CAPED CRUSADER

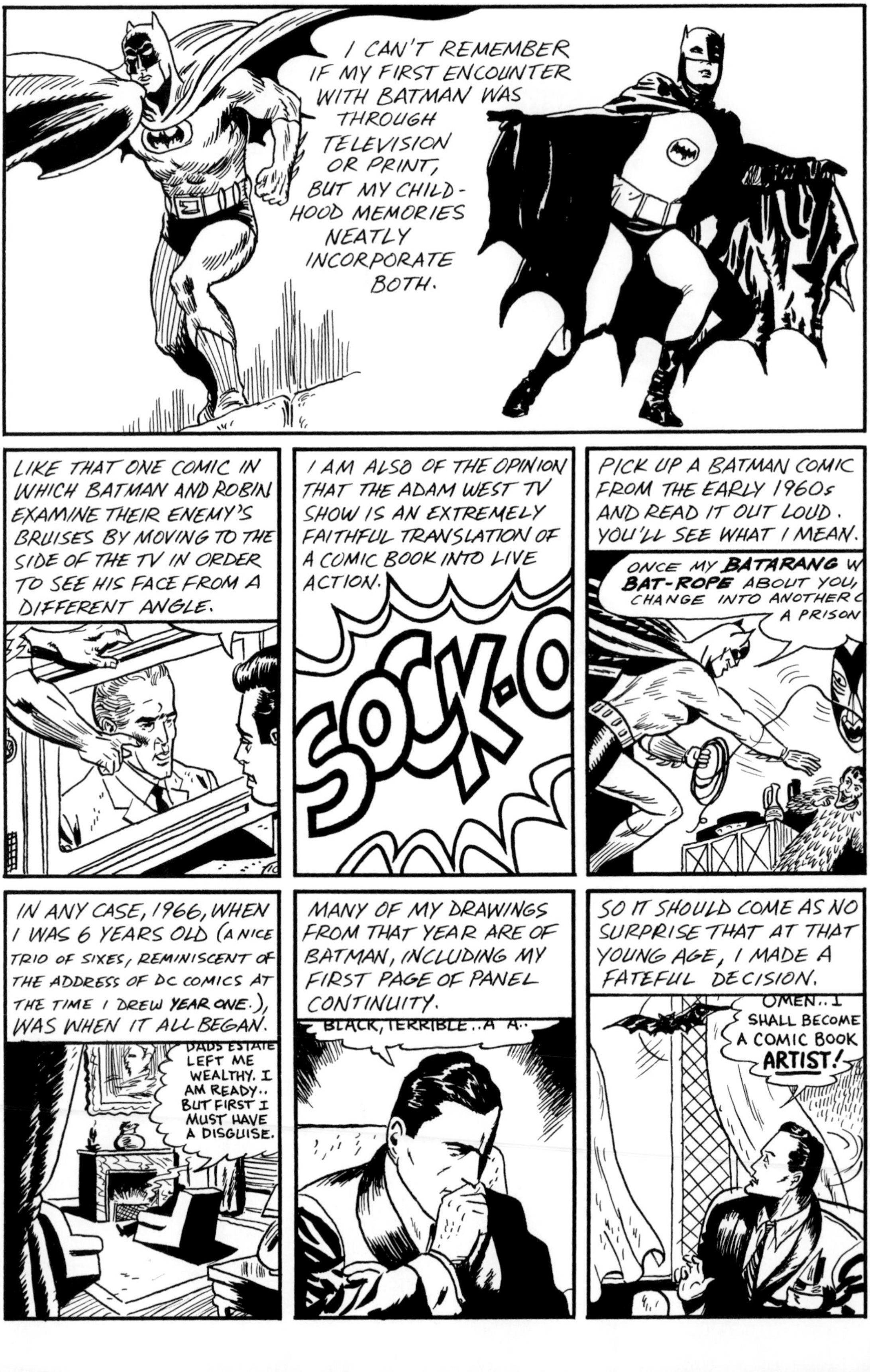

I CAN'T REMEMBER IF MY FIRST ENCOUNTER WITH BATMAN WAS THROUGH TELEVISION OR PRINT, BUT MY CHILD-HOOD MEMORIES NEATLY INCORPORATE BOTH.
LIKE THAT ONE COMIC IN WHICH BATMAN AND ROBIN EXAMINE THEIR ENEMY'S BRUISES BY MOVING TO THE SIDE OF THE TV IN ORDER TO SEE HIS FACE FROM A DIFFERENT ANGLE.
I AM ALSO OF THE OPINION THAT THE ADAM WEST TV SHOW IS AN EXTREMELY FAITHFUL TRANSLATION OF A COMIC BOOK INTO LIVE ACTION.
SOCK-O
PICK UP A BATMAN COMIC FROM THE EARLY 1960s AND READ IT OUT LOUD. YOU'LL SEE WHAT I MEAN.
ONCE MY BATARANG BAT-ROPE ABOUT YOU, CHANGE INTO ANOTHER A PRISON
IN ANY CASE, 1966, WHEN I WAS 6 YEARS OLD (A NICE TRIO OF SIXES, REMINISCENT OF THE ADDRESS OF DC COMICS AT THE TIME I DREW YEAR ONE.), WAS WHEN IT ALL BEGAN.
DADS ESTATE LEFT ME WEALTHY. I AM READY.. BUT FIRST I MUST HAVE A DISGUISE.
MANY OF MY DRAWINGS FROM THAT YEAR ARE OF BATMAN, INCLUDING MY FIRST PAGE OF PANEL CONTINUITY.
BLACK, TERRIBLE..A A..
SO IT SHOULD COME AS NO SURPRISE THAT AT THAT YOUNG AGE, I MADE A FATEFUL DECISION.
OMEN..I SHALL BECOME A COMIC BOOK ARTIST!

THE WEIRD CREATURE OF DARKNESS

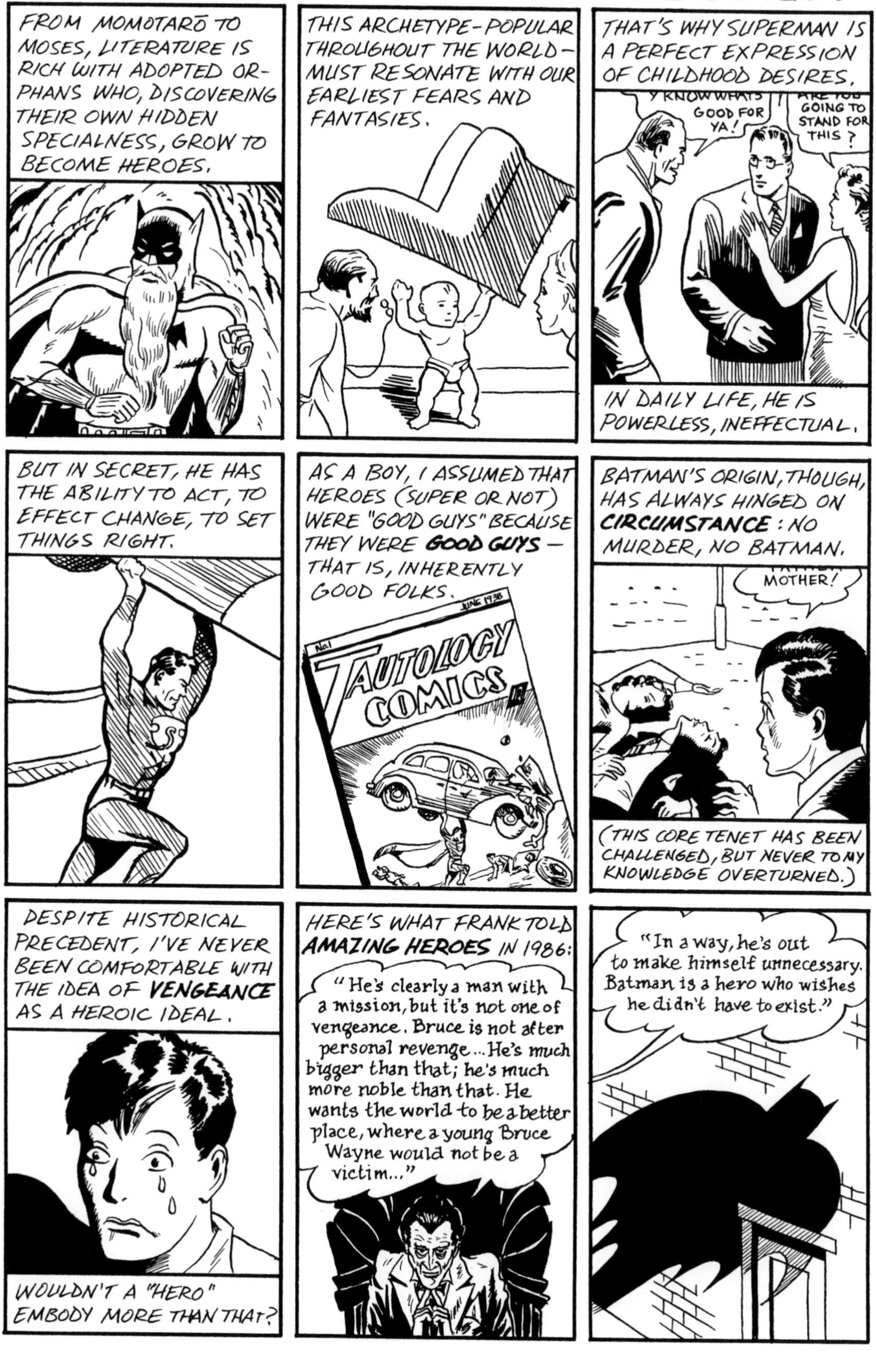

FROM MOMOTARŌ TO MOSES, LITERATURE IS RICH WITH ADOPTED OR-PHANS WHO, DISCOVERING THEIR OWN HIDDEN SPECIALNESS, GROW TO BECOME HEROES.
THIS ARCHETYPE — POPULAR THROUGHOUT THE WORLD — MUST RESONATE WITH OUR EARLIEST FEARS AND FANTASIES.
THAT'S WHY SUPERMAN IS A PERFECT EXPRESSION OF CHILDHOOD DESIRES.
GOOD FOR YA!
GOING TO STAND FOR THIS ?
IN DAILY LIFE, HE IS POWERLESS, INEFFECTUAL.
BUT IN SECRET, HE HAS THE ABILITY TO ACT, TO EFFECT CHANGE, TO SET THINGS RIGHT.
AS A BOY, I ASSUMED THAT HEROES (SUPER OR NOT) WERE "GOOD GUYS" BECAUSE THEY WERE **GOOD GUYS** — THAT IS, INHERENTLY GOOD FOLKS.
JUNE 1938
No. 1
TAUTOLOGY COMICS
BATMAN'S ORIGIN, THOUGH, HAS ALWAYS HINGED ON **CIRCUMSTANCE**: NO MURDER, NO BATMAN.
MOTHER!
(THIS CORE TENET HAS BEEN CHALLENGED, BUT NEVER TO MY KNOWLEDGE OVERTURNED.)
DESPITE HISTORICAL PRECEDENT, I'VE NEVER BEEN COMFORTABLE WITH THE IDEA OF **VENGEANCE** AS A HEROIC IDEAL.
WOULDN'T A "HERO" EMBODY MORE THAN THAT?
HERE'S WHAT FRANK TOLD **AMAZING HEROES** IN 1986:
"He's clearly a man with a mission, but it's not one of vengeance. Bruce is not after personal revenge... He's much bigger than that; he's much more noble than that. He wants the world to be a better place, where a young Bruce Wayne would not be a victim..."
"In a way, he's out to make himself unnecessary. Batman is a hero who wishes he didn't have to exist."

THE DYNAMIC DUO

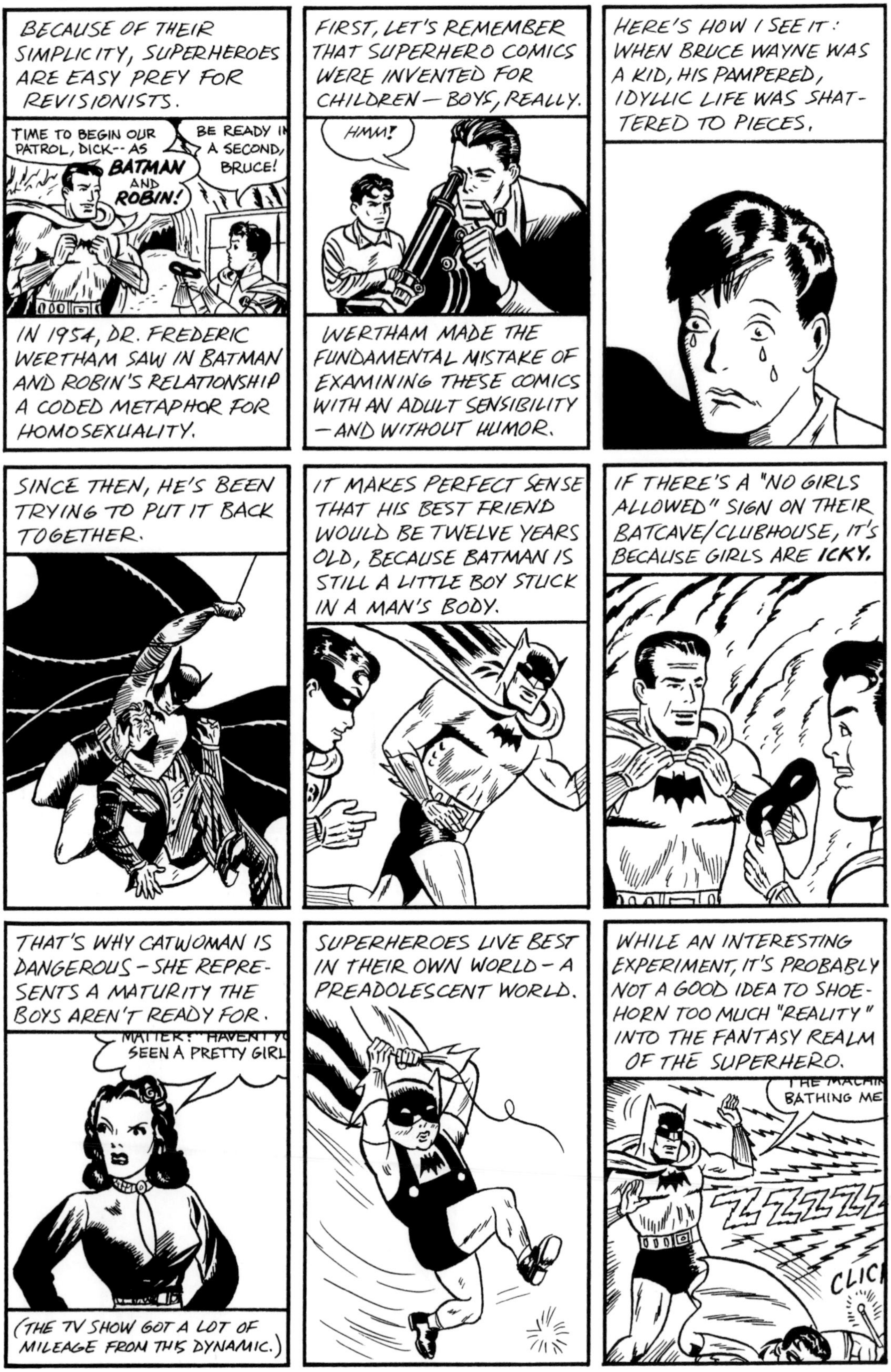
BECAUSE OF THEIR SIMPLICITY, SUPERHEROES ARE EASY PREY FOR REVISIONISTS.
TIME TO BEGIN OUR PATROL, DICK-- AS BATMAN AND ROBIN!
BE READY IN A SECOND, BRUCE!
IN 1954, DR. FREDERIC WERTHAM SAW IN BATMAN AND ROBIN'S RELATIONSHIP A CODED METAPHOR FOR HOMOSEXUALITY.
FIRST, LET'S REMEMBER THAT SUPERHERO COMICS WERE INVENTED FOR CHILDREN — BOYS, REALLY.
HMM!
WERTHAM MADE THE FUNDAMENTAL MISTAKE OF EXAMINING THESE COMICS WITH AN ADULT SENSIBILITY — AND WITHOUT HUMOR.
HERE'S HOW I SEE IT: WHEN BRUCE WAYNE WAS A KID, HIS PAMPERED, IDYLLIC LIFE WAS SHATTERED TO PIECES.
SINCE THEN, HE'S BEEN TRYING TO PUT IT BACK TOGETHER.
IT MAKES PERFECT SENSE THAT HIS BEST FRIEND WOULD BE TWELVE YEARS OLD, BECAUSE BATMAN IS STILL A LITTLE BOY STUCK IN A MAN'S BODY.
IF THERE'S A "NO GIRLS ALLOWED" SIGN ON THEIR BATCAVE/CLUBHOUSE, IT'S BECAUSE GIRLS ARE ICKY.
THAT'S WHY CATWOMAN IS DANGEROUS — SHE REPRESENTS A MATURITY THE BOYS AREN'T READY FOR.
SEEN A PRETTY GIRL
(THE TV SHOW GOT A LOT OF MILEAGE FROM THIS DYNAMIC.)
SUPERHEROES LIVE BEST IN THEIR OWN WORLD — A PREADOLESCENT WORLD.
WHILE AN INTERESTING EXPERIMENT, IT'S PROBABLY NOT A GOOD IDEA TO SHOEHORN TOO MUCH "REALITY" INTO THE FANTASY REALM OF THE SUPERHERO.
BATHING ME
ZZZZZZ
CLIC

...OOPS

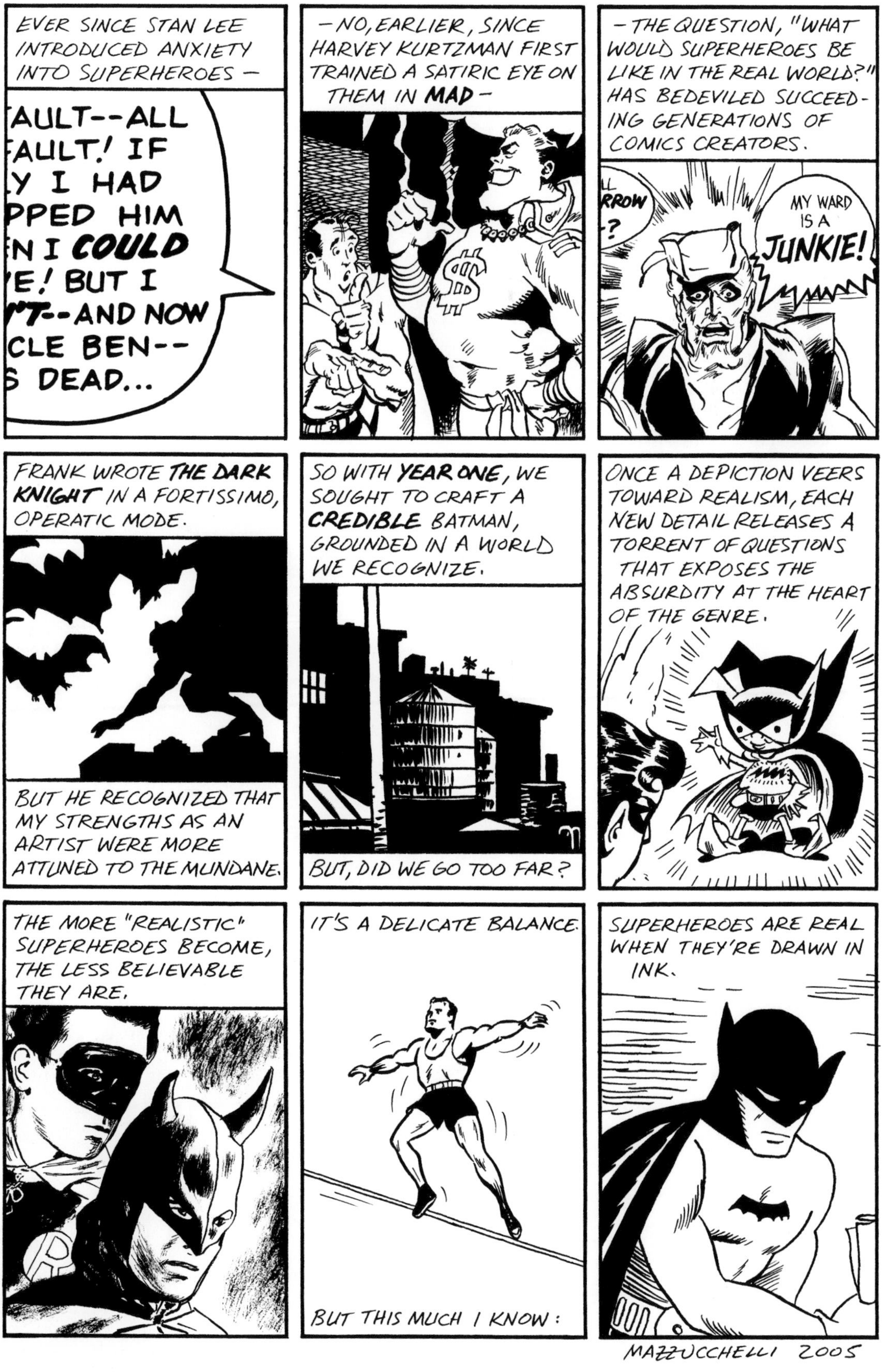
EVER SINCE STAN LEE INTRODUCED ANXIETY INTO SUPERHEROES –
AULT--ALL
AULT! IF
Y I HAD
PPED HIM
N I COULD
E! BUT I
'T--AND NOW
CLE BEN--
S DEAD...
–NO, EARLIER, SINCE HARVEY KURTZMAN FIRST TRAINED A SATIRIC EYE ON THEM IN MAD –
–THE QUESTION, "WHAT WOULD SUPERHEROES BE LIKE IN THE REAL WORLD?" HAS BEDEVILED SUCCEEDING GENERATIONS OF COMICS CREATORS.
MY WARD IS A JUNKIE!
FRANK WROTE THE DARK KNIGHT IN A FORTISSIMO, OPERATIC MODE.
BUT HE RECOGNIZED THAT MY STRENGTHS AS AN ARTIST WERE MORE ATTUNED TO THE MUNDANE.
SO WITH YEAR ONE, WE SOUGHT TO CRAFT A CREDIBLE BATMAN, GROUNDED IN A WORLD WE RECOGNIZE.
BUT, DID WE GO TOO FAR?
ONCE A DEPICTION VEERS TOWARD REALISM, EACH NEW DETAIL RELEASES A TORRENT OF QUESTIONS THAT EXPOSES THE ABSURDITY AT THE HEART OF THE GENRE.
THE MORE "REALISTIC" SUPERHEROES BECOME, THE LESS BELIEVABLE THEY ARE.
IT'S A DELICATE BALANCE.
BUT THIS MUCH I KNOW:
SUPERHEROES ARE REAL WHEN THEY'RE DRAWN IN INK.
MAZZUCCHELLI 2005

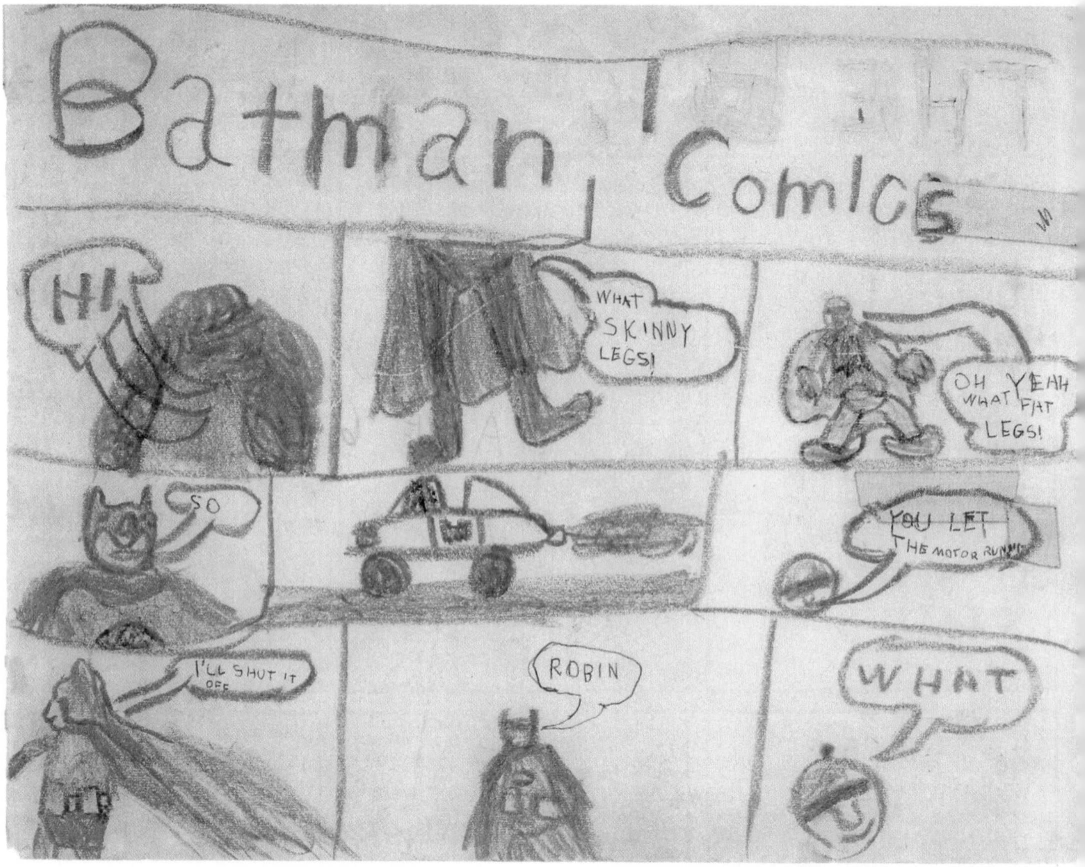

Batman Comics
HI
WHAT SKINNY LEGS!
OH YEAH WHAT FAT LEGS!
SO
YOU LET THE MOTOR
I'LL SHUT IT OFF
ROBIN
WHAT

"Batman Comics," 1966 (above). My first comic page.
Submission sample, 1983 (facing page).
Submission sample, c. 1981 (below).

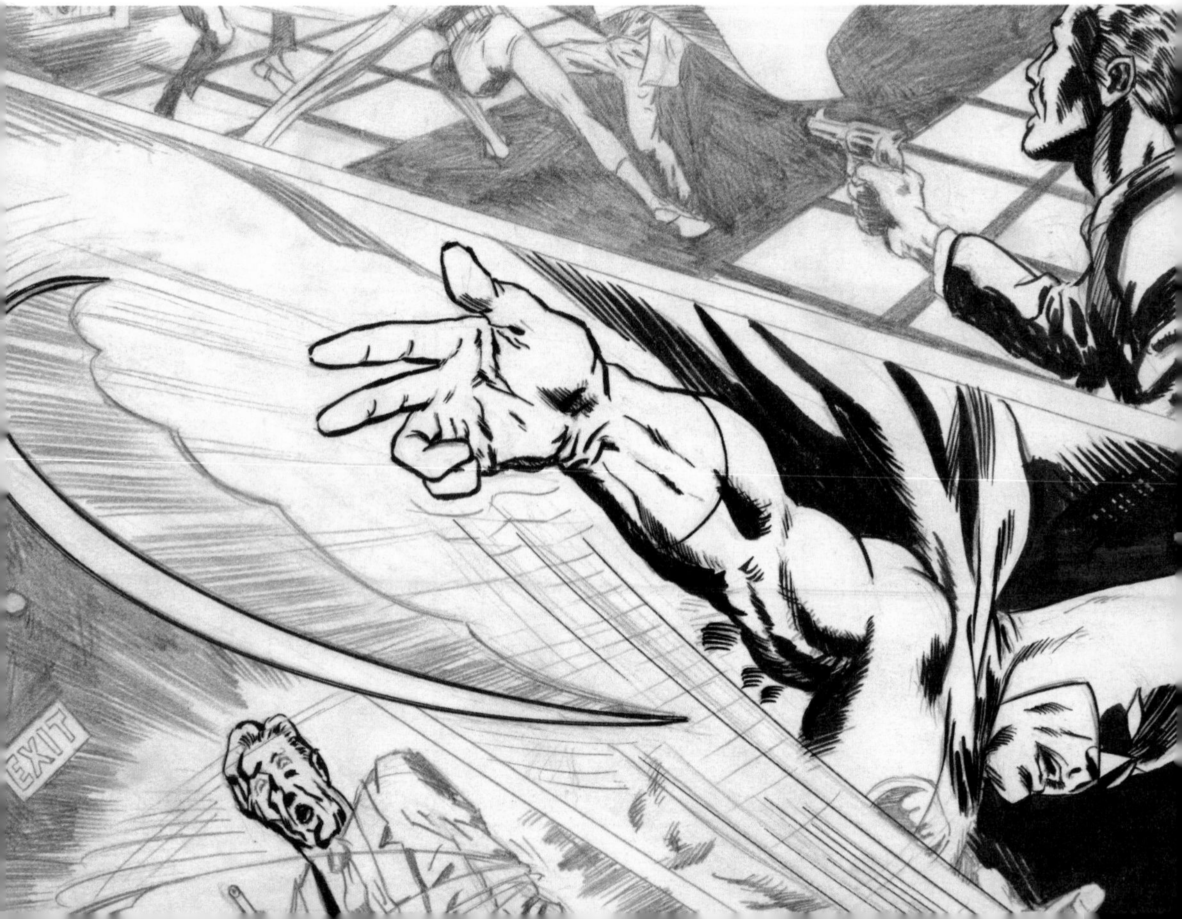

EXIT

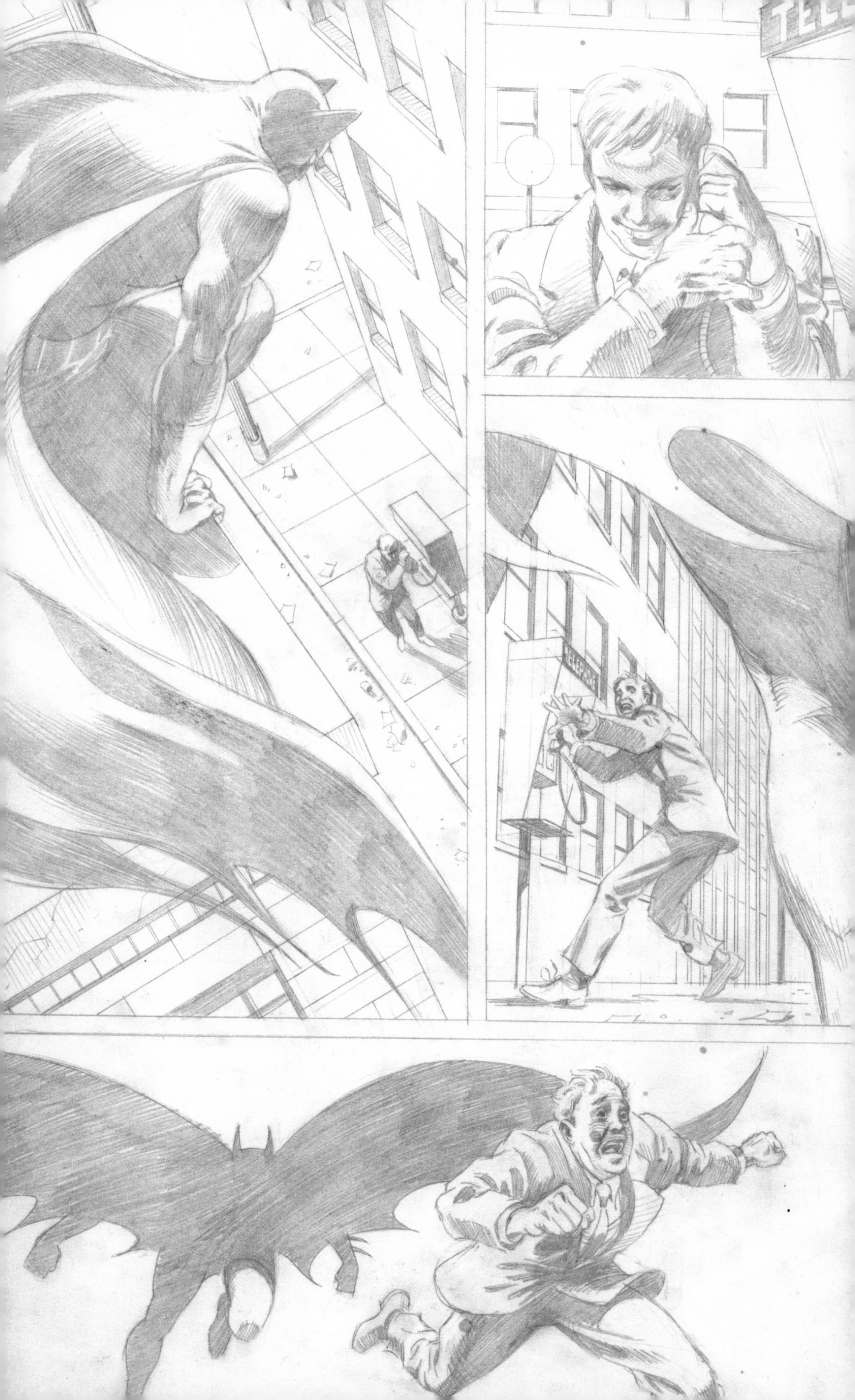

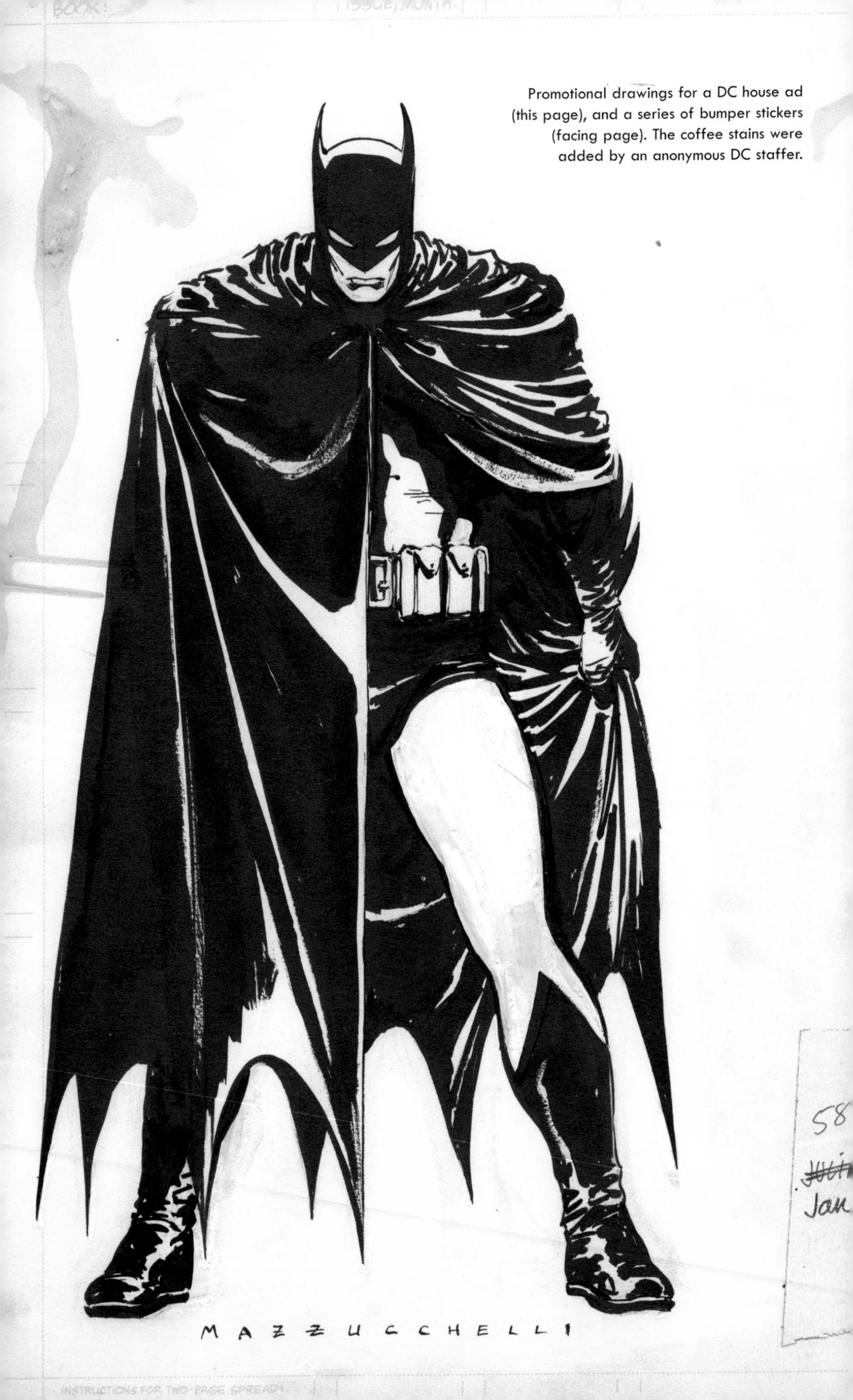
MAZZUCCHELLI

Promotional drawings for a DC house ad (this page), and a series of bumper stickers (facing page). The coffee stains were added by an anonymous DC staffer.

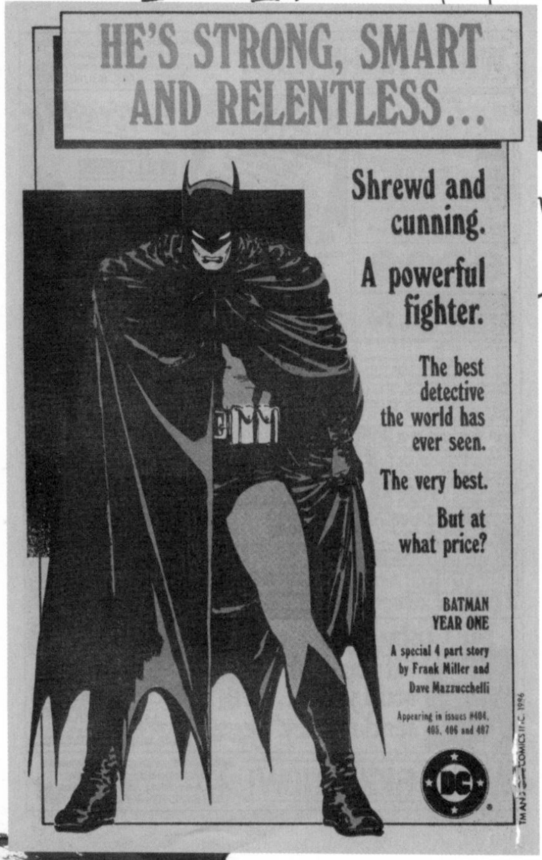
HE'S STRONG, SMART AND RELENTLESS...
Shrewd and cunning.
A powerful fighter.
The best detective the world has ever seen.
The very best.
But at what price?
BATMAN YEAR ONE
A special 4 part story by Frank Miller and Dave Mazzucchelli
Appearing in issues #404, 405, 406 and 407

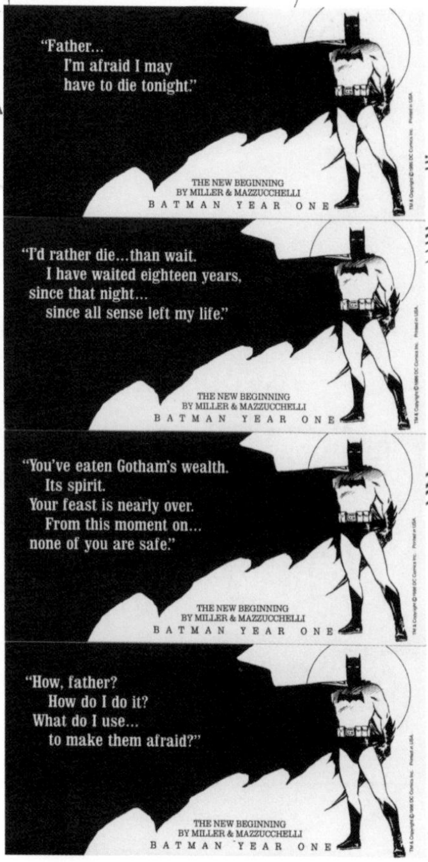
"Father...
I'm afraid I may
have to die tonight."
THE NEW BEGINNING
BY MILLER & MAZZUCCHELLI
BATMAN YEAR ONE
"I'd rather die...than wait.
I have waited eighteen years,
since that night...
since all sense left my life."
THE NEW BEGINNING
BY MILLER & MAZZUCCHELLI
BATMAN YEAR ONE
"You've eaten Gotham's wealth.
Its spirit.
Your feast is nearly over.
From this moment on...
none of you are safe."
THE NEW BEGINNING
BY MILLER & MAZZUCCHELLI
BATMAN YEAR ONE
"How, father?
How do I do it?
What do I use...
to make them afraid?"
THE NEW BEGINNING
BY MILLER & MAZZUCCHELLI
BATMAN YEAR ONE

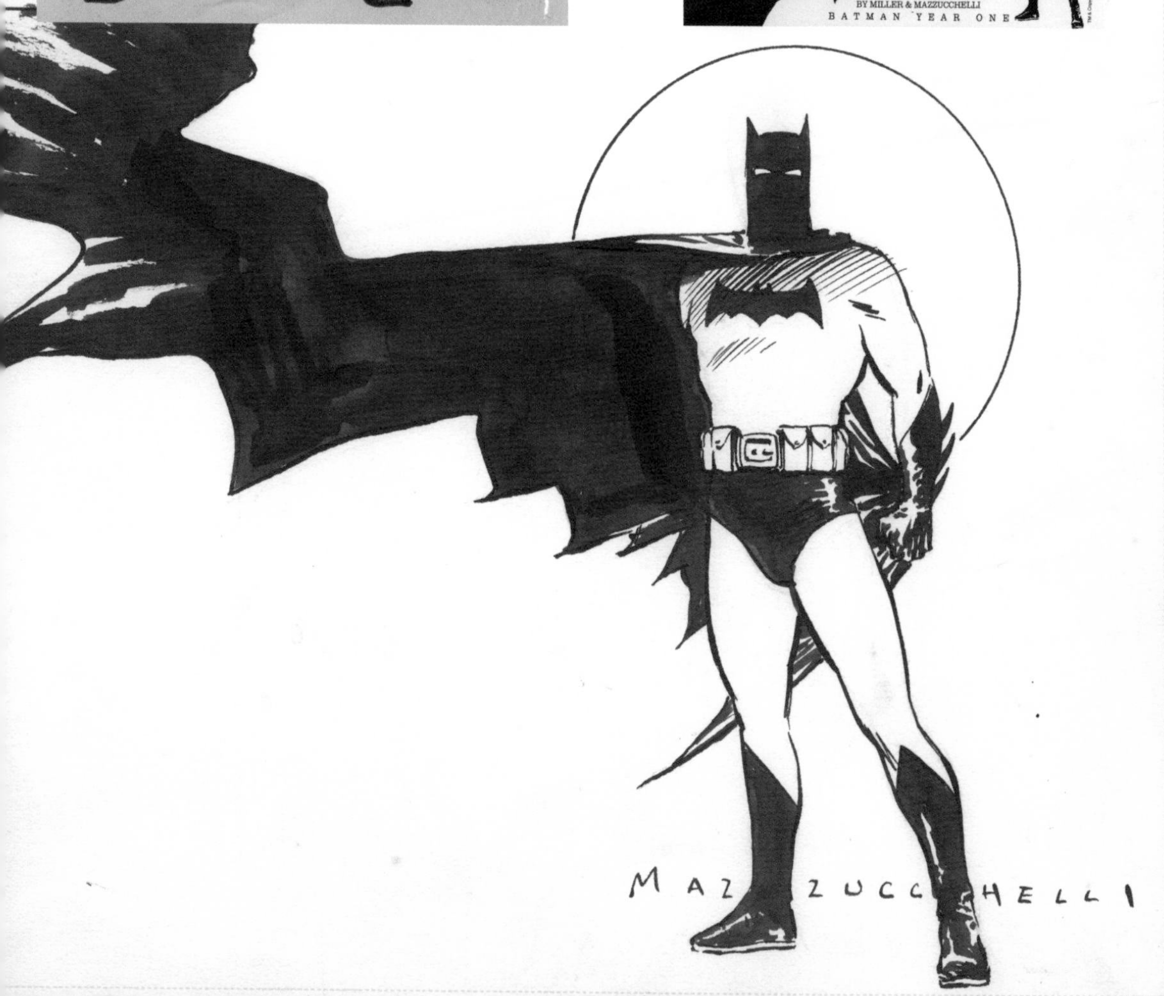
MAZZUCCHELLI

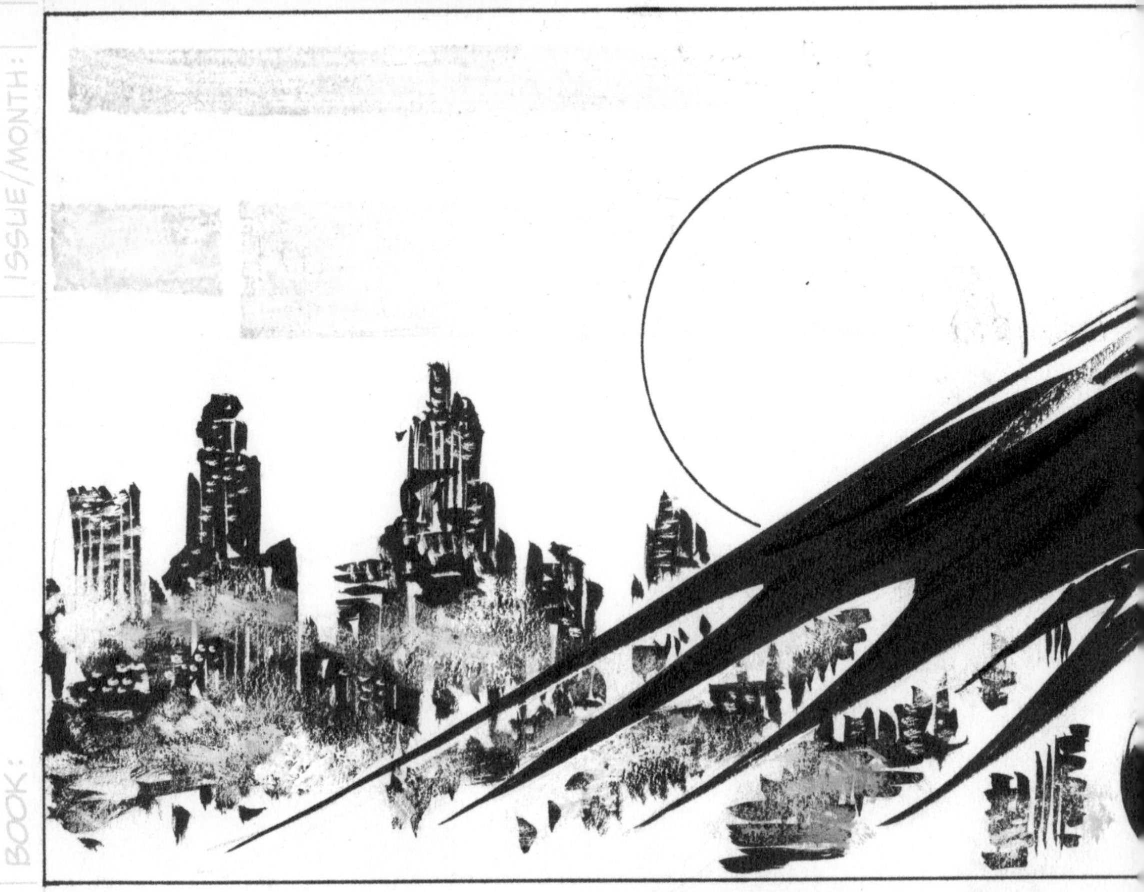
ISSUE/MONTH:
BOOK:

My first rendering of a "Year One" Batman (above), used for a DC house ad (note the bat-like ears).

Sketches of Bruce Wayne, after photos of Gregory Peck (below).

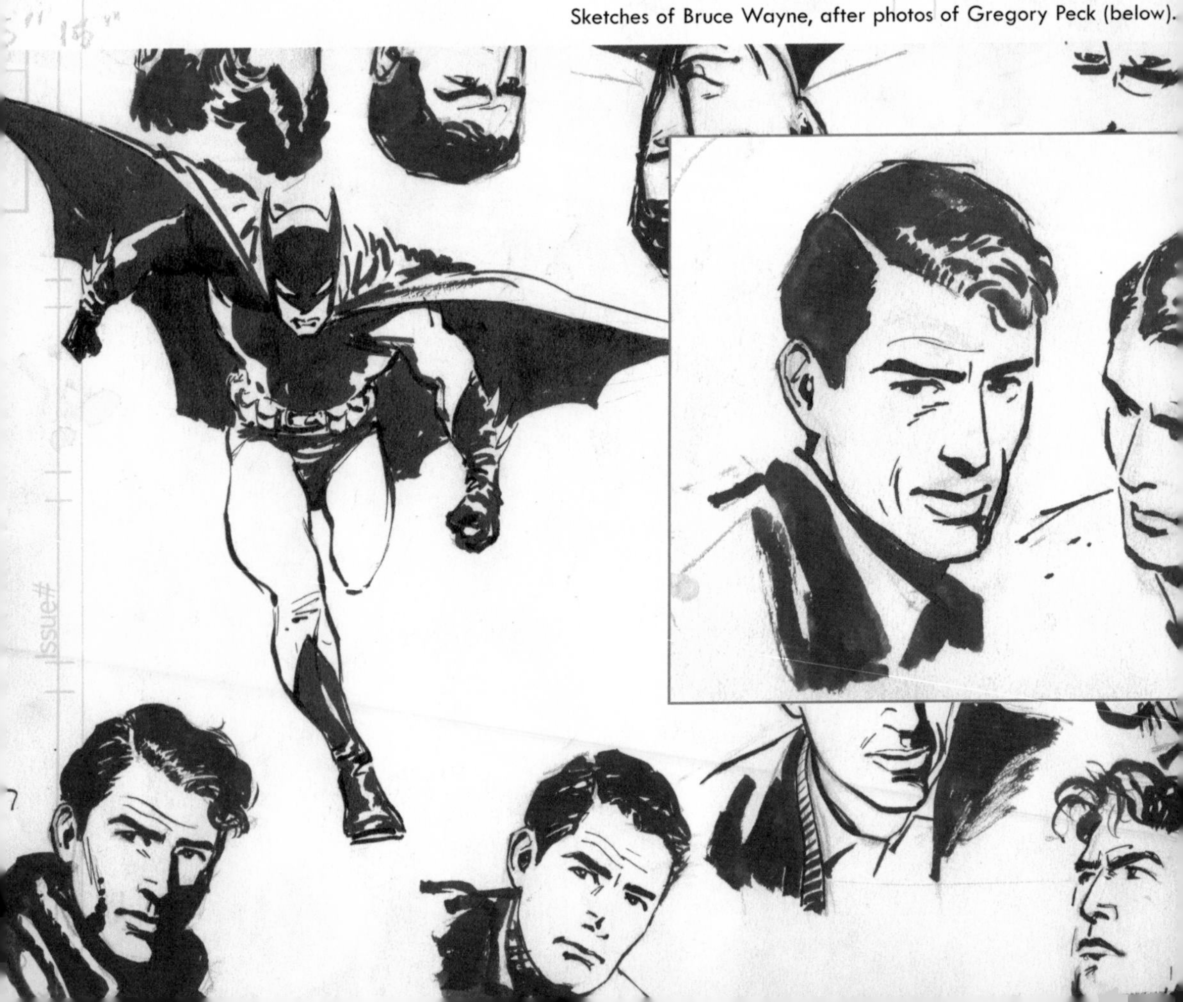
Issue#

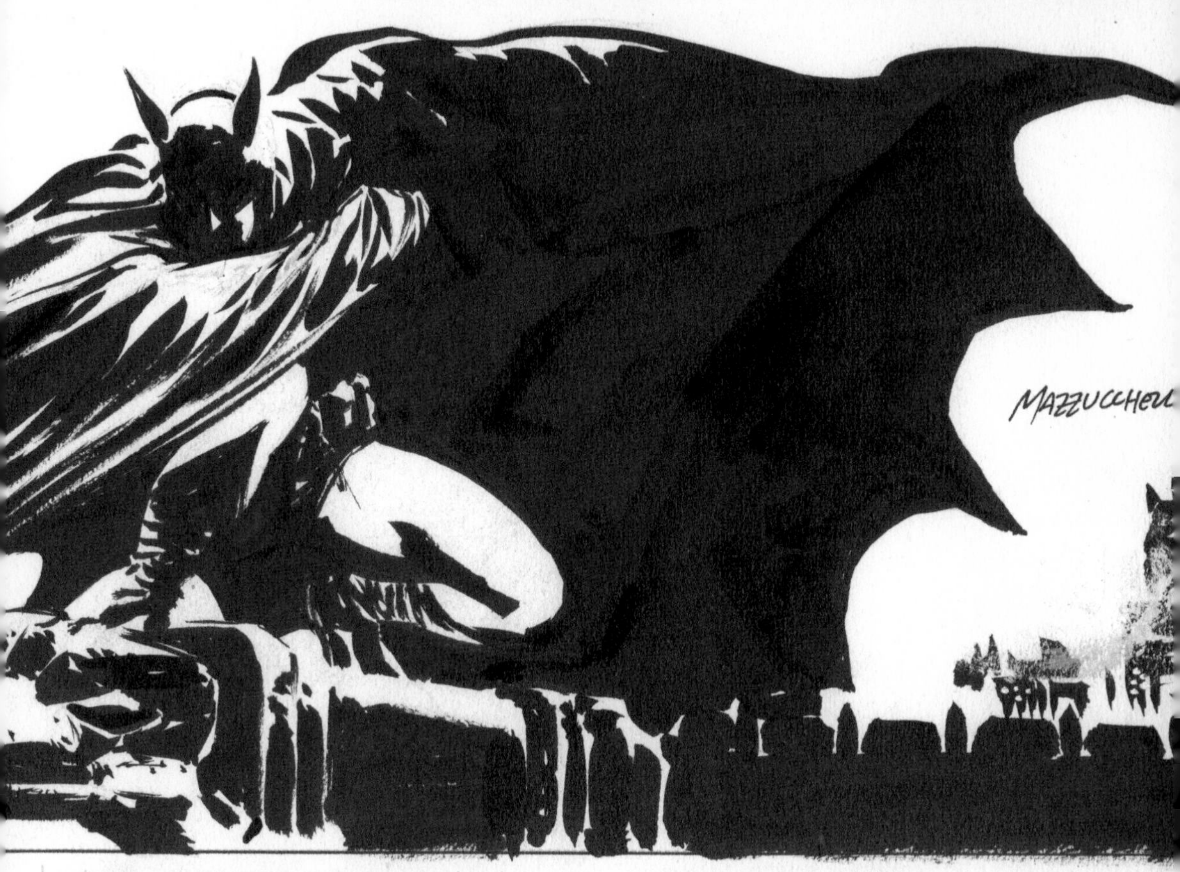

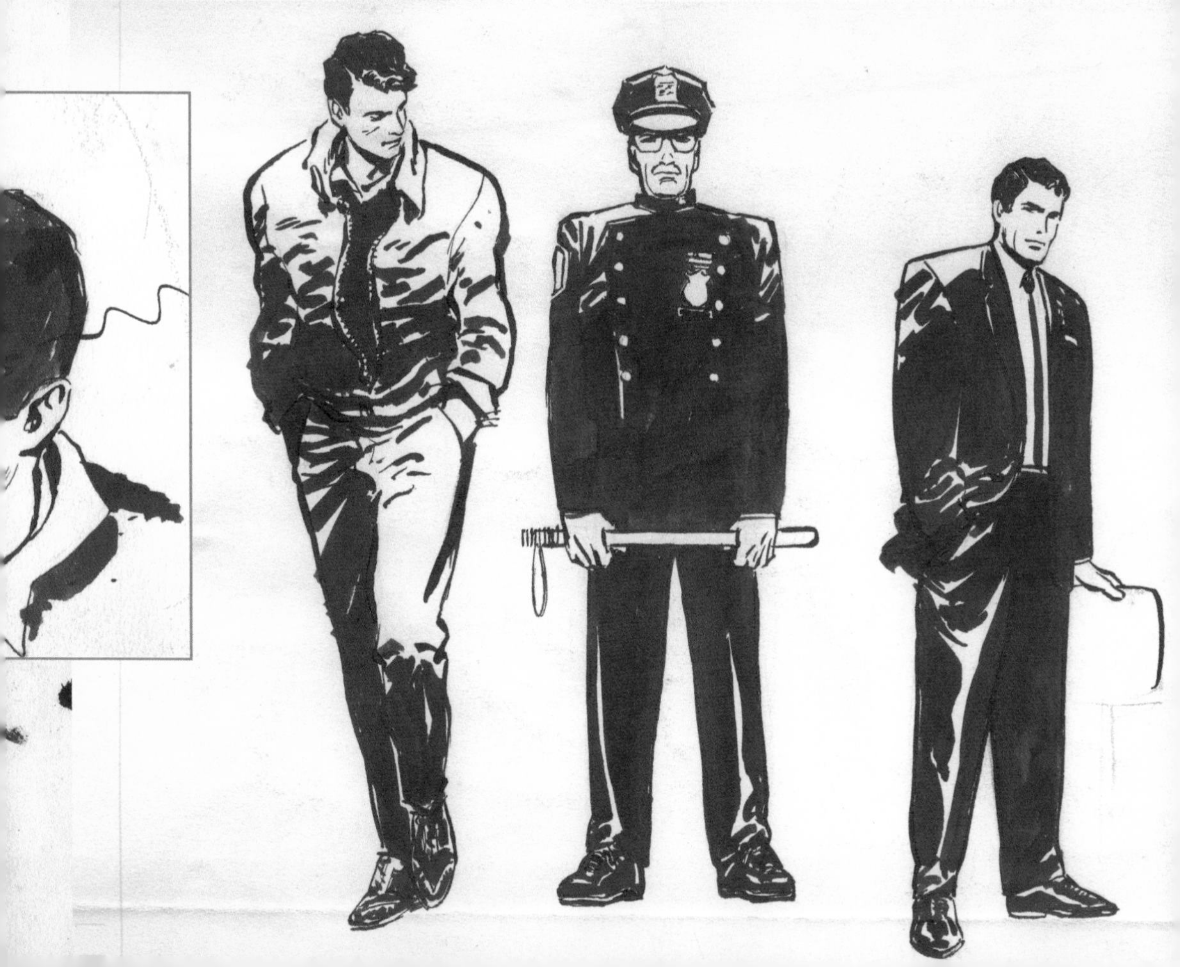

BATMAN/p8

1.
BIG PANEL. INTERIOR A LARGE PARKING GARAGE. THE SIDES OF THE GARAGE ARE EXPOSED, MAKING VISIBLE GOTHAM ROOFTOPS. THE GARAGE IS DARK, AND ONLY A FEW CARS, ALL OF EXPENSIVE MAKE, ARE VISIBLE. PROMINENT IN THE FOREGROUND IS A GLEAMING BLACK PORSCHE, ITS HEADLIGHTS ON, ITS WINDSHIELD TINTED BLACK.

1 TITLE (AS ON PAGE 2): MARCH 11
2 CAP(B): The engine hums, gently, not quite convinced it should stop.
3 CAP(B): Everything is in PLACE. The ATTENDANT was even obliging enough to ask me for my AUTOGRAPH. My ALIBI is SET.
4 CAP(B): BRUCE WAYNE has been SIGHTED at the ~~most expensive hotel in town~~ the same HOTEL as a visiting Hollywood SEX QUEEN. That should generate sufficient RUMORS --
5 CAP(B): -- to account for my WHEREABOUTS, for the next few hours.

2.
CLOSE ON BRUCE, UNDERLIT BY THE DASHBOARD, SPREADING GREY MAKE UP ON HIS CHEEK. HIS FACE IS CALM.

6 CAP(B): This is a RECONNAISSANCE mission. Until I know MORE, I must avoid combat. Until I'm READY...
7 CAP(B): ...My ANONYMITY is an OBVIOUS priority. The murder of my PARENTS is a matter of public RECORD.

3.
CLOSE ON BRUCE, ADHERING A HIDEOUS FAKE SCAR TO HIS CHEEK AND NECK.

8 CAP(B): All it requires is a change in CLOTHING and COMPLEXION --
9 CAP(B): -- and a single, memorable, distracting DETAIL.

[MORE]

BATMAN/p8, continued

~~1.~~
[4.]
MEDIUM ON GORDON, IN HIS GARAGE, OPENING THE DOOR TO HIS CHEAP, BATTERED SEDAN [A RUST PATCH ON ITS SIDE WOULDN'T HURT]. HE LOOKS BACKWARD, OVER HIS SHOULDER, AS HE HEARS A VOICE. [DAVID -- GARAGE MUST BE IDENTIFIABLY DIFFERENT THAN THE ONE BRUCE IS IN.]

PARKING GARAGE? DOES HE LIVE IN AN APT OR A HOUSE?

10 CAP[G]: Requested OFF this NIGHT SHIFT four times now -- damn it, Barbara NEEDS me at night, these days, Barbara, and little JAMES ...
11 CAP[G]: ... so I hope it's a BOY. So WHAT.
12 CAP[G]: FOUR TIMES and no REPLY. I'm not making FRIENDS in the department --
13 VO: Going to WORK, Lieutenant?

[5.]
MEDIUM LONG ON GORDON, STANDING. HUGE IN FOREGROUND ARE SEVERA ARMS, HOLDING BASEBALL BATS.

14 VO: Going to be LATE.
15 [2]: May have to skip the whole NIGHT.

REVERSE? GORDON UP CLOSE - LINE OF SILHOUETTES IN COCKY POSES W/ BATS IN BG?

BATMAN/p10

1.
STREET SCENE, IN FRONT OF A HOTEL THAT ADVERTISES HOURLY RATES. ONE OR TWO HOOKERS STAND ON THE SIDEWALK. A PIMP, WHITE, VERY TOUGH LOOKING, STANDS IN A DOORWAY. VARIOUS PEOPLE, NONE DRESSED WELL, COME AND GO, INCLUDING A COUPLE OF TEENAGERS WHO OGLE THE WHORES. PROMINENT IN THE FOREGROUND, HIS BACK TO US, WALKING, IS BRUCE. HE'S DRESSED IN ARMY SURPLUS BOOTS, BLUE JEANS, AND A WEATHERED ARMY JACKET.
(DAVID -- THIS IS THE MASTER SHOT FOR THE ACTION ON THE NEXT FEW PAGES. WE NEED A STRONG SENSE OF LOCALE. IT SHOULD DOMINATE THE PAGE.)

1 CAP(B): It's a twenty block walk to the enemy camp.
2 CAP(B): It's been EDUCATIONAL. I was sized up like a piece of MEAT by the LEATHER boys in ROBINSON PARK. I waded through PLEAS and half-hearted THREATS from JUNKIES at the FINGER MEMORIAL. I stepped across a field of human RUBBLE that lay sleeping in front of the overcrowded SPRANG MISSION.
3 CAP(B): Finally, the WORST of it.
4 CAP(B): The EAST END.

2.
MEDIUM CLOSE ON BRUCE, CROPPED AT THE CHEST, LOOKING DOWN AS HE HEARS A VOICE. THE SCAR, AND THE CLOTHES SHOULD MAKE HIM LOOK LIKE HE'S TRYING OUT FOR THE TRAVIS BICKLE LOOK ALIKE CONTEST.

5 CAP(B): Hard to believe it's gotten WORSE.
6 BALLOON FROM BELOW: Cheer you up.

3. MEDIUM LONG
~~FULL FIGURES~~ ON BRUCE AND HOLLY, A PRETTY, THIRTEEN YEAR OLD WHORE. SHE STANDS FACING BRUCE, LOOKING UP AT HIM, HER HANDS CLASPED BEHIND HER BACK, HER HEAD TILTED COQUETTISHLY. (DAVID -- THROUGHOUT THIS SEQUENCE, TREAT HER AS A LITTLE GIRL, NOT AS A TOUGH URBAN WHORE. SHE SHOULDN'T SNEER OR ACT SLUTTY; SHE HAS NO IDEA THAT THERE'S ANYTHING WRONG WITH WHAT SHE'S DOING. SHE JUST WANTS TO PLEASE HER PIMP.)

BRUCE HAS HIS HANDS IN HIS POCKETS. HE STANDS CASUALLY, SMILES AT HER A LITTLE PAINFULLY. THE PIMP APPROACHES THEM FROM BEHIND.

7 BRUCE: I doubt it. How old are you?
8 HOLLY: Young as you WANT me to be.
9 PIMP: Stupid B -- thas all WRONG, Holly. You doin it WRONG.

PIMP WEARING RED?

[MORE]

BATMAN/p11

1.
MEDIUM ON ACTION AS THE PIMP TURNS, IRRITATED, TO SEE HOLLY STILL STANDING BESIDE HIM. BRUCE WATCHES.

1 PIMP: You still HERE? TOLD you to GO, Holly.
2 HOLLY: He hadn't SAID.

2.
CLOSE AS THE PIMP GRABS HOLLY'S HAIR, ROUGHLY. HER MOUTH OPENS WIDE IN PAIN.

3 PIMP: We talk this over LATER, sweet chunks.
4 VO: No ...

3.
CLOSE ON BRUCE, SMILING CHEERFULLY, VERY EAGER.

5 BRUCE: ... I think you're FINISHED with her.
6 CAP[B]: I'm PROVOKING him.
7 CAP[B]: I really shouldn't.

4.
MEDIUM LONG, LOOKING DOWN AT BRUCE AND THE PIMP. THE PIMP STANDS, SIZING BRUCE UP, ANGRY. BRUCE REMAINS STILL, HIS HANDS STILL IN HIS POCKETS.

8 PIMP: Man, you PUSHIN. You on the EDGE.
9 (2): You lookin for NEW scar. THAS right. Jus tell me WHERE, man ...
~~BALLOON FROM ABOVE: Oh, Christ...~~

5.
LOOKING UP AT A HOTEL WINDOW. SELINA KYLE, YOUNG, DARK, EXOTIC, AND SLEAZY, LEANS ON THE SILL, LOOKING OUT. SHE WEARS A LEATHER CORSET. HER HAIR IS SHORT, CUT CLOSE TO HER HEAD. SHE HOLDS A CIGARETTE IN ONE HAND; A RIDING CROP IN THE OTHER. SHE'S IRRITATED.

10 SELINA: ... can't be VICE. We're paid UP. Just some IDIOT out to get himself KILLED.
11 VOICE FROM INSIDE WINDOW (SMALL LETTERS, LARGE, WOBBLY BALLOON): Selina ... don't stop NOW ...

6.
SAME ANGLE. SELINA LEANS FORWARD, DROPS AN ASH

12 SELINA: Shut up, Skunk.
13 (2): You know what I hate MOST about MEN, Skunk?
14 VOICE FROM INSIDE WINDOW (SAME AS PREVIOUS PANEL): PLEASE, Selina ... TELL me ... why you HATE us so ... oh, PLEASE ...

7.
CLOSE ON SELINA, LOOKING DOWN, DISGUSTED.

15 SELINA: Never met one.
16 VO (AS BEFORE): Say it AGAIN ...

[MORE]

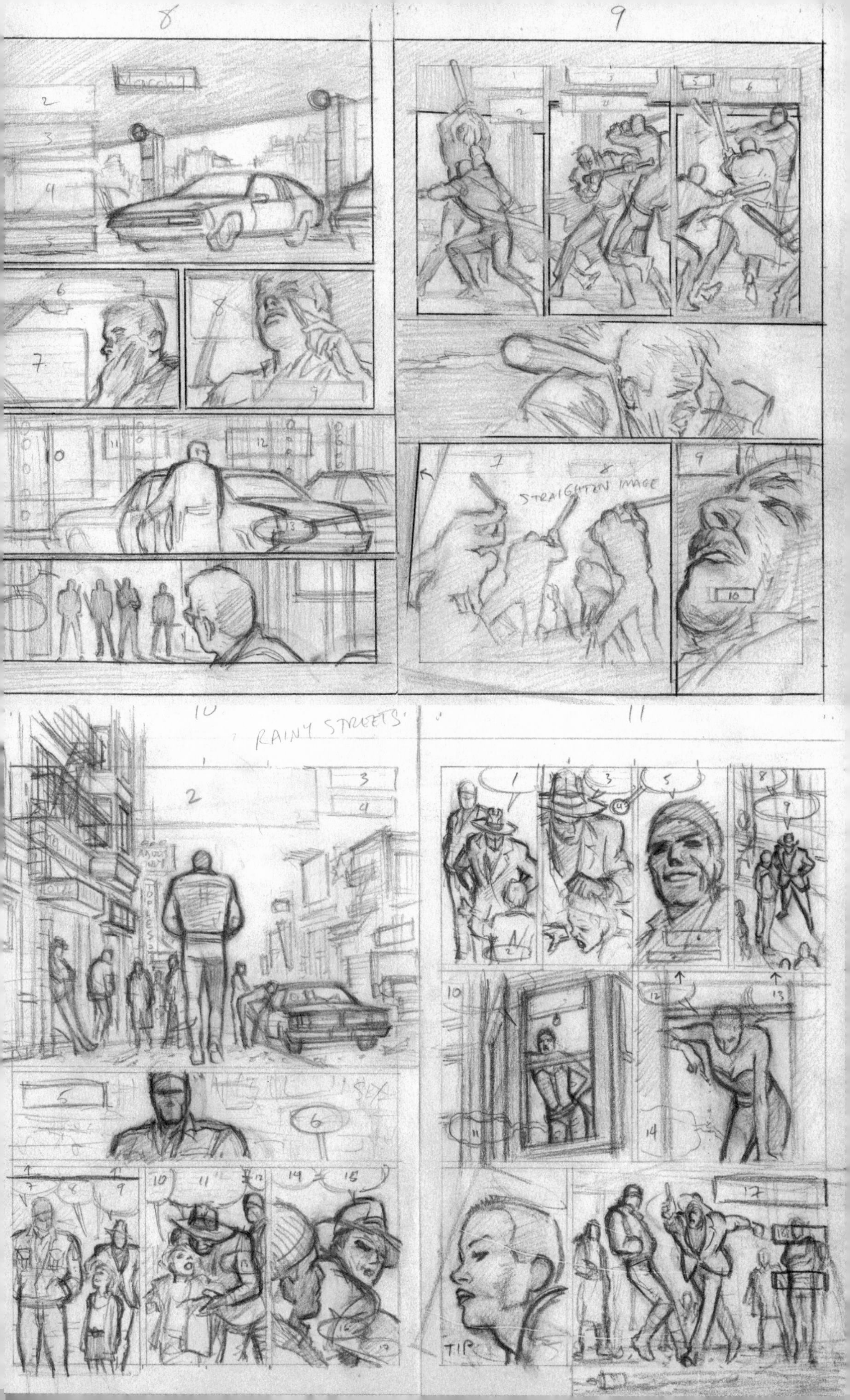

8
9
STRAIGHTEN IMAGE
10
RAINY STREETS
SEX
11
TIP

BATMAN/p12

1.
SAME ANGLE AS BRUCE STEPS INSIDE THE PIMP'S GUARD, GRABS HIS WRIST WITH ONE HAND, TWISTING IT, FORCING THE PIMP TO DROP THE KNIFE; WITH HIS OTHER ARM, BRUCE BRINGS HIS ELBOW INTO THE PIMP'S STERNUM. THE PIMP IS STARTLED, IN PAIN.

1 CAP(B): -- I won't say he has a CHANCE --
2 CAP(B): -- but he's fast.
3 CAP(B): This is getting a little too GOOD to me -- better wrap it UP --

2.
[redacted] FULL FIGURES AS BRUCE DEMOLISHES THE PIMP WITH A SPINNING KICK. THE PIMP IS KNOCKED BACKWARD, INTO THE CROWD. SOMEWHERE IN SHOT, HOLLY PICKS UP THE PIMP'S SWITCHBLADE FROM THE SIDEWALK.
NO COPY

3.
CLOSE ON BRUCE, HIS MOUTH OPEN IN SUDDEN PAIN.

4 CAP(B): IDIOT -- NEVER should have done this --
5 CAP(B): -- have to get OUT of here before I draw [redacted] ATTENTION --
6 BRUCE: AAAA

4.
MEDIUM ~~LONG~~ ON ACTION AS HOLLY HOLDS TIGHT TO BRUCE'S LEG WITH ONE ARM; THE OTHER HAS DRIVEN THE SWITCHBLADE DEEP INTO BRUCE'S THIGH.

7 HOLLY: Come ON you GUYS -- I GOT him --

5.
MEDIUM LONG AS: HOLLY DRAWS THE KNIFE OUT, BACK, TO STAB AGAIN; BRUCE GRABS HER WRIST; ANOTHER HOOKER, WITH ANOTHER KNIFE, TRIES TO STAB BRUCE; HE KICKS HER IN THE STOMACH WITH HIS FREE LEG; A THIRD HOOKER, A HUGE BULL OF A WOMAN WITH INHUMANLY LARGE BREASTS, TALLER THAN BRUCE, TUNDERS AT HIM FROM BEHIND, HER ARMS REACHING AROUND HIS HEAD IN AN ATTEMPT TO GRAB HIM.

8 CAP(B): Very GOOD, Bruce.
9 CAP(B): You've really put the fear of GOD into them.

6.
LOOKING UP AT THE HOTEL WINDOW AS SELINA LEAPS TO THE SILL, VAULTING FORWARD, ANGRY, THROWING HER CIGARETTE AWAY.

10 SELINA: [redacted] DAMN it --

BATMAN/p13

1.
FULL FIGURE OF SELINA, WEARING KNEE HIGH BLACK LEATHER BOOTS, THE CORSET, AND SKIN TIGHT BLACK LEATHER PANTS, WITH A PAIR OF HANDCUFFS DANGLING FROM HER BELT, SWINGS ACROBATICALLY ON THE LADDER OF A FIRE ESCAPE.

1 SELINA: -- NOBODY hurts HOLLY --

2.
FULL FIGURES AS: HOLLY SITS ON THE SIDEWALK, HOLDING HER WRIST, HOWLING IN PAIN; BRUCE FLIPS THE BIG ONE OVER HIS BACK, FORWARD; THE SECOND ONE WITH A KNIFE HOLDS HER STOMACH, IS ON HER KNEES AND ONE HAND ON THE SIDEWALK, GASPING FOR BREATH.

2 HOLLY: HURTS bet he broke my WRIST --
3 CAP(B): MESS -- made a MESS of it --
4 CAP(B): -- no EXCUSE -- didn't CONTROL myself --

3.
THE BIG ONE FLIES INTO A ROW OF GARBAGE CANS; BESIDE HER, SELINA LANDS ON THE PAVEMENT, CROUCHED FORWARD, FURIOUS.

5 CAP(B): -- ANOTHER one -- hissing like a CAT --
6 CAP(B): -- looks like she KNOWS what she's doing -- be CAREFUL --

4.
MEDIUM LONG AS SELINA THROWS A KARATE KICK AT BRUCE'S FACE; BRUCE BLOCKS IT WITH A FOREARM.

7 CAP(B): -- that's GOOD -- she's had KARATE training --
8 CAP(B): -- but ONLY karate --

5.
MEDIUM CLOSE AS BRUCE PUNCHES SELINA IN THE FACE. HER HEAD TWISTS AROUND, HER MOUTH IS LOOSE; SHE'S BEEN KNOCKED SENSELESS.

9 SE (RUNNING ACROSS BACKGROUND): EEEEEEEEEEEE
10 CAP: -- oh, NO --

6.
LONG ON ACTION AS A POLICE CAR SCREECHES TO A HALT AT THE CURB, LIGHTS FLASHING, COPS LEAPING FROM EITHER SIDE, GUNS DRAWN. BRUCE WHEELS, MOVING TOWARD THE COPS. SELINA LIES FLAT ON HER BACK, DAZED, WITH A CONCUSSION. HOLLY LEANS OVER SELINA, TERRIFIED.

SE: EEEEE SKREEECHH
11 12 COP: FREEZE --
13 HOLLY: SeLINa get UP -- SeLINa --
14 CAP(B): -- if I'm CAUGHT -- it's OVER --

BATMAN/p18

[1.]
SILHOUETTE OF FLASS, HUGE, UNSTEADY, A BEER IN HIS HAND.

1 CAP[G]: Finally.
2 CAP[G]: Flass.

[2.]
MEDIUM ON GORDON, LEANING FORWARD IN HIS SEAT AS HE STARTS THE ENGINE.

3 CAP[G]: He staggers to his STATION WAGON and gets in. It only takes him two tries.
4 CAP[G]: I hear his engine start and watch him pull out. He almost [redacted] flattens the MAILBOX [redacted] before he remembers to turn his LIGHTS on.

[3.]
ON A STRETCH OF DIRT ROAD, SURROUNDED BY TREES, GORDON'S SEDAN SIDESWIPES FLASS' STATION WAGON. SPARKS FLY.

5 CAP[G]: I keep mine off and follow.
6 CAP[G]: I haven't seen a house in three minutes when I [redacted] pull up beside him and jerk the wheel.
7 CAP[G][AT BOTTOM]: He's ten miles over the speed limit.

[4.]
FLASS STEPS OUT OF HIS CAR, HIS GUN DRAWN. THE FRONT END OF HIS CAR IS CRUMPLED INTO A LARGE TREE. LARGE IN FOREGROUND, GORDON'S HAND POINTS HIS .38 AT FLASS.

8 CAP[G][AT TOP]: Not fast [redacted] enough to KILL him when he hits the TREE.
9 CAP[G][AT BOTTOM]: I show him my GUN. He says my NAME and drops his.

[5.]
MEDIUM LONG ON GORDON AND FLASS, STANDING A FEW YARDS APART. FLASS HAS DROPPED HIS GUN, LOOMS A FULL HEAD TALLER THAN GORDON. GORDON HOLD THE BASEBALL BAT IN BOTH HANDS, ONE HAND ON EACH END, HORIZONTALLY ACROSS HIS WAIST.

10 CAP[G]: He's BIG.
11 CAP[G]: GREEN BERET training.
12 CAP[G]: It's been FIFTEEN YEARS since I had to take out a GREEN BERET.

[6.]
MEDIUM ON GORDON AS HE TOSSES THE BAT FORWARD, IN FLASS' DIRECTION.

13 CAP[G]: Even so --
14 CAP[G]: -- he deserves a HANDICAP.

BATMAN/p19

[1.]
MEDIUM AS FLASS CHARGES, SWINGING THE BAT WITH BOTH HANDS. GORDON DUCKS PAST THE BAT, PUNCHES FLASS ACROSS ONE EYE, DRAWING BLOOD.

1 CAP[G]: I don't crack his skull.

[2.]
MEDIUM CLOSE AS GORDON FOLLOWS THROUGH WITH A STRAIGHT-FINGERED BLOW TO FLASS' THROAT.

2 CAP[G]: I don't crush his larynx.

[3.]
FULL FIGURES AS GORDON LIFTS FLASS FROM THE GROUND WITH AN UPPERCUT TO HIS SOLAR PLEXUS. FLASS DROPS THE BAT.

3 CAP[G]: I don't break his RIBS or punch my hand through his CHEST.

[4.]
MEDIUM ON ACTION AS: FLASS, ON HIS KNEES, FALLS BACKWARD AS GORDON KICKS HIM IN THE FACE.
NO COPY

[5.]
MEDIUM CLOSE ON GORDON, HIS HAND LIFTED FROM A PUNCH, BLOODY.

4 CAP[G]: I do just ENOUGH --
5 CAP[G]: -- to keep him out of the HOSPITAL.

[6.]
FULL FIGURES AS GORDON HANDCUFFS FLASS'S ARMS BEHIND HIS BACK. FLASS IS FACE DOWN ON GRASS, COMPLETELY NAKED.

6 CAP[G]: [redacted] I toss his GUN into the WOODS. It should be RUSTY by MORNING.
7 CAP[G]: I take his CLOTHES off and leave him in his own CUFFS by the side of the ROA
8 CAP[G][AT BOTTOM]: He'll never REPORT it. Not FLASS. He'll make up some STORY that involves at least TEN attackers and NEVER admit I DID it.

[7.]
CLOSE ON GORDON, DRIVING, LOOKING BACK, DISGUSTED.

9 CAP[G]: But he'll KNOW. And he'll stay away from BARBARA.
10 CAP[G]: Thanks, Flass.
11 CAP[G]: You've shown me what it TAKES to be a COP in GOTHAM CITY.

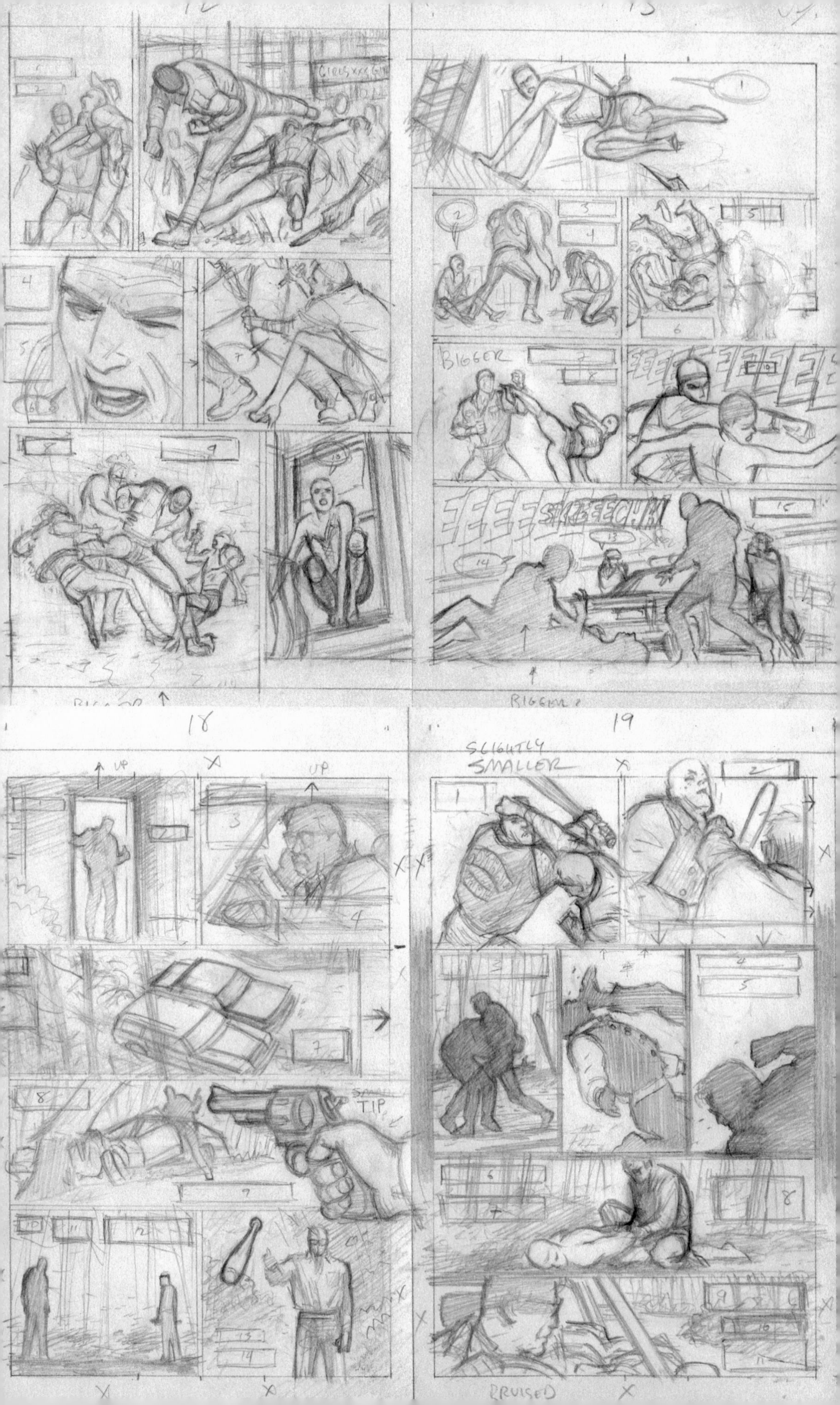
GIRLS XXX GIR
BIGGER
EEEE SKREEECH!!
BIGGER
18
19
SLIGHTLY SMALLER
UP
UP
TIP
BRUISED

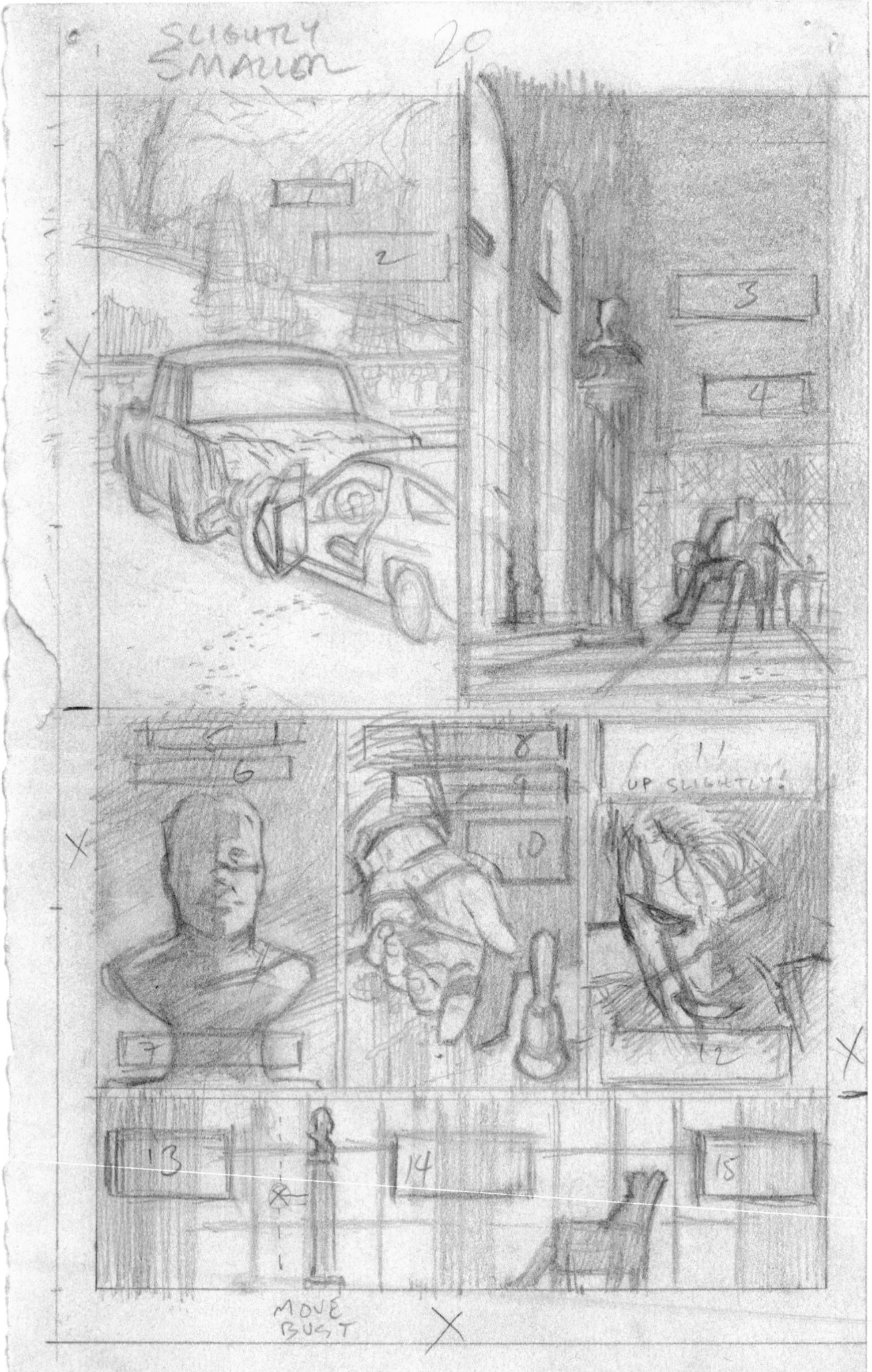
SLIGHTLY SMALLER
20
1
2
3
4
5
6
7
8
9
10
11
UP SLIGHTLY!
12
13
14
15
MOVE BUST

More roughs, actual size.

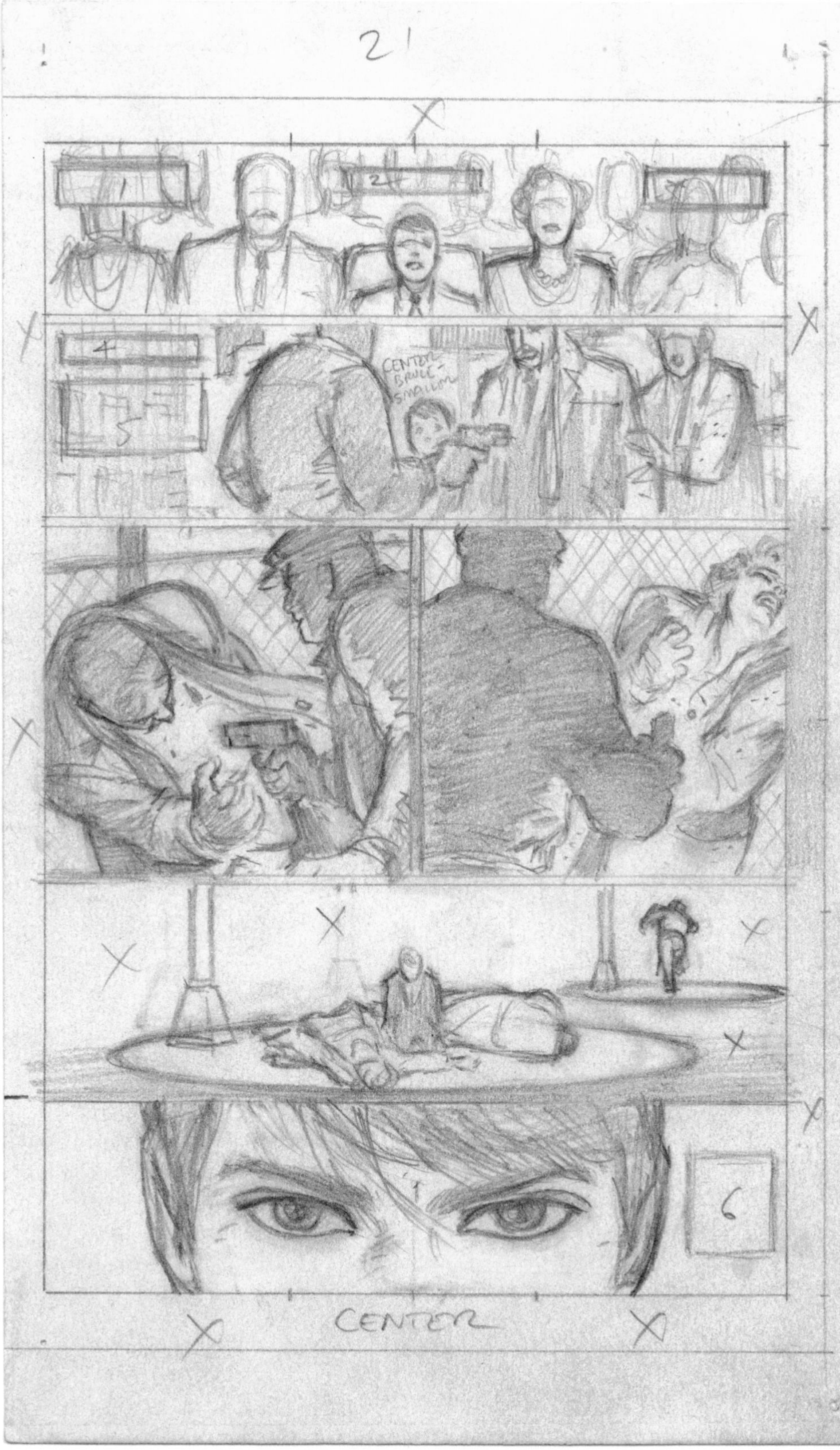
21
CENTER

BATMAN/p6

[redacted] [1.]
INTERIOR GORDON'S BEDROOM. BARBARA LIES, ASLEEP, IN BED, THE SHEETS TWISTED AND SPREAD, COVERING HER UPPER BODY, AS IF SHE HASN'T SLEPT PEACEFULLY, WEARING ONLY PANTIES. GORDON SITS, TENSE, TROUBLED, ON THE FOOT OF THE BED, HOLDING AN ASHTRAY IN ONE HAND, SMOKING WITH THE OTHER. THROUGH A WINDOW BEHIND HIM GOTHAM TENEMENTS RISE, ALMOST OBSCURING A FULL MOON, WHICH LIGHTS THE SCENE.

1 CAP[G]: ... I pray he's VERY strong. And SMART enough to stay ALIVE.
2 CAP[G]: How did I let this happen?
3 CAP[G]: How did I screw up so BADLY ... to bring an X innocent CHILD to life ...
4 CAP[G]: ... in a city without hope ...

[redacted] [2.]
BIG PANEL. LOOKING MXXX ACROSS TENEMENT ROOFTOPS THAT STRETCH BACK TO A CLEAR BLUE SKY. [redacted] STRETCHED BETWEEN BUILDINGS ON A CORD, LAUNDRY WAVES WILDLY, CAUGHT IN A FIERCE WIND. SEVERAL PIGEONS SCATTER, AS IF FRIGHTENED. THE MOON, NOT IN THE SHOT, CASTS XXXXXXXXXXXX LONG SHADOWS ACROSS THE ROOFTOPS. SMALL IN SHOT, SILHOUETTED, HIS CAPE SPREAD TO RESEMBLE WINGS, BATMAN RUNS, TOWARD US. [NO COPY]

[redacted] [3.]
INTERIOR GORDON'S APARTMENT, AT NIGHT. FULL FIGURES ON GORDON AND BARBARA. GORDON LIES ON HIS STOMACH, SHIRTLESS. BARBARA STRADDLES HIS BACK, XXXX MASSAGING HIS SHOULDERS AND TRAPEZIUS, HER HAIR TIED UP, ATTRACTIVELY. SHE WEARS A SATIN TEDDY THAT FIT HER BETTER BEFORE SHE BECAME PREGNANT. THEY ARE ON THE FLOOR OF THEIR LIVING ROOM. NEAR THEM IS A CHECKERED TABLECLOTH, WITH PLATES AND SILVER FOR TWO, AS WELL AS WINE GLASSES AND A BOTTLE OF WINE IN AN ICE BUCKET. LIGHTING THE SCENE ARE TWO TALL CANDLES IN SIMPLE CANDLE HOLDERS. THEY HAVEN'T EATEN YET; IT'S GORDON'S NIGHT OFF, AND THIS IS SUPPOSED TO BE THE BEGINNING OF A ROMANTIC EVENING. [KEEP IN MIND THAT THE XXXXXXXX GORDONS ARE STRUGGLING TO GET BY. NOTHING IN THE APARTMENT SHOULD LOOK EXPENSIVE.]

5 TITLE: APRIL 9
6 CAP[G]: They CALL it my night OFF.
7 CAP[G]: It starts OUT well enough, with the smell of Barbara's LEMON CHICKEN --
8 CAP[G]: -- and her FINGERS, kneading BABY OIL into my SHOULDERS ...
9 CAP[G]: ... RACHMANINOFF, played soft ... her idea ... corny, but it works ...
10 BARBARA: Don't have to go to METROPOLIS ...
11 [2]: ... for a man of STEEL ...
12 [3]: ... could use a JACKHAMMER on your BACK ...
13 GORDON: XXXX Feels GREAT, honey ...

[MORE]

BATMAN/[redacted] 6

[redacted] [1.]
LOOKING DOWN THE SIDE OF A TENEMENT AT A FIRE ESCAPE, ON WHICH THREE SPANISH YOUTHS SCRAMBLE TO CARRY A STEREO AND LARGE TELEVISION SET FROM AN OPEN APARTMENT WINDOW. THEY'RE FROZEN IN POSITION, ONE HOLDING THE TV IN BOTH ARMS, ALL LOOKING UP IN ABSOLUTE HORROR. [redacted]

1 CAP[B]: The costume WORKS -- better than I'd HOPED.
2 CAP[B]: They FREEZE and STARE and give me all the time in the WORLD ...

[redacted] [2.]
[redacted] WAIST-LEVEL VIEW, FULL FIGURES, AS BATMAN, LIT BY LIGHT FROM THE APARTMENT WINDOW, LANDS ON THE FIRE ESCAPE, FACING OUTWARD, SNARLING AT THE YOUTH WITH THE TELEVISION SET. THE YOUTH INVOLUNTARILY LEAPS BACKWARD, HORRIFIED, DROPPING THE TV, PITCHING BACKWARD OVER THE XXXX FRON OF THE FIRE ESCAPE, ABOUT TO FALL INTO SPACE. ANOTHER OF THEM LEAPS NIMBLY TO THE SIDE OF THE FIRE ESCAPE, CROUCHING ON IT LIKE SPIDER-MAN. THE THIRD FALLS BACK, SITTING ON THE FLOOR OF THE FIRE ESCAPE, XXX AGAINST THE WALL OF THE BUILDI SCREAMING IN TERROR. GOTHAM CITY STRETCHES BACK INTO THE NIGHT.

3 CAP[B]: ... I come in CLOSE onx the one who looks the STRONGEST -- throw him a GROWL [redacted] I've brought all the way from AFRICA --
4 CAP[B]: -- and suddenly everything falls to PIECES.
5 CAP[B]: The one to my LEFT calls for his MOTHER -
6 CAP[B]: -- to my RIGHT the OTHER collects his SENSES and leaps to POSITION -- XXX he'll be TROUBLE --
7 CAP[B]: -- the STRONG one gets SCARED -- TOO scared --

[redacted] [3.]
EXTREME CLOSE ON BATMAN, DESPERATE, REACHING FORWARD.

8 CAP[B]: -- NO --
9 CAP[B]: -- I'm no KILLER --

[redacted] [4.]
LOOKING UP AT THE FIRE ESCAPE AS THE YOUTH STARES TOWARD US, MOUTH OPEN, SCREAMING. BATMAN IS PITCHED PARTWAY OVER THE SIDE, HOLDING THE YOUTH BY THE ANKLE. SPIDER-MAN BALANCES HIMSELF BY HOLDING ONTO A LADDER WITH ONE HAND, MOVES CLOSER, READY TO KICK BATMAN. THE REMAINING YOUTH IS WATCHING, RISING TO HIS FEET, BOTH HANDS ON THE TV SET.

10 CAP[B]: -- he SCREAMS -- like a GIRL --
11 CAP[B]: -- can't be older than FIFTEEN --
12 CAP[B]: -- a CHILD -- just a CHILD --

[MORE]

BATMAN/p18

[1.]
MEDIUM CLOSE ON BATMAN, WHIRLING, ALERT. [HE'S ON A ROOFTOP; BACKGROUND SHOULD BE A NIGHT SKY, PERHAPS A TOUCH OF ROOF DETAIL.]

NO COPY

[2.]
CLOSE ON GORDON, LOOKING UP THROUGH THE CAR WINDOW, CIGARETTE FLYING FROM HIS MOUTH, SHOULDER RAISED AS HE WRENCHES THE WHEEL.

1 CAP[G]: Maybe it's PILLS --
2 CAP[G]: -- maybe it's a HEART ATTACK --

[3.]
LOOKING UP THROUGH THE TRUCK WINDOW AT THE TRUCK'S DRIVER, WHO'S LURCHED BACK IN HIS SEAT, RIGID, EYES WIDE.

3 CAP[G]: -- maybe it's BOTH XX but that doesn't MATTER --
4 CAP[G]: -- he's out of CONTROL -- his FOOT must be pressed to the ACCELERATOR --

[4.]
PULL BACK TO SHOW: IN FOREGROUND, XXX A BAG LADY STANDS IN THE MIDDLE OF THE STREET, STRAINING TO TUG A SHOPPING CART FULL OF GARBAGE, WHICH HAS A BROKEN WHEEL AND WON'T MOVE; IN BACKGROUND, THE TRUCK CAREENS TOWARD HER; GORDON'S CAR SWERVES BEHIND THE TRUCK, PIVOTING TO FOLLOW THE TRUCK.

5 CAP[G]: -- oh, NO -- that old WOMAN --
6 CAP[G]: -- can't LET this HAPPEN --
7 SE[FROM GORDON'S CAR]: SKREEEE
8 CAP[G]: -- come ON you heap MOVE --

[5.]
SILHOUETTE OF BATMAN, LEAPING FROM A ROOFTOP INTO SPACE.

NO COPY

[6.]
INTERIOR GORDON'S CAR. MEDIUM CLOSE ON ACTION AS ESSEN LOOKS ON, STARTLED, TO SEE GORDON HAS OPENED THE CAR DOOR AND IS STEPPING OUT [THE CAR IS, OF COURSE, MOVING].

9 ESSEN: LIEUTENANT --
10 GORDON: Take the WHEEL. OFF PANEL

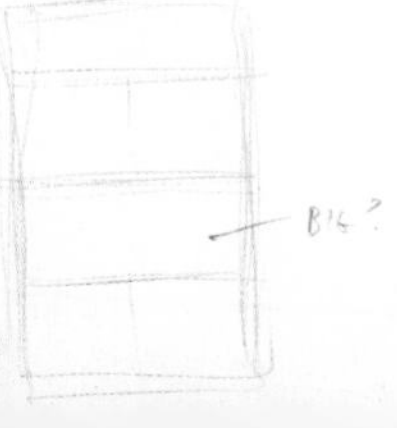

BATMAN/p19

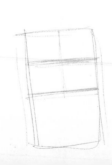

[1.]
MEDIUM CLOSE ON THE BAG LADY, LOOKING UP, CONFUSED.

NO COPY

[2.]
FULL FIGURE AS GORDON LEAPS FROM HIS CAR, GRABS THE RIDER SIDE DOOR OF THE RUSHING TRUCK. ESSEN GRABS THE STEERING WHEEL OF GORDON'S CAR.

1 CAP[G]: -- DAMN -- no TIME --
2 CAP[G]: -- no TIME --

FRONT VIEW OF CAR

[3.]
FULL FIGURE, LOOKING UP AT ACTION, AS BATMAN BOUNDS FROM A STREETLIGHT, CURLED, FLIPPING THROUGH SPACE TOWARD THE STREET.

NO COPY

SWINGING AROUND LAMPPOST

[4.]
MEDIUM ON ACTION AS GORDON REACHES IN THROUGH THE RIDER'S SIDE WINDOW OF THE TRUCK, DESPERATELY TRYING TO GRAB THE STEERING WHEE THE DRIVER'S EXPRESSION AND POSITION HAVE NOT CHANGED.

3 CAP[G]: -- can't REACH --
4 CAP[G]: -- no TIME --
5 CAP[G]: -- it's OVER I've BLOWN it --

[5.]
LONG ON ACTION AS: BATMAN TACKLES THE BAG LADY, CARRYING HER OUT X OF THE PATH OF THE TRUCK; THE TRUCK SMASHES THE SHOPPING CART, SPREADING GARBAGE ALL OVER; THE TRUCK HITS A GARBAGE DUMPER, KNOCKING IT SIDEWAYS; GORDON FLIES FROM THE SIDE OF THE TRUCK, ROLLING ACROSS THE PAVEMENT.

NO COPY

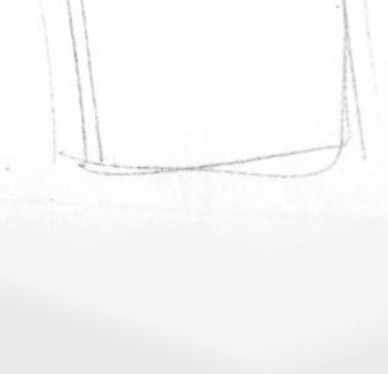

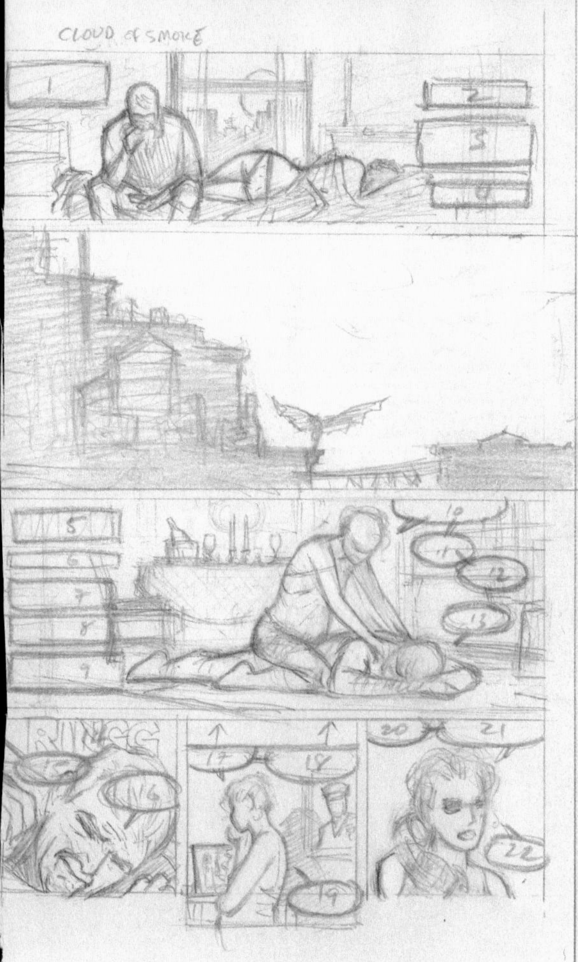
CLOUD OF SMOKE

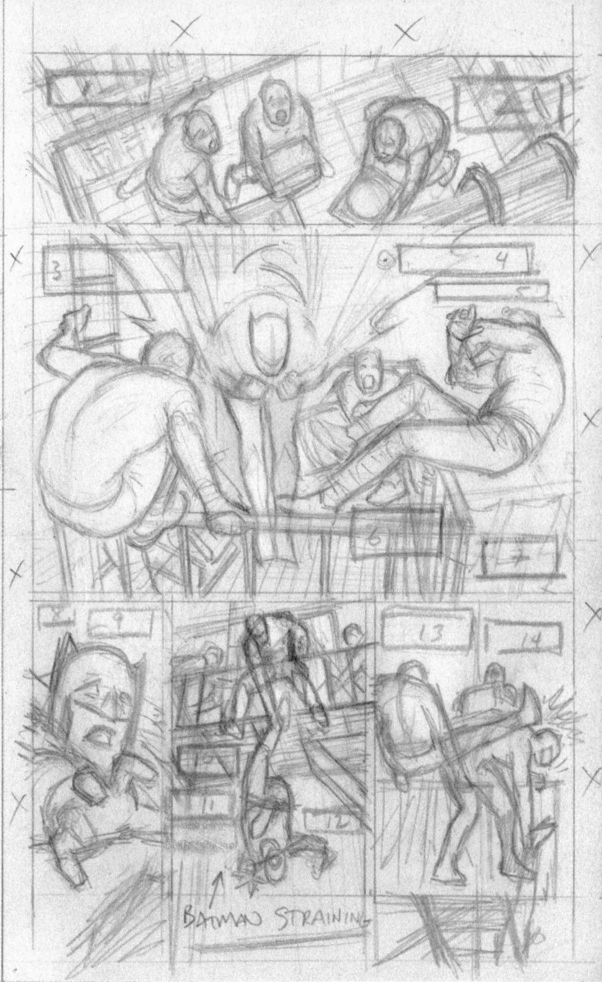
BATMAN STRAINING

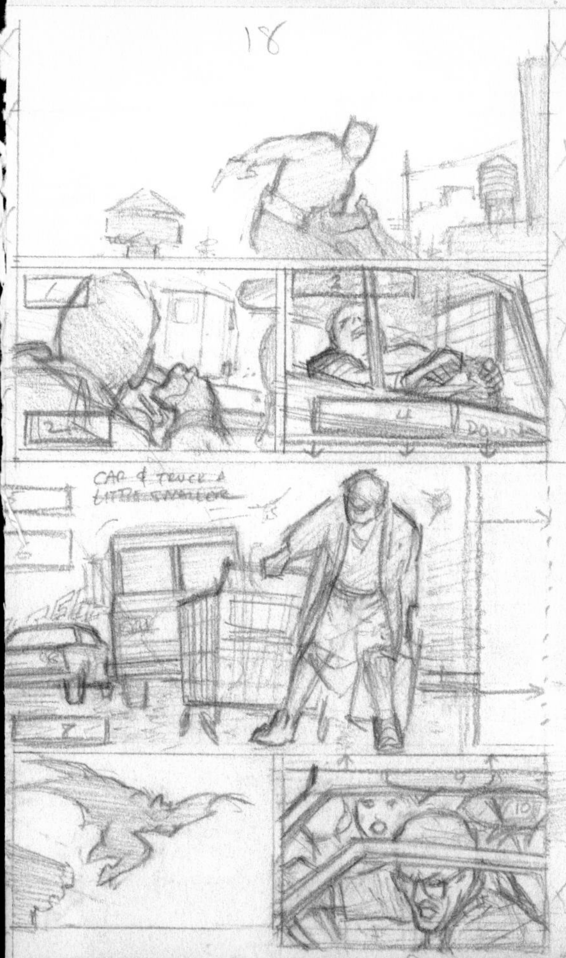
18
DOWN
CAR & TRUCK A
LITTLE SMALLER

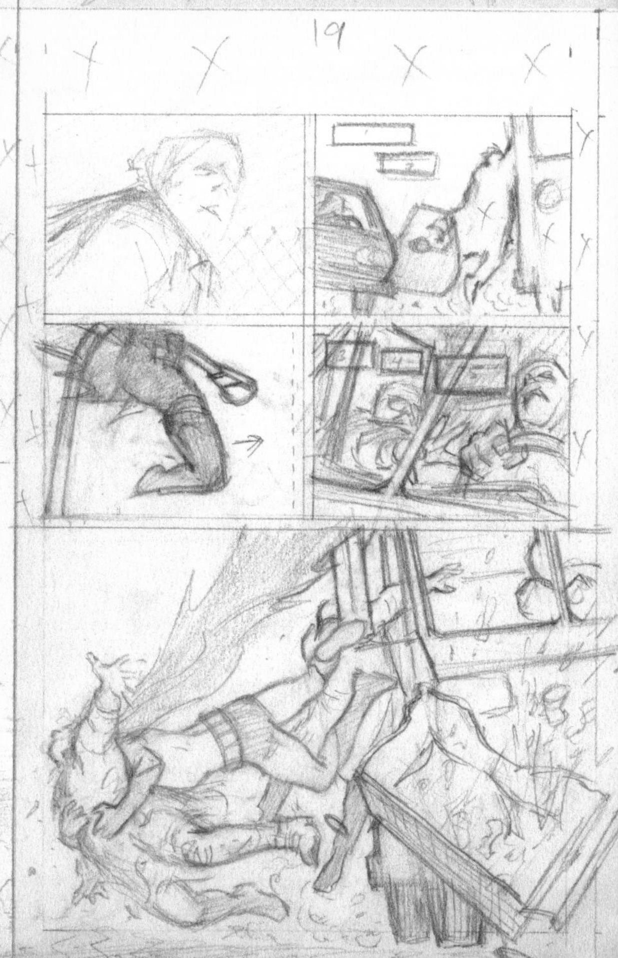
19

BATMAN/p2

[1.]
BIG PANEL. FULL FIGURE OF BATMAN, BACKLIT, TUMBLING DOWN A COLLAPSING STAIRWELL DOWN WHICH FIRE IS STREAMING. A WINO, CROUCHED IN THE STAIRWELL, WAKES, SCREAMING, FINDING HIMSELF ON FIRE. PATCHES OF FIRE ARE ON BATMAN'S CAPE.

1 CAP[BATMAN]: -- stairwell's COLLAPSING -- fall WITH --
2 CAP[B]: -- get away from the FIRE --
3 CAP[B]: -- that old MAN -- doesn't have a CHANCE -- can't HELP him --
4 CAP[B]: -- can't HELP him --

[2.]
FIGURE OF BATMAN, UPSIDE DOWN. FLAME, AND PIECES OF THE STAIRWELL, JUST FRAGMENTS, SURROUND HIM. BREAKING HIS SILHOUETTE, PART OF HIS UTILITY BELT CATCHES FIRE. HE'S REACHING FOR HIS BELT BUCKLE.

5 CAP[B]: -- SCREAMING -- can't HELP him --
6 CAP[B]: -- oh no --
7 CAP[B]: -- THERMITE -- in my BELT -- catching --
8 CAP[B]: -- get it OFF--

[3.]
CLOSE ON BATMAN'S BELT, IN FLAME, EXPLODING, NO LONGER ON BATMAN. FLAME IN BACK GROUND.

9 CAP[B]: -- still have XXXXX WEAPONS -- in CAPE -- and BOOTS --
10 CAP[B]: -- NEED them -- if I XXXXX survive this --

[4.]
LOOKING PAST A METAL TRAPDOOR, ON THE FLOOR, AS BATMAN LANDS ON THE FLOOR. THE DOOR IS MARKED "DANGER ELECTRICITY 80,000 WATTS". FLAMING RUBBLE IS FALLING, ALL ROUND. BATMAN'S CAPE IS SERIOUSLY ON FIRE. THE DOOR IS LOCKED BY A CHAIN AND PADLOCK.

11 CAP[B]: -- METAL --
12 CAP[B]: -- trap door's METAL --
13 CAP[B]: -- might be ENOUGH -- to PROTECT me ---
14 CAP[B]: -- provided that WARNING -- is a LIE --

[5.]
CLOSE ON BATMAN'S HANDS, SLIDING A PICKLOCK INTO THE LOCK.

15 CAP[B]: -- LUCKY -- keep the PICK in my GLOVE --
16 CAP[B]: -- LUCKY --

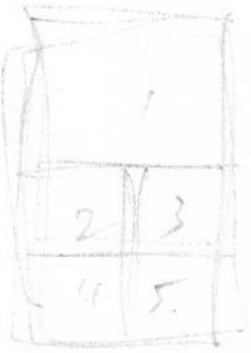

1
2
3
4
5

BATMAN/p[redacted] 3

[1.]
XXXXXXXXXXX -- GREY DAYBREAK OVER GOTHAM CITY. SMALL IN THE SKY, A HELICOPTER DROP A PAYLOAD TOWARD BUILDING

1 TITLE: JUNE 7
2 VO [FROM BELOW]: Nffmgmm
XXXX 3 [2]: Gox way, Otto. You don eat fr n hour.

[2.]
CLOSE ON SELINA KYLE, IN BED, TRYING NOT TO WAKE UP, AS A [redacted] SIAMESE CAT TRIES TO SQUIRREL ITS NOSE UNDER HER CHIN. CRANKY AS SELINA IS, SHE'S ALWAYS NICE TO HER CATS, SO THIS IS HER AT HER SOFTEST.

4 SE [FROM CAT]: Mroww
5 XSELINA: Mmfgg
6 [2]: Siamese. Too noisy. Should've left you at the market.

[3.]
INTERXXIOR A SMALL TENEMENT. THE ROOM IS CLUTTERED WITH MOVIE MAGAZINE EMPTY PACKS OF CIGARETTES, AND SELINA'S CLOTHING, STREWN ABOUT -- A FAIR AMOUNT OF WHICH SHOULD BE STRAIGHT FROM FREDRICK'S OF HOLLYWOOD. SEEMINGLY OUT OF PLACE, A SMALL PUNCHING BAG XX HANGS IN XX THE MIDDLE OF THE ROOM, OVER A SMALL PAIR OF ONE-HAND BARBELLS. SELINA LIES IN A LARGE, ORNATE, ANTIQUE BRASS BED. SHE'S CURLED, WRAPPING HERSELF IN BLACK SATIN SHEETS. CONVERGING ON HER ARE A DOZEN CATS, ALL COLORS AND SIZES. LINING THE WALLS ARE POSTERS OF MARLENE DIETRICH, BARBARA STANWYCK, GRETA GARBO, XXXXXXXXXXXXX MARILYN MONROE, AND ANY OTHER CLASSIC SCREEN SEX SYMBOLS YOU CARE TO THROW IN. THE POSTERS ARE INTERRUPTED ONLY BY EXPOSED PIPES, AND ONE WINDOW. HOLLY, WEARING ONE OF SELINA'S BLOUSES AS A NIGHTSHIRT, WHICH HANGS DOWN NEARLY TO HER KNEES, LEANS AGAINST THE WINDOW SILL, POINTING OUTWARD, EXCITED AND A LITTLE SCARED. HEY. NO PROBLEM. I MEAN, THROW A MARCHING BAND IN WHILE YOU'RE AT IT. HOW ABOUT A MURAL OF THE TAKING OF TROY AND A COMPLETE MAP OF THE WORLD? MAYBE SOME DANCING ELEPHANTS?

7 SE [FROM CATS]: Mrowwrr RRwreOWW Rroww
8 SELINA: Whole CREW now. Ganging UP. It's MUTINY.
9 [2]: Holly. What the hell time is it?
10 HOLLY: SeLINa -- outSIide --

[4.]
MEDIUM ON SELINA, SITTING UP IN BED, CATS CRAWLING ALL OVER HER, HOLDING A PORTABLE ALARM CLOCK IN ONE HAND, PETTING ONE OF THE CATS WITH THE OTHER HAND. HER HEAD IS CRANED FORWARD. SHE SQUINT AT THE CLOCK. SHE'S WEARING A BLACK LACE BRA.

11 VO: -- exPLOsions --
12 SELINA: GGnff
13 [2]: Christ. Not even LIGHT out.
14 [3]: Christ. Five in the morning.
15 SE [FROM CATS]: MMREeeoww Mrrowwwrrr

[MORE]

(3)

1
2
3
4
5
6

BATMAN/p12

[1.]
FULL FIGURES AS: IN FOREGROUND, BATMAN LEAPS BEHIND COLUMNS, IN THE DIRECTION OF THE CAT, WHO RUNS, BULLETS STRIKING BEHIND HIM. THE SWAT TEAM IS IN THE BACKGROUND FIRING, HITTING COLUMNS. ONE SWAT IS TRYING TO SHOOT THE CAT.

1 SE: BRAKABRAKABRAKABRAKA
2 BALLOONS[NOT TAILS, NEAR SWATS]: -- THERE -- 1
-- can't SEE him -- where -- 2
-- moves so FAST -- 3
-- dark -- 4
-- could be ANYWHERE -- 5
3 SE[NEAR CAT]: reeOWWWWWRrr
4 SWAT SHOOTING AT CAT: Wha --
5 [2]: -- DAMN that cat --

[2.]
FULL FIGURE OF BATMAN, ROLLING ACROSS THE FLOOR, HOLDING THE CAT IN BOTH HANDS. HE'S ROLLING TOWARD A SHATTERED WINDOW. BULLET HOLES MARK HIS PATH, RIPPING PLASTER FROM THE WALL.

6 SE: BRAKABRAKABRAKABRAKA
7 BALLOONS[NOT TAILS]: -- THERE -- -- so FAST --
8 SE[NEAR CAT]: WREEOWWWWW

[3.]
MEDIUM ON ACTION AS BATMAN FLINGS THE CAT BACKWARD, OVER HIS HEAD, OUT THE WINDOW. BULLETS STRIKE THE WALL, AT WINDOW LEVEL. ONE HITS BATMAN BELOW THE ELBOW.

9 SE: BRAKABRAKABRAKA
10 SE[NEAR CAT]: WREEEEE
11 SE[NEAR BATMAN]: NGG

[4.]
THE CAT RUNS ACROSS A STRETCH OF PAVEMENT OUTSIDE THE BUILDING.
XXXXXXXXXXXXXXXXXXXX

12 VO[FROM DIRECTION OF BUILDING]: -- TAGGED him -- -- close IN --
13 VO[FROM OPPOSITE DIRECTION]: COMMISSIONER -- for God's SAKE -- come IN --

[5.]
MEDIUM ON ACTION AS THE CAT XXX LEAPS TO THE TOP OF A SQUAD CAR, PAST GORDON AND MERKEL, XXXXXXXXXXXXXXXXXXXXXXXXXXX WHO ARE OUTSIDE THE CAR. GORDON SCREAMS INTO THE CAR MICROPHONE. MERKEL XXXXX JERKS BACKWARD AGAINST THE CAR, CLUTCHING HIS SHOULDER, HIS HAT TOPPLING FROM HIS HEAD. A BULLET HOLE APPEARS IN THE CAR WINDOW.

14 GORDON: -- those IDIOTS are firing X out the WINDOWS -- for God's --
15 [2]: -- MERKEL! --
16 SE[NEAR MERKEL]: NGGAAH

[6.]
MEDIUM ON ACTION AS THE CAT LEAPS INTO SELINA'S OUTSTRETCHED XXXXX HANDS. SELINA LOOKS FIERCE. SHE'S THE ONLY ONE STANDING. HOLLY X DUCKS, TERRIFIED.

NO COPY

BATMAN/p13

[redacted]
[1.] FULL FIGURES AS: THE ENTIRE SWAT TEAM RUSHES TOWARD BATMAN, WHO CROUCHES, XXXXXXXXXX LEANING AGAINST A COLUMN, HOLDING HIS ARM, GETTING A LITTL GROGGY FROM LOSS OF BLOOD. NOBODY'S FIRING.

1 BALLOON[NO TAIL]: GOT him --
2 BALLOON[NO TAIL]: -- get in CLOSE -- cut that bastard in HALF --
3 BALLOON[NO TAIL]: -- GOT him man we've GOT him --
4 CAP[B]: GROGGY -- losing -- too much BLOOD --
5 CAP[B]: -- had to -- put a BULLET -- in my GOOD leg -- didn't they..

[2.]
[redacted]
MEDIUM LONG ON ACTION AS BATMAN KICKS THE PILLAR WITH HIS WOUNDED LEG [I SUGGEST YOU REPEAT THE LAYOUT OF PANEL 3, PAGE 7, CHAPTER ONE]. THE PILLAR SHATTERS.

6 CAP[B]: -- FORGET it -- IGNORE it --
7 → [redacted] 8 SE: KKRAAAKKKK ← 7 CAP[B]: ..put what's LEFT.. INTO it..

[3.]
BIG PANEL. BATMAN LEAPS CLEAR AS A SECTION OF CEILING COLLAPSES, INCLUDING A LARGE BEAM THAT HITS TWO OF THE SWATS. WOOD, PLASTER, ETC., CRACK AND BREAK ACROSS THE REST. A BATHTUB COMES XXXXXXXXXXX TUMBLING DOWN, DEMOLISHING ONE OF THEM. PLASTER FLIES THROUGH THE AIR. DUST BLOWS UP. ONE OF THEM, THE ONE WHO SHOT AT THE CAT, ROLLS OFF TO THE SIDE, HOLDING HIS MACHINE GUN, RELATIVELY OUT OF HARM'S WAY.

NO COPY

[4.]
XXXXXXXXCLOSE ON BATMAN, TURNING HIS HEAD, LOOKING OVER HIS SHOULDER, SEVERE.

9 BATMAN: XXXXX YOU'RE the one --

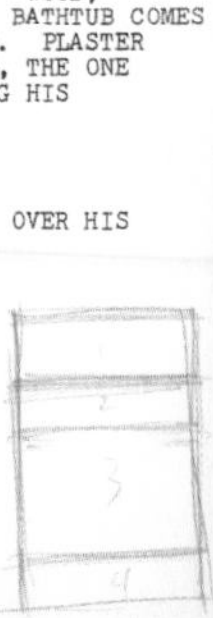

DC Comics, Inc.

BOOK: (2) ISSUE/MONTH: STORY PAGE #: (3)

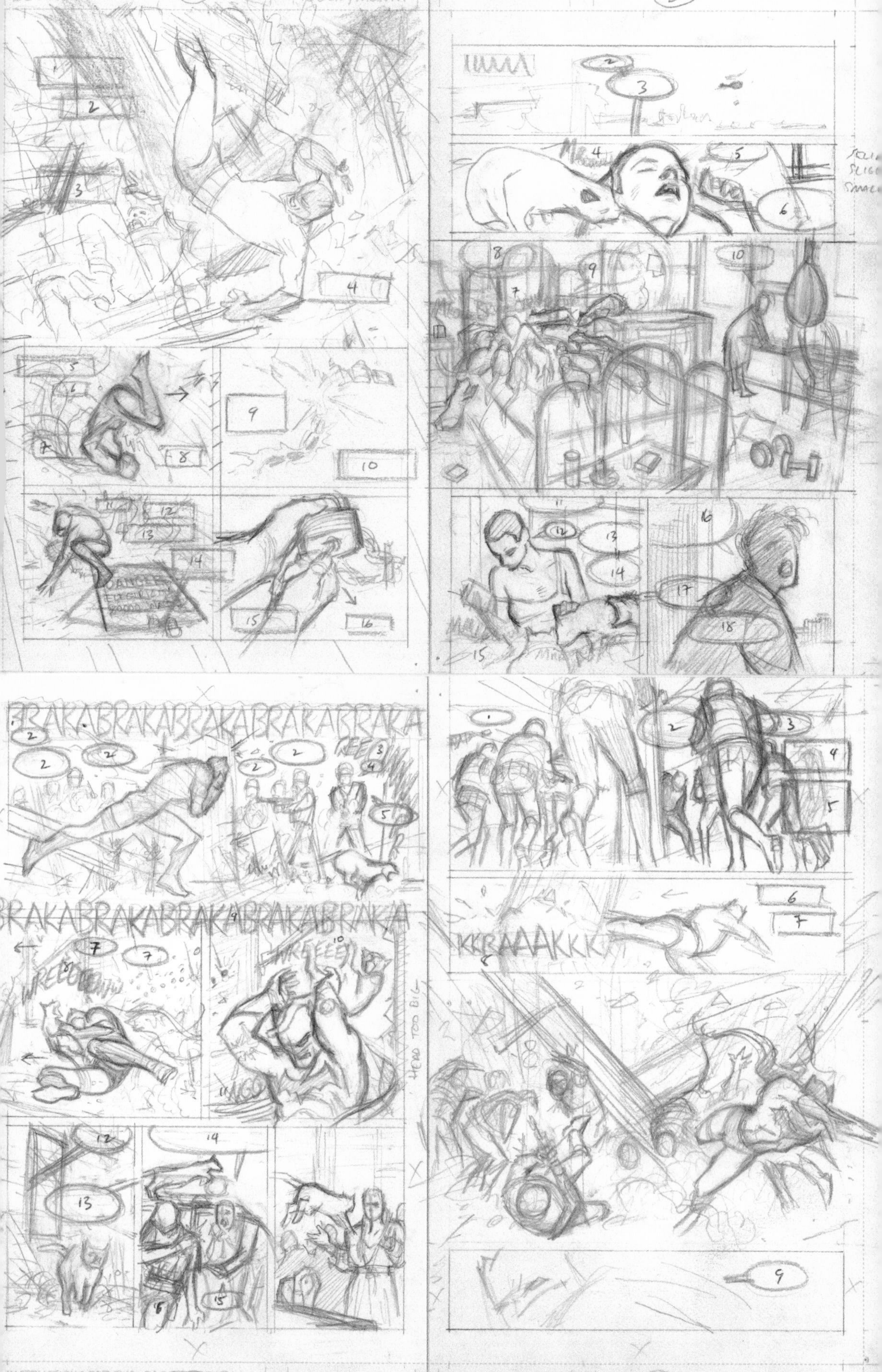

DANGER
BRAKABRAKABRAKABRAKA
BRAKABRAKABRAKABRAKA
KKRAAAKKK

INSTRUCTIONS FOR TWO-PAGE SPREAD:
BUTT PAPER AT EDGES, TAPE ON BACK. **DO NOT OVERLAP AT CENTER!** EACH HALF SHOULD MEASURE

DC Comics, Inc. 18

BOOK: ISSUE/MONTH:

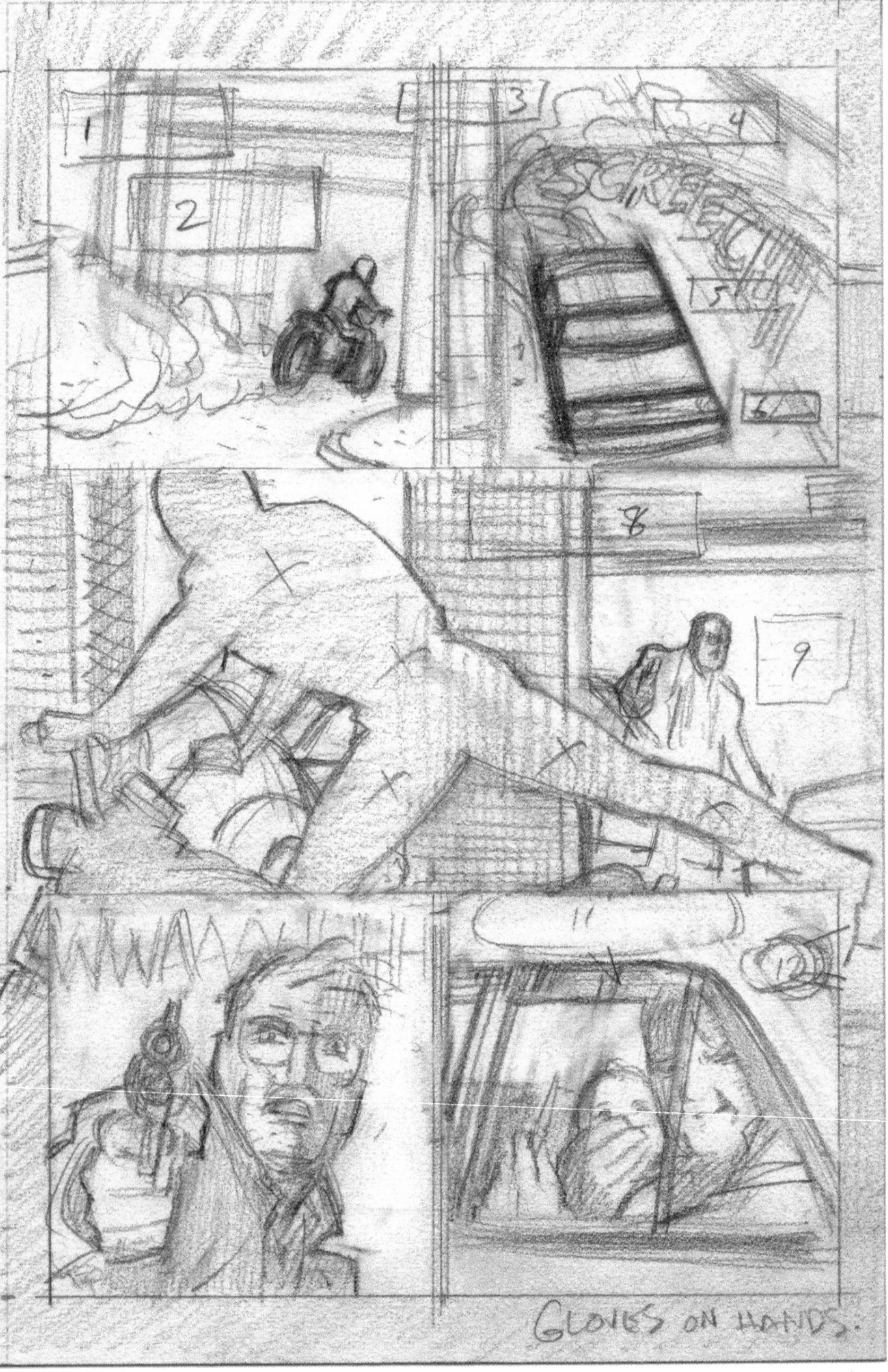

GLOVES ON HANDS.

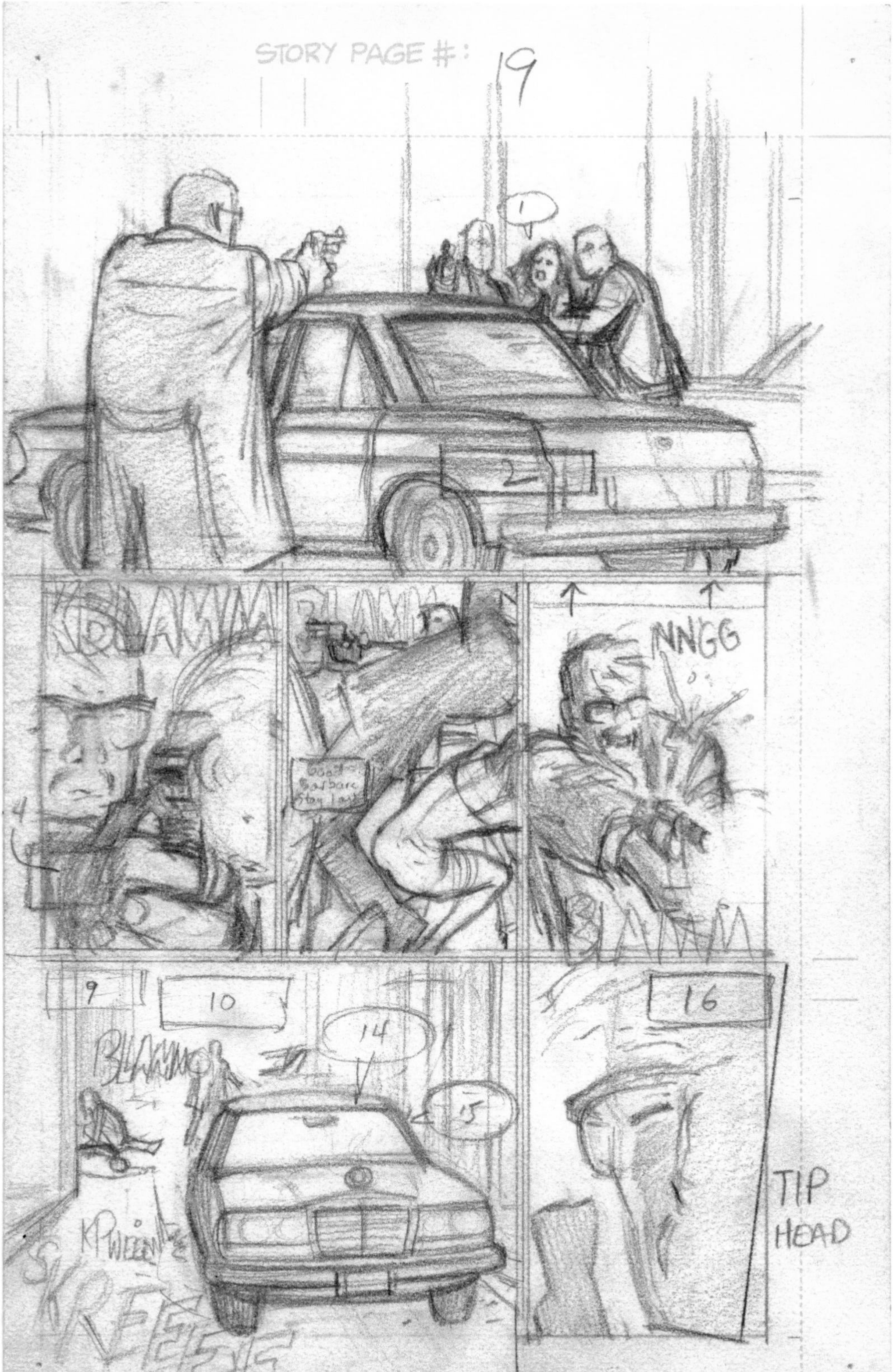
STORY PAGE #: 19
1
2
BLAMM
NNGG
9
10
14
15
16
TIP
HEAD

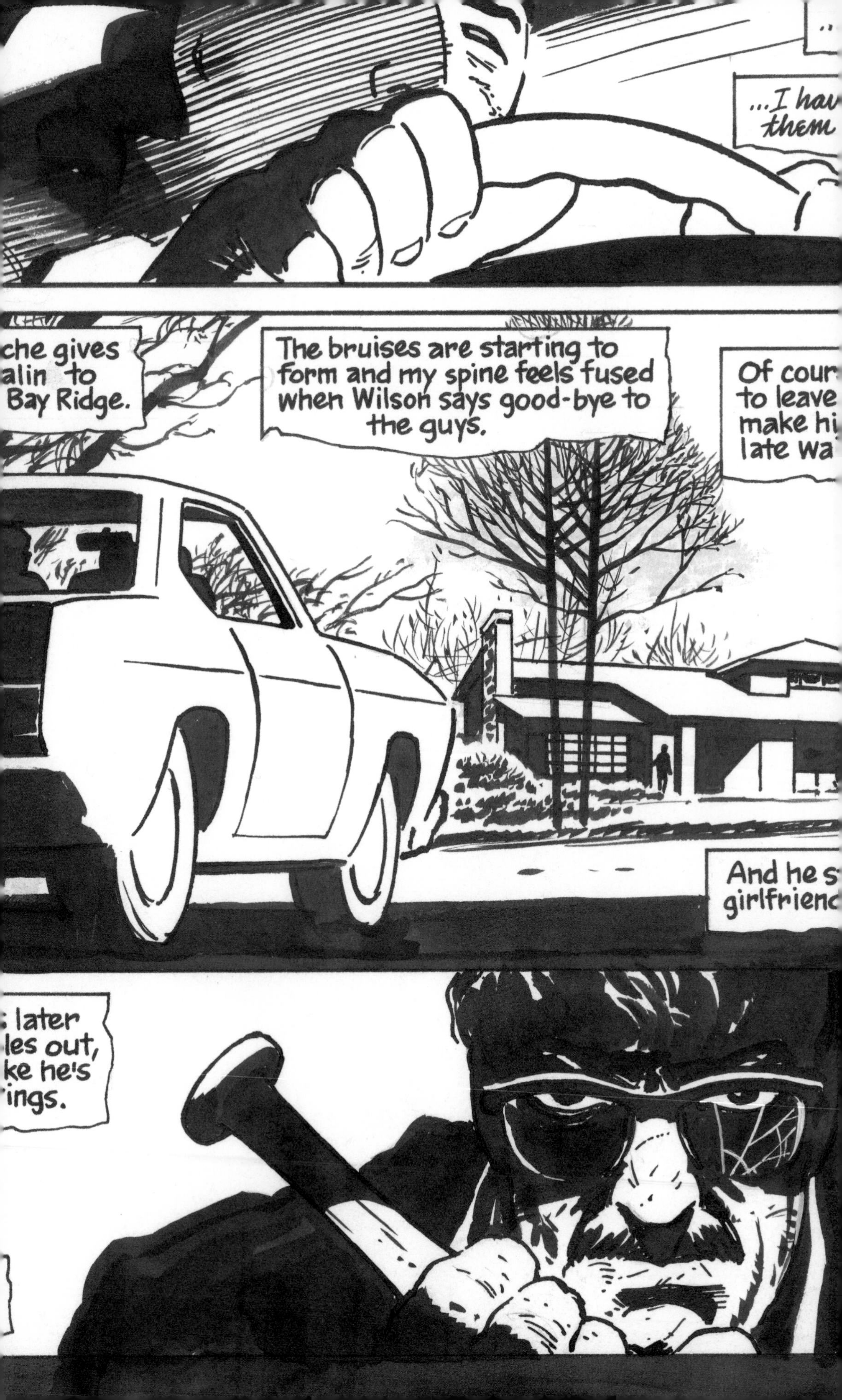

...I hav
them
che gives
alin to
Bay Ridge.
The bruises are starting to form and my spine feels fused when Wilson says good-bye to the guys.
Of cour
to leave
make hi
late wa
And he s
girlfrienc
later
les out,
ke he's
ings.

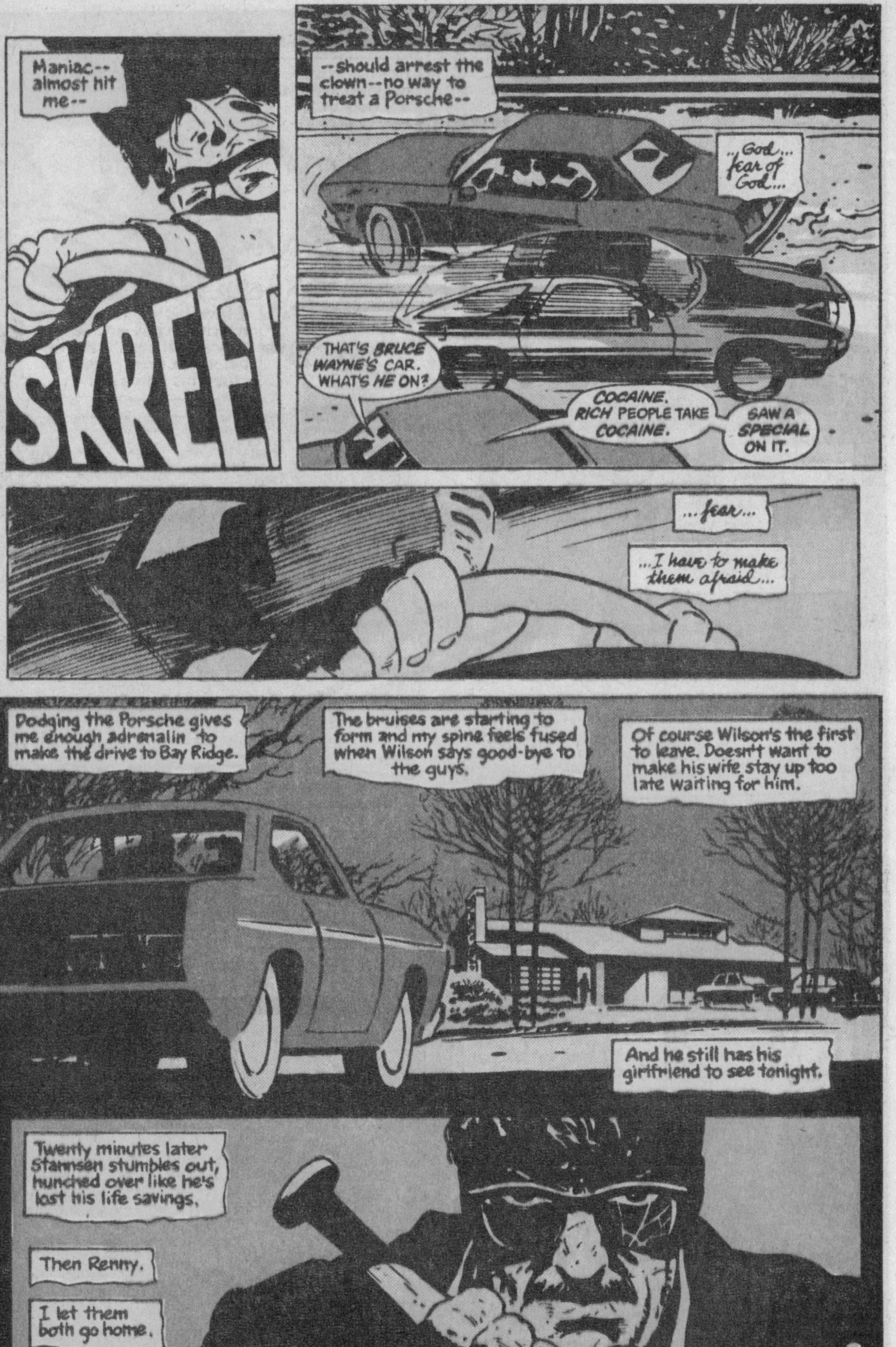
Maniac--
almost hit
me--
SKREE
--should arrest the
clown--no way to
treat a Porsche--
...God...
fear of
God...
THAT'S BRUCE
WAYNE'S CAR.
WHAT'S HE ON?
COCAINE.
RICH PEOPLE TAKE
COCAINE.
SAW A
SPECIAL
ON IT.
...fear...
...I have to make
them afraid...
Dodging the Porsche gives
me enough adrenalin to
make the drive to Bay Ridge.
The bruises are starting to
form and my spine feels fused
when Wilson says good-bye to
the guys.
Of course Wilson's the first
to leave. Doesn't want to
make his wife stay up too
late waiting for him.
And he still has his
girlfriend to see tonight.
Twenty minutes later
Stannsen stumbles out,
hunched over like he's
lost his life savings.
Then Renny.
I let them
both go home.
17

Final ink artwork, actual size (facing page), and the same page in color from the newsprint version. Comics printed on newspaper had an available palette of only about sixty colors, which Richmond utilized brilliantly.

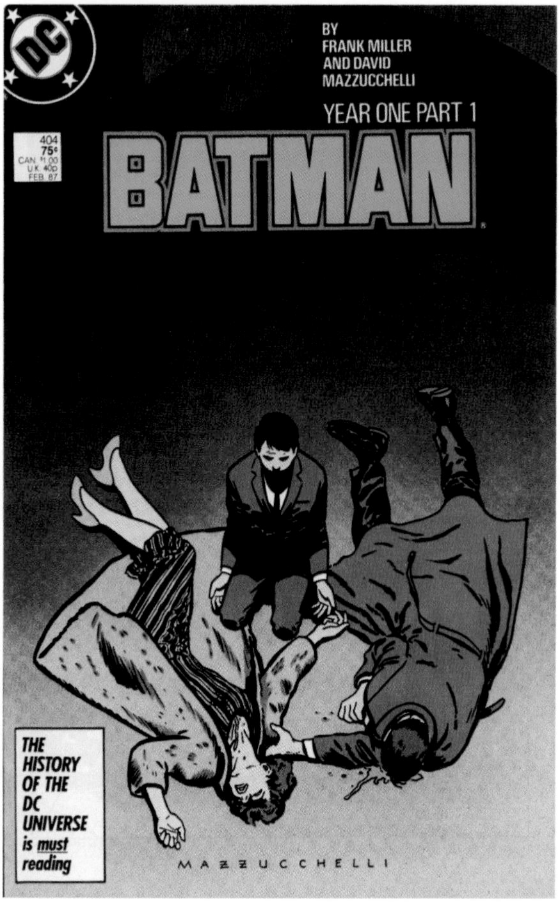
BY
FRANK MILLER
AND DAVID
MAZZUCCHELLI
YEAR ONE PART 1
404
75¢
CAN. $1.00
U.K. 40p
FEB. 87
BATMAN
THE HISTORY OF THE DC UNIVERSE is must reading
MAZZUCCHELLI

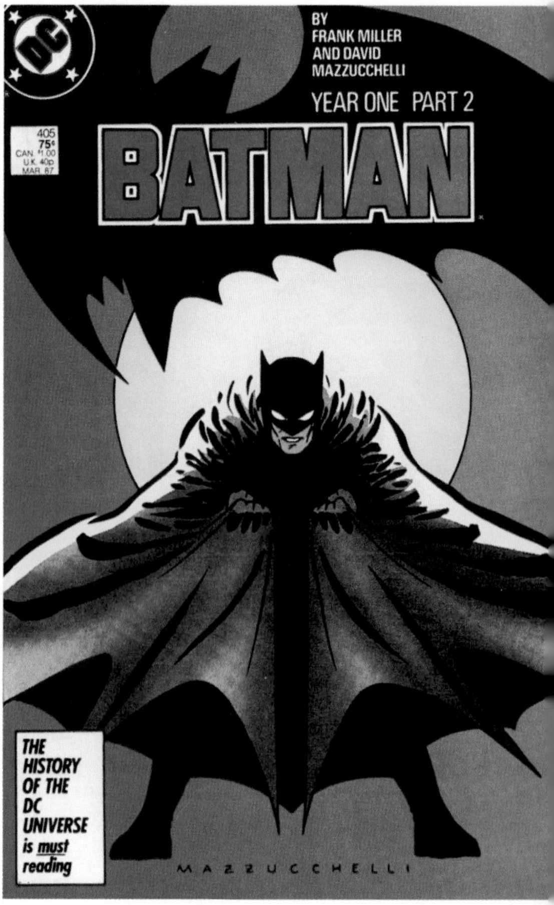
BY
FRANK MILLER
AND DAVID
MAZZUCCHELLI
YEAR ONE PART 2
405
75¢
CAN. $1.00
U.K. 40p
MAR. 87
BATMAN
THE HISTORY OF THE DC UNIVERSE is must reading
MAZZUCCHELLI

The four issues of Batman in which Year One was first published (this page), and some interior pages (opposite).

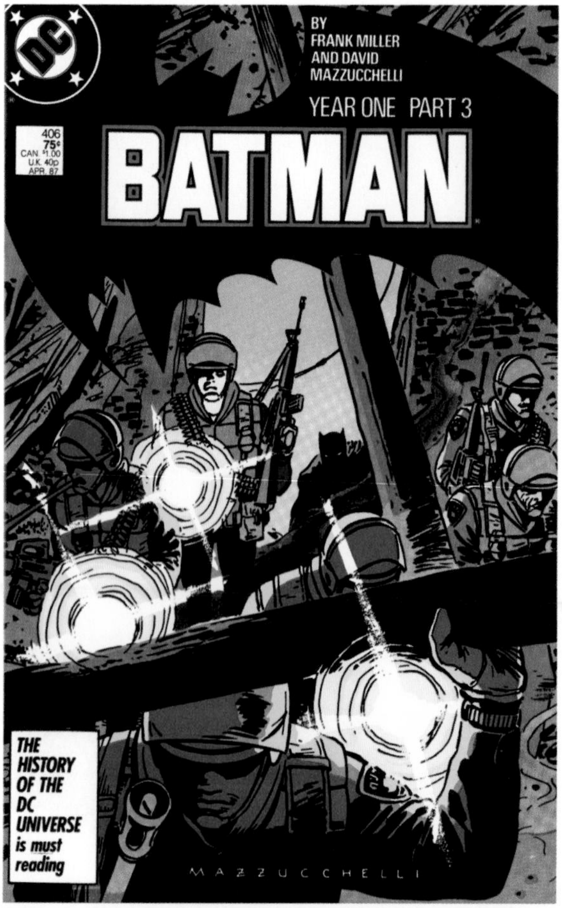
BY
FRANK MILLER
AND DAVID
MAZZUCCHELLI
YEAR ONE PART 3
406
75¢
CAN. $1.00
U.K. 40p
APR. 87
BATMAN
THE HISTORY OF THE DC UNIVERSE is must reading
MAZZUCCHELLI

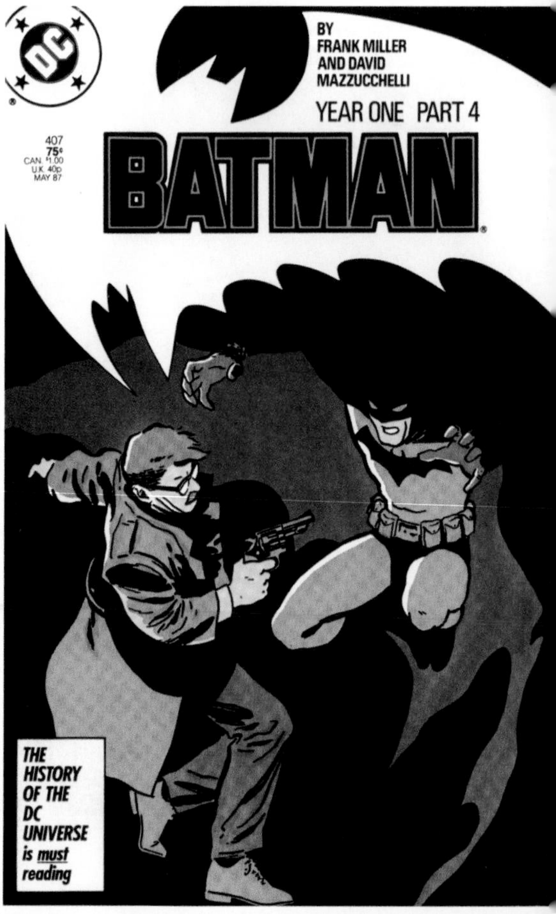
BY
FRANK MILLER
AND DAVID
MAZZUCCHELLI
YEAR ONE PART 4
407
75¢
CAN. $1.00
U.K. 40p
MAY 87
BATMAN
THE HISTORY OF THE DC UNIVERSE is must reading

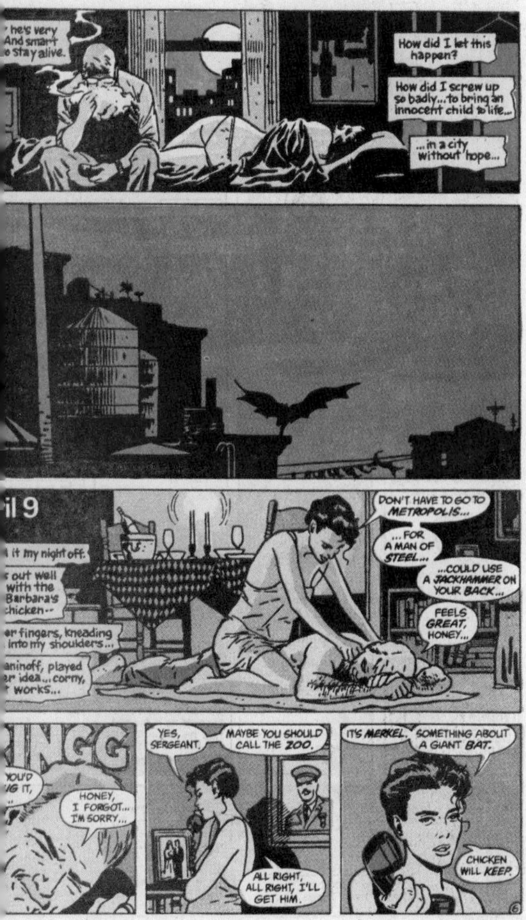

How did I let this happen?
How did I screw up so badly...to bring an innocent child to life...
...in a city without hope...
DON'T HAVE TO GO TO METROPOLIS...
...FOR A MAN OF STEEL...
...COULD USE A JACKHAMMER ON YOUR BACK...
FEELS GREAT, HONEY...
HONEY, I FORGOT... I'M SORRY...
YES, SERGEANT.
MAYBE YOU SHOULD CALL THE ZOO.
ALL RIGHT, ALL RIGHT, I'LL GET HIM.
IT'S MERKEL.
SOMETHING ABOUT A GIANT BAT.
CHICKEN WILL KEEP.
6

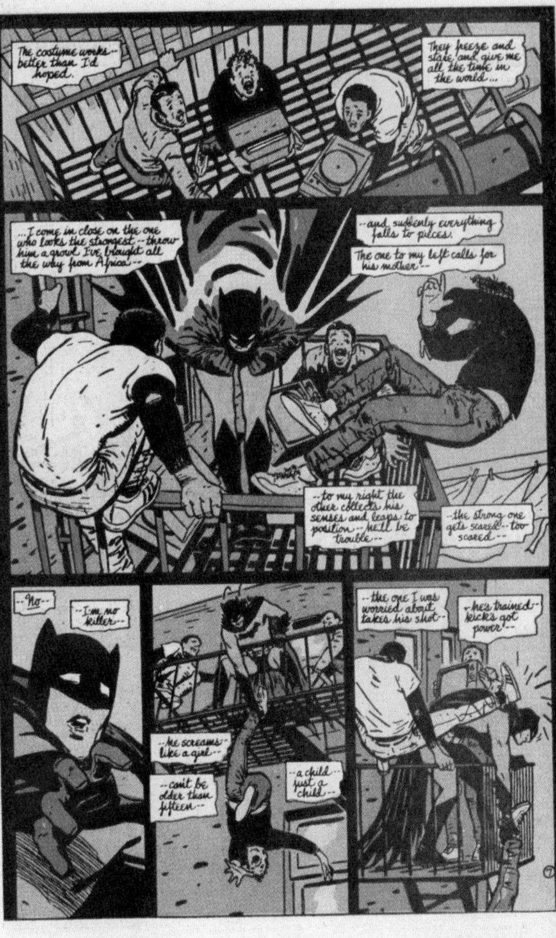

The costume works-- better than I'd hoped.
They freeze and stare and give me all the time in the world...
...I come in close on the one who looks the strongest --throw him a growl I've brought all the way from Africa--
--and suddenly everything falls to pieces.
The one to my left calls for his mother--
--to my right the other collects his senses and leaps to position--he'll be trouble--
--the strong one gets scared--too scared--
--No--
--I'm no killer--
--he screams like a girl--
--can't be older than fifteen--
--a child-- just a child--
--the one I was worried about takes his shot--
--he's trained-- kick's got power--
7

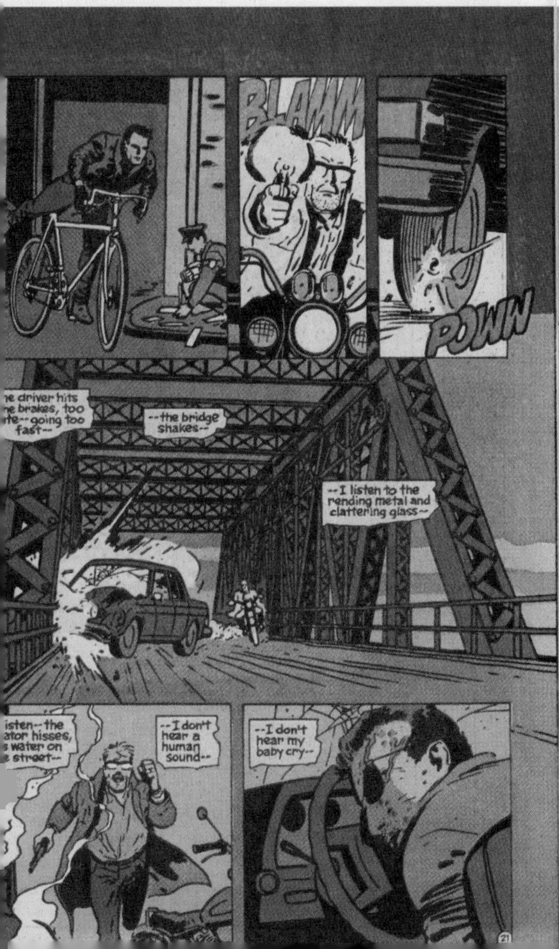

POWW
--the bridge shakes--
--I listen to the rending metal and clattering glass--
--I don't hear a human sound--
--I don't hear my baby cry--
21

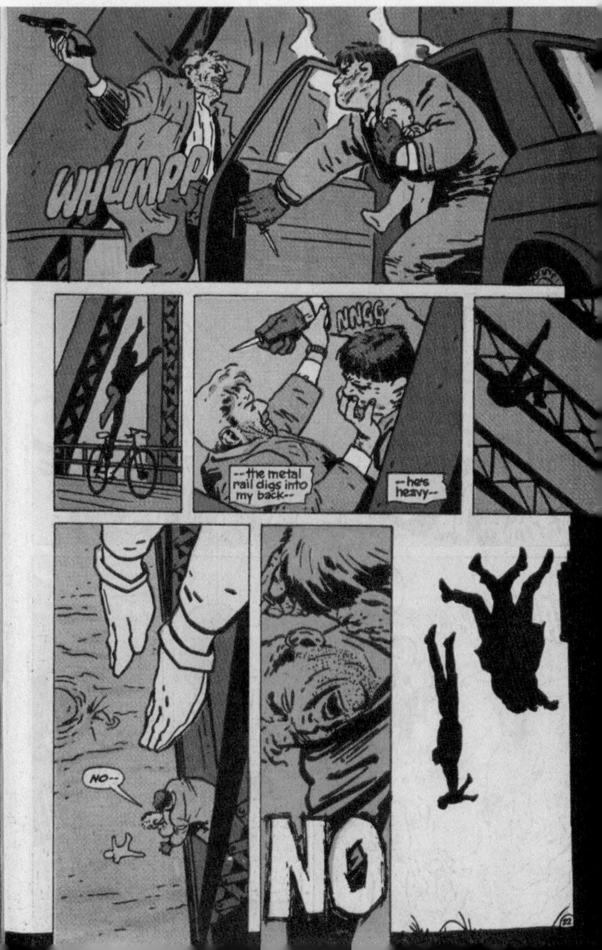

WHUMPP
NNGG
--the metal rail digs into my back--
--he's heavy--
NO--
NO
22

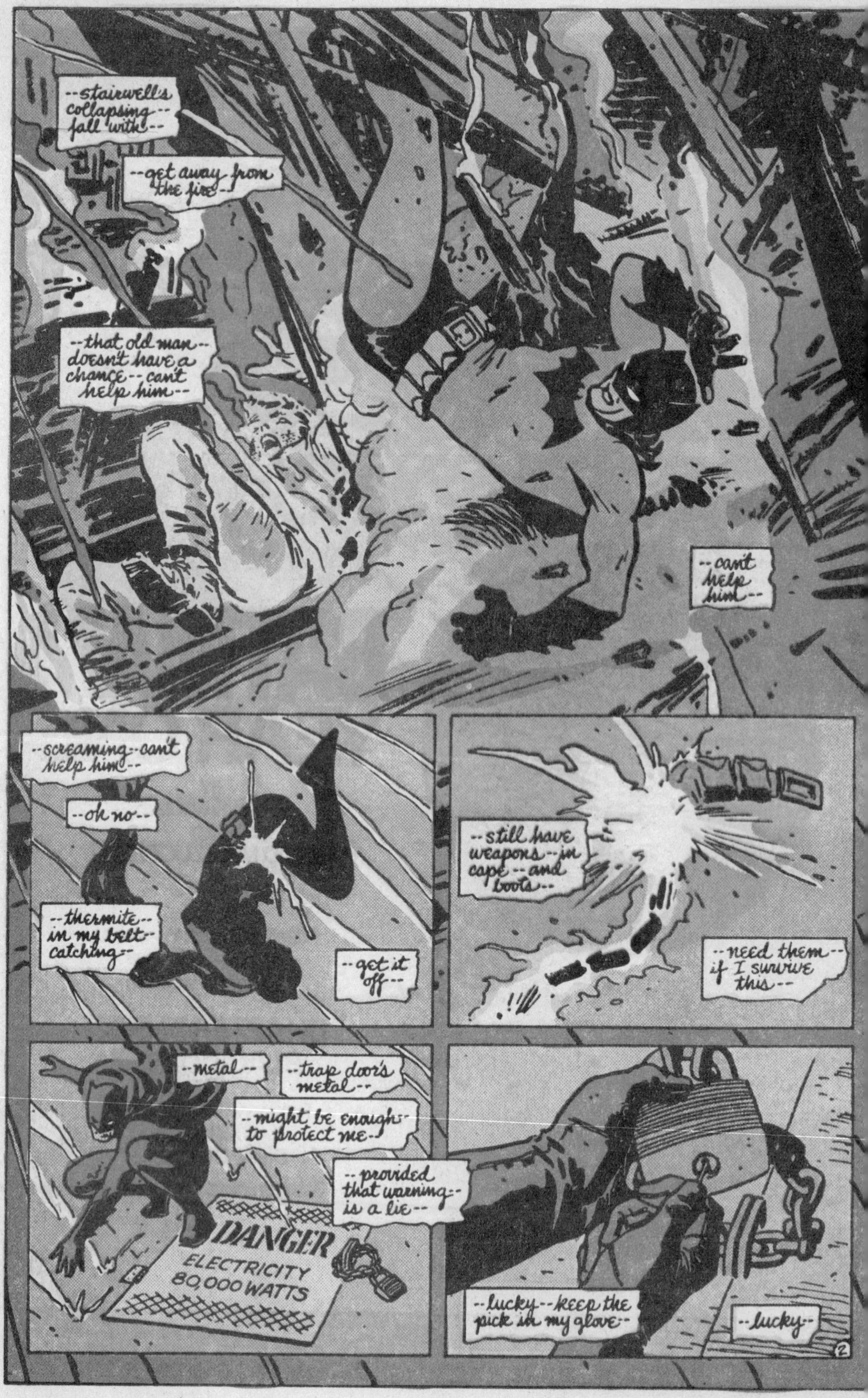
--stairwell's collapsing--fall with--
--get away from the fire--
--that old man--doesn't have a chance--can't help him--
--can't help him--
--screaming--can't help him--
--oh no--
--thermite--in my belt--catching--
--get it off--
--still have weapons--in cape--and boots--
--need them--if I survive this--
--metal--
--trap door's metal--
--might be enough--to protect me--
--provided that warning--is a lie--
DANGER
ELECTRICITY
80,000 WATTS
--lucky--keep the pick in my glove--
--lucky--
2